DICTIONARY OF INDUSTRIAL ORGANIZATION

Dictionary of Industrial Organization

George Norman

Cummings Family Chair of Entrepreneurship and Business Economics, Tufts University, USA

Darlene C. Chisholm

Professor of Economics, Suffolk University, USA

Edward Elgar
Cheltenham, UK • Northampton, MA, USA

Published by
Edward Elgar Publishing Limited
The Lypiatts
15 Lansdown Road
Cheltenham
Glos GL50 2JA
UK

Edward Elgar Publishing, Inc.
William Pratt House
9 Dewey Court
Northampton
Massachusetts 01060
USA

A catalogue record for this book
is available from the British Library

Library of Congress Control Number: 2013946794

This book is available electronically in the ElgarOnline.com Economics Subject Collection, E-ISBN 978 1 78347 198 0

ISBN 978 1 84376 914 9 (cased)

Typeset by Servis Filmsetting Ltd, Stockport, Cheshire
Printed and bound in Great Britain by T.J. International Ltd, Padstow

CONTENTS

INTRODUCTION

The branch of economics that is commonly referred to as "industrial organization" has undergone several major revolutions over the past 100 or so years. At its heart, industrial organization is the study of firms and of the markets in which they operate. This simple idea, however, raises a host of complex questions.

What do we mean by a "firm"? The view that has emerged in answer to this question in the past few decades is that we should think of the firm as a "nexus of contracts".[1] This approach provides a useful organizing framework. Some of the contracts are internal to the firm, relating to the ways in which intra-firm relationships can be organized. An important question that arises with these contracts is how to formulate them in order to align the interests of agents employed by the firm to act on the firm's behalf, with principals who "own" the firm. Other contracts are between the firm and outside agents, such as suppliers or buyers. One important issue with these contracts relates to the appropriate form of contract – short-term, longer-term, relational. Another relates to the choice of activities that should be left outside the firm and those that should be internalized to the firm, essentially asking the question first posed explicitly by Ronald Coase (1937): What is the "nature of the firm"?

Then, what do we mean by a "market" and how might we measure the structure of markets? The underlying principle is that markets of different types can be expected to evolve in very different ways. In addition, firms operating in different types of market face competitive pressures that vary in nature and degree and so have to deal with issues that depend on the specific market context. This variety in competitive environments introduces important strategic questions, for example on pricing policy, product design, or product and process innovation. It also introduces complex econometric questions. Theory is useful in providing us with testable hypotheses with respect to the behavior of firms and markets. But how are these hypotheses to be tested? What models are appropriate and what econometric techniques need to be applied?

The remainder of this introduction to the *Dictionary of Industrial Organization* builds on these questions and provides a rationale for the choices we have made with respect to the range of entries we have included.

---

[1] This concept was first suggested by Jensen and Meckling (1976).

EARLY INDUSTRIAL ORGANIZATION:
STRUCTURE–CONDUCT–PERFORMANCE

The "structure–conduct–performance" (SCP) paradigm provided some of the earliest empirically grounded analysis of industrial organization. This paradigm was first developed in the early work of Edward Mason (1939, 1957) and his colleagues at Harvard, and was further developed in the work of Joe Bain (1956). The SCP paradigm begins with the idea that basic economic conditions determine market structure, defined as a spectrum along which all real-world markets lie. At one extreme are heavily concentrated markets dominated by a small number of firms, close to the monopoly end of the spectrum. At the other are markets containing many firms, none with any significant market power and lying nearer to the perfectly competitive end of the spectrum. The analysis of an industry begins with determining where on this spectrum the industry lies, using factors such as the number and size of sellers, the degree of product differentiation, and barriers to entry.

Market structure, it was hypothesized, determines market conduct, as captured by pricing behavior, product and process innovation, and advertising. Finally, market structure and conduct together determine the market performance of the industry being studied, as measured by, for example, economic efficiency, consumer welfare and profitability.

Much of the analysis in the SCP paradigm was based on empirically rich case studies and large-scale cross-section econometric analysis, and exhibited a remarkable ability to interpret institutional details and identify stylized facts. This approach suffered, however, from two major defects. First, there is the explicit assumption that structure affects conduct, which affects performance, implicitly assuming that market structure is exogenous. Recent developments suggest, by contrast, that there may well be important feedback loops from conduct to structure, and from performance to conduct and structure, with the result that all three elements of the paradigm are endogenous. Second, the paradigm implicitly characterizes an industry in terms of the mix of perfect competition and monopoly it exhibits. The problem with this characterization is that there is no role for strategic decision-making. At the competitive end of the spectrum there are so many firms that no one firm can affect anything. At the other end there is only one firm that need not worry about any other firms. As a result, the SCP paradigm suppressed any explicit consideration of firms thinking and behaving strategically.

Bain (1956) developed an analysis that was something of an exception, introducing the notion that industry and firm performance cannot be analyzed independently of a consideration of the ability of new firms to enter the market. This idea is important. Indeed, it subsequently re-emerged in the "contestability" theory developed by William Baumol et al. (1982). In Bain's analysis, however, entry barriers were largely taken as existing independently of the strategic actions of firms, whereas more recent developments treat barriers to entry as being partly structural but also potentially strategic: see, for example, Steven Salop (1979a) and Harold Demsetz (1982).

THE THEORY OF THE FIRM

Just as the SCP paradigm was developing, another strand in industrial organization was also emerging, based on the seminal 1937 article by Ronald Coase, "The Nature of the Firm". The SCP paradigm takes "the firm" as a given – almost a black box – and asks us to look from the firm outwards to its markets. Coase took a very different view, asking that we look inside the firm. He asked a truly fundamental question: Why do firms exist? If we consider the firm as a set of transactions mediated by contracts, bringing a transaction inside a firm means that the firm is replacing the market as a mechanism for undertaking that transaction. If markets are perfect, this implies a loss of efficiency, so why do this?

Coase answered this question by arguing that traditional economic analysis ignores an important set of costs: the transaction costs of using markets. He went further. If transaction costs of using markets are significant, why do we not see a small set of very large firms? The implication is that there must also be transaction costs of bringing activities inside the firm. The implication is that the boundaries of the firm, sometimes referred to as the resolution of the "make-or-buy" decision, or the degree of vertical integration, is the result of the firm balancing these two sets of transaction costs.

Subsequent development of this approach to the firm by, for example, Oliver Williamson (1985), Paul Milgrom and John Roberts (1992) and Oliver Hart and John Moore (1990) added much-needed additional detail to the concept of transaction costs.[2] These authors suggested that transaction costs of using the market take two broad forms. First, there are the costs of search, negotiation, contract formation, monitoring and enforcement as firms seek to attract and retain customers and suppliers. Second, in some cases one, or the other, or both parties to a transaction has to make a relationship-specific investment to support the transaction. Making such an investment creates quasi-rents and opens the door to the

---

[2]   An accessible review of these ideas is provided by Besanko et al. (2013). The central role of contracts as mediators of transactions is discussed in detail in Hart (1995) and Bolton and Dewatripont (2005).

possibility of *ex post* opportunistic renegotiation of the original contract in order to extract the quasi-rents. This is referred to as the "hold-up problem", based on what Williamson (1979) referred to as "self-interest seeking with guile": see, for example, Victor Goldberg (1976), Benjamin Klein et al. (1978) and Klein (1996).

If the contract in question perfectly delineated every possible contingency, there would be no scope for opportunism. However, contracts are inevitably incomplete as a result of bounded rationality and asymmetric information. The immediate implication is that we are more likely to see an activity conducted inside the firm when that activity requires significant investment in relationship-specific assets.

The question that remains is: What limits the degree of vertical integration? Why not replace the market completely? The answer to these questions rests on another set of transaction costs, those that arise within firms. These take two broad forms. First, there are agency costs:[3] the costs of slack effort by employees in the firm and the costs associated with deterring and/or detecting slack effort. Second, there are influence costs:[4] the costs of activities intended to affect the firm's internal allocation of scarce resources (lobbying, internal politicking) and the costs of inefficient decisions that arise as a result of influence activities.

The argument is that agency and influence costs are proportionately more significant in large, vertically integrated firms. Monitoring employee performance in such firms is difficult, less effective and more costly as a result of the very size of these firms. Similarly, aligning the interests of employees (agents) with those of the firm (or its principals) is more difficult in large, vertically integrated firms. In addition, such firms contain more operating divisions, each of which is competing for resources within the firm, making the integrated firm more vulnerable to costly influence activities.

So again we return to a deceptively simple proposition. The firm resolves the make-or-buy decision with respect to a particular activity by balancing the external transaction costs against the internal transaction costs associated with that activity.

MONOPOLY

While, as we noted above, monopoly lies at one extreme on the spectrum of market structures, the analysis of a monopolist's decision-making does raise many interesting issues for industrial organization. Far from being

---

[3]   Jensen and Meckling (*op. cit.*).
[4]   Milgrom and Roberts (1990).

insulated from strategic concerns, real-world monopolists have to worry about potential entrants, and entry deterrence is an explicit strategic act. Moreover, a monopolist may well in some circumstances be competing with itself, for example if the monopolist produces a durable good, and so again has to think strategically.

Suppose, for example, that the monopolist does indeed produce a durable good such as a software package, an automobile or capital equipment.[5] Suppose further that the monopolist sells this good in a market that lasts for multiple periods, and that the monopolist sells to consumers who live for multiple periods. The result is that the monopolist actually faces competition – from its own product. This introduces the Coase conjecture (Coase 1972). Since the monopolist cannot credibly commit to withholding supply in later periods, goods sold in later periods effectively compete with goods sold in earlier periods. The durability of a good thus erodes the monopolist's market power. Coase conjectured that in the limit, as the period between sales decreases, the monopolist will be constrained to price at marginal cost.

The underlying idea is simple enough (the analysis is much more complex). The monopolist need not charge the same price in every period and it is to be expected that price will fall over time; after all, the monopolist in later periods actually faces competition from sales by consumers who have purchased in earlier periods. As a result, consumers will tend to postpone their purchase decisions in order to take advantage of the lower future prices. This forces the monopolist to charge lower prices in the earlier periods, weakening the monopolist's market power. While the generality of the Coase conjecture has been called into question,[6] the basic point remains: the monopoly provider of a durable good faces competition from itself.

The analysis of durable goods implies that the monopolist can charge different prices for goods that are differentiated by the time at which they are sold – intertemporal price discrimination. We can also consider situations in which the monopolist charges different prices for goods sold at the same time. Price discrimination in this context is defined by Louis Phlips as "implying that two varieties of a commodity are sold (by the same seller) to two buyers at different *net* prices, the net price being the price (paid by the buyer) corrected for the cost associated with the product

---

[5] The literature on durable goods monopoly essentially began with Coase (1972). See also Bulow (1982) and Schmalensee (1979a).

[6] The literature providing exceptions is too large to cite here. For a recent analysis, see McAfee and Wiseman (2008).

differentiation" (Phlips 1983, p. 6). Thus the large difference between first-class and economy airline fares is probably an example of price discrimination, as is a firm that sells a product produced in London to consumers in Paris, New York and Singapore at the same price.

Several interesting questions arise with price discrimination. First, what makes price discrimination feasible and profitable? This requires three conditions: (a) the monopolist knows that it is serving consumers of different types; (b) the monopolist either has an exogenous signal of a consumer's true type or is able to design a pricing mechanism that encourages consumers to self-select into their true types; and (c) the monopolist can prevent arbitrage from consumers charged lower prices to consumers charged higher prices.

Second, what form of price discrimination should be applied? The language here is that developed by Arthur Pigou (1920): first-, second- or third-degree price discrimination, referred to more recently by Carl Shapiro and Hal Varian (1999) as personalized pricing, menu pricing and group pricing.

Third, what are the efficiency properties of price discrimination? Are there circumstances in which price discrimination increases total surplus, and if so, what are these? Standard analysis (see, for example, Lynne Pepall et al. 2008; Richard Schmalensee 1981) tells us that a necessary condition for third-degree price discrimination to increase social welfare is that it increases total output.[7] It follows that one obvious way in which price discrimination will increase total surplus is if such discrimination leads to markets being served that would otherwise not be served. More complex examples rest on the convexity/concavity of demand functions in the different markets.

Just as a monopolist can discriminate in prices, the monopolist can also discriminate in product quality by designing goods or services some of which are of high quality and some of which are of lower quality.[8] As with durable goods, offering goods of different qualities means that the monopolist is effectively competing with itself. The firm has to design and price its different products to satisfy an incentive compatibility constraint with respect to its consumers, such that consumers are able to choose the product quality they will buy. Thus in pricing the high-quality good, for

---

[7]   Pepall et al. (2008) show that the same condition applies to second-degree price discrimination. First-degree price discrimination always maximizes social welfare.

[8]   The seminal contribution is Mussa and Rosen (1978). Extension of their analysis to oligopolistic market structures was made by Shaked and Sutton (1982, 1983).

example, the monopolist must recognize that the consumers for whom this product is designed – those who place a high value on quality – can always choose instead to purchase a lower-quality good.

Quality differentiation implies that the monopolist is offering more than one good; in this case, multiple goods differentiated by quality, or vertically differentiated. Monopolists often also offer multiple goods that are horizontally differentiated: goods of similar qualities but with different characteristics. This is particularly relevant as a strategy when the monopolist knows that its market contains consumers with similar willingness to pay for quality but with very different tastes for the characteristics of the goods being offered.

The question to be answered now is: How many product variants should the monopolist bring to market? In answering this question, the firm must balance three forces. First, having additional product variants implies that each variant is more closely aligned with a particular group of consumers' tastes and so is more attractive to those consumers. Second, adding another product means that the monopolist is competing with its existing products, cannibalizing sales of the existing products. Third, introducing additional products can sacrifice economies of scale. There is yet another more strategic consideration. Once we recognize that a monopolist is not necessarily free from the threat of entry, the ability to offer multiple product variants to supply a market, containing consumers with very diverse tastes, introduces the strategic possibility that the monopolist will seek to "cover the market" in order to leave no "holes" that a potential entrant might exploit.[9]

Resolving these issues raises the question of whether the monopolist offers too much or too little product variety in a social welfare sense. There is no settled answer to this question, the conclusion being dependent upon the specific modeling assumptions. One set of analyses indicates that the monopolist offers excess variety, another that there is too little variety, and the third that there is socially optimal variety. In other words, theory offers us little guidance on this question.

STRATEGIC OLIGOPOLY PRICING AND GAME THEORY
We noted in our discussion of the SCP paradigm that it pays little or no attention to the strategic dimension of firms' decisions when they are operating in markets that are imperfectly competitive. Explicitly recognizing

---

[9] For one of the first formal analyses of product proliferation as a strategic entry deterrence strategy see Schmalensee (1979b). For a critique of this strategy see Judd (1985).

the interdependence that characterizes decision-making in such markets is a distinctive feature of what is often called the new or modern industrial organization.[10] Firms try to influence their market environment rather than take that environment as exogenously given.

The language now becomes that of game theory. The final outcome of any particular game will be dependent upon the strategy space, firms' beliefs and information sets, the sequence of moves and the ability to make strategic commitments, the time horizon and players' time preferences. The limitation of this approach is that we can no longer develop a general theory covering the full range of industrial behavior. However, the advantage of this approach is that we can address a wide range of important questions that were beyond the capabilities of theorists steeped in the SCP paradigm.

Game theory allows us to analyze the relationship between market power and pricing, using, for example, the workhorses of Cournot and Bertrand competition. We can build on the seminal Harold Hotelling (1929) analysis of spatial competition, addressing his hypothesis that competing oligopolists will offer horizontally differentiated products characterized by what he termed an "excessive sameness". By contrast, firms offering vertically differentiated products are likely to offer highly differentiated products.

Hotelling's analysis of spatial competition has provided us with a theoretical approach that can be applied to a wide range of apparently non-spatial questions. The effects of deregulation of airline transport routes, the implications of introducing flexible manufacturing systems, and the choice of movie exhibition programming might seem to be unrelated questions, but they can be and have all been addressed using the spatial model that Hotelling first introduced.

Returning to some of our comments in the previous section on monopoly, a game-theoretic approach allows us to analyze whether competition will lead to excess product variety. William Vickrey (1964) was the first to coin the "excess entry theorem", that in a circle model of horizontal product differentiation[11] consumers will be offered too much product variety. More recent analyses can be found in, for example, Yiquan Gum and Tobias Wenzel (2009) and Toshihiro Matsumara and Makoto Okamura (2006). A contrasting result holds in models of vertical differentiation, referred to as the "finiteness property" (Jaskold Gabszewicz and Jacques-François Thisse 1980; Avner Shaked and John Sutton 1983). Even

---

[10]   See, for example, Carlton and Perloff (2005), Pepall et al. (2008, 2011) and Waldman and Jensen (2013). Essential reading continues to be Tirole (1988).
[11]   This model actually predates the Salop (1979b) analysis.

if firms offering vertically differentiated products have zero fixed costs, the market will only support a finite number of firms with positive revenues.

An important distinction in game theory more generally is between static and repeated games. This distinction is particularly important when we apply game theory to questions such as price setting, location strategies and product line competition. Take an extreme example of Bertrand competition between firms offering essentially identical products. If this is posed as a static game, then the only price equilibrium with two or more firms in the market is marginal cost pricing. When we extend this to a two-stage entry-price game, the only subgame perfect equilibrium is monopoly. By contrast, if the game is indefinitely repeated, we can apply the "folk theorem" (James Friedman 1971) to conclude that any set of prices between the competitive and the monopoly price is sustainable for some discount factor sufficiently close to unity. In the two-stage entry game we can now see the potential for multiple-firm entry, even in the seemingly aggressive Bertrand context.

Repeated games typically support a non-competitive outcome by means of tacit cooperation based upon a trigger strategy. We should, however, be aware of the fact that firms in imperfectly competitive markets have an incentive to explicitly cooperate if they can possibly do so, forming cartels. This is far from a new idea. Indeed, one of its earliest statements is to be found in Adam Smith's *Wealth of Nations* (1776) where he wrote, "People of the same trade seldom meet together, even for merriment and diversion, but the conversation ends in a conspiracy against the public, or in some contrivance to raise prices" (Book 1, Chapter X, Part II).

Some of the simpler analyses of cartels suggest that we need not be concerned about their impact on market efficiency: they will fall apart of their own volition as a result of the temptation to cheat on the cartel's agreed prices or market quotas. At first sight this appears encouraging. However, it ignores the repeated game context in which cartels operate. The same trigger strategy that can sustain tacit cooperation is even more effective in sustaining explicit cartels. The question then is: Can we offer reasonably simple tests by which cartels can be discovered? According to Ronald Harstad and Phlips (1994) and Phlips (1996), we cannot. They formulated the indistinguishability theorem, stating that cartel members can exploit their information advantages with respect to the antitrust authorities to make the cartel behavior appear to be competitive.

One mechanism to ease cartel detection that the antitrust authorities have adopted in the United States, the European Union and Australia, among others, is to offer a simple amnesty program that can be paraphrased something along the following lines: "If you are the member of a cartel and you provide us with information that leads to successful prosecution of the cartel, you go free. Everyone else faces heavy fines."[12] This would appear to present the cartel members with a classic prisoners' dilemma. However, careful application of game theory indicates that matters are not quite so simple.[13] Yes, once a cartel is suspected to exist it should be easier to detect at law as a result of at least one firm asking for amnesty in return for evidence of the workings of the cartel. On the other hand, the cost of being a member of a cartel that is detected and prosecuted is now much lower provided that you can defect to the antitrust authorities first.

Further strategic considerations arise with respect to such issues as entry deterrence and innovation. We noted above that a monopolist may have an incentive to employ product proliferation as an entry-deterring device. The same strategy applies to oligopolists, for example, by installing excess capacity, or by offering exclusive contracts, or by adopting strategies such as advertising and creating consumer loyalty that raise the costs of potential entrants.

With respect to innovation, the techniques that we can draw from game theory allow us to answer questions such as whether a monopolist has a greater incentive to innovate than a competitive firm. The Schumpeterian hypothesis suggests that this is, indeed, the case (Joseph Schumpeter 1942). We can also consider the optimal design of a patent system. For example, under what circumstances should patents be "short and broad" rather than "long and narrow" (Richard Gilbert and Carl Shapiro 1990; Paul Klemperer 1990)? What are the efficiency implications of the patent system? On the one hand, it may encourage innovation. On the other hand, it creates at least local monopolies. Moreover, given the "first-past-the-post" nature of the patent system, where being second to file is of no benefit, the patent system may well encourage wasteful patent races, implying that encouraging research joint ventures might well be efficiency enhancing.[14]

INFORMATION, AGENCY AND CONTRACTS

Turning once again from looking from the firm to its outside markets, to looking inside the firm, modern developments in industrial organization research have given us important insights by applying the language and techniques of game theory. These developments are rooted in two

---

[12]   The precise conditions under which amnesty might be granted are given in a speech by the Assistant Attorney General at http://www.usdoj.gov/atr/public/speeches/2247.htm.

[13]   For details of this analysis see Motta and Polo (2003) and Motta (2004).

[14]   Scotchmer (2004) gives an excellent overview of the literature on innovation. On patent races see Loury (1979) for the early research and Reinganum (1989) for an excellent survey.

fundamental propositions: first, that contracts are inevitably incomplete; and second, that parties to a transaction have asymmetric information. This opens up the possibility of opportunistic behavior by the parties to a contract and raises the question of what type of contract should actually be formulated.

Suppose that agents have private information, for example with respect to their true nature or the true quality of a good or service that they are offering for sale. Suppose further that agents' actions can be observed only imperfectly. In other words, it is not clear whether or not an agent has abided by the terms of a contract. Two potential market failures arise, one pre-contract and the other post-contract.

Pre-contract, there is the potential for adverse selection. In insurance markets, for example, potential buyers are privately informed of their true risk characteristics, with the result that those who actually purchase insurance are a biased sample of the population of potential buyers. Moreover, raising insurance premiums drives out good risks, worsening the risk class that actually buys the insurance.

In markets that contain both new and pre-owned goods, similar biases emerge, as demonstrated by George Akerlof's Nobel prize-winning work (Akerlof 1970). Consider the market for automobiles and suppose that there is a small, but finite, probability that a new automobile is a low-quality "lemon". Now consider a typical buyer. Having bought a new car, the buyer is privately informed regarding whether or not he has a lemon. Suppose that he does, indeed, have such a lemon. Then the owner will be tempted to sell the lemon and replace it with a new car that is likely not to be a lemon. Suppose, by contrast, that the buyer finds that his new car is perfect. Then he will prefer to hold on to it since selling it and replacing it with a new car exposes him to the risk that he purchases a lemon. The implication is that the second-hand market will contain a much higher proportion of lemons than the new market.

Post-contract, if an agent's actions cannot be perfectly observed, there is the potential for moral hazard. Having insurance can bias risk-taking behavior, as was seen rather spectacularly in the United States savings and loan scandal. When the true quality of the goods or services being offered is difficult to observe – for example advertising, management or financial consulting, or maintenance services – there is the potential for the agent providing the goods or services to renege on the actual quality offered as compared to the quality that is contracted.

Moral hazard is particularly problematic in principal–agent settings.[15]

---

[15]   See Hart and Holmström (1987) and Laffont and Martimort (2001).

Here a principal delegates the performance of an activity to an agent who is supposed to work on the principal's behalf. Such settings are common: shareholders of publicly traded companies delegate the management of such companies to senior management; senior management delegates to middle management; clients delegate to consultants, and so on. The interests of the principal and those of the agent are not necessarily fully aligned, which would of itself not be a problem if the actions of the agent could be perfectly observed by the principal and so could be made the subject of an enforceable contract. However, the principal can only imperfectly observe the actions of the agent, opening up the possibility that the agent will act opportunistically post-contract.

The challenge in such principal–agent settings is finding mechanisms that can control, at least partly, the temptation of the agent to renege on the true spirit of the contract with the principal. One possibility is for the principal to offer the agent an incentive-based contract. Such a contract has to satisfy two constraints. The first is the participation constraint: the agent must be willing to accept the contract – a necessary condition for which is that it is better than the agent's next-best contract. The second is the incentive compatibility constraint: the contract must make it in the self-interest of the agent to behave "well" – exert optimal effort, for example – rather than behave badly.

Incentive-based compensation is not always appropriate. First, note that an incentive contract results in an inefficient allocation of risk. Risk is moved from the principal, the firm, which is roughly risk neutral, to the agent, who is typically risk averse. As a result, an incentive contract must offer the agent a risk premium to compensate for the risk associated with the contract. The literature (see, for example, Paul Milgrom and John Roberts 1992, Chapter 7) suggests that such incentive-based compensation schemes are more likely to be effective when:

- the value of output is sensitive to the agent's effort;
- the agent is not very risk averse;
- the level of risk beyond the agent's control is low;
- the agent's effort is sensitive to increased incentives;
- the agent's output can be measured at low cost.

Another possibility is to place the contract in a repeated game setting or, equivalently, to tie the agent's reputation to the agent's measured performance. Now the agent recognizes that reneging on a contract gives a short-term gain but, if reneging is detected, results in a long-term loss. This requires, of course, that it is feasible and desirable to offer the possibility of a long-term contract. Japanese major assembly companies such as Mitsubishi, Toyota and Hitachi, for example, traditionally offered "life-time employment" contracts to their employees. They continue to use negotiation with long-term suppliers rather than competitive tendering in the sourcing of critical inputs. In addition, for reputation to be effective in controlling moral hazard, there must be a finite, non-trivial probability that opportunism by the agent will be detected by the principal.

A third possibility is to give the agent "ownership" of the value the agent creates. Commission-based contracts that are typical in some retail settings and which are characteristic of contracts with sales teams have some of this property. Management buyouts of publicly traded companies change the status of managers from agents to principals. In many upscale hairdressing salons the top stylists are self-employed, renting space from the owner of the salon.

Franchising is a very common method by which a principal, the franchisor, gives ownership to an agent, the franchisee. In the typical franchise contract the franchisee gains the right to operate under the franchisor's name in return for a fixed up-front fee and a royalty based on some measurable performance criterion such as sales or turnover. Such a contract makes the franchisee the residual claimant on the returns generated by the franchise, aligning the interests of the franchisee with those of the franchisor.[16]

Note, however, that not everything can be franchised. There remains the potential for moral hazard if the franchisee can increase their returns by reneging on the agreed quality with the franchisor. In other words, franchising is most likely to be found when the quality of the good or service being franchised can be easily defined and measured, and when the reputational costs to the franchisor of underperformance by a franchisee are relatively small.

The issues that we have been discussing in this section have direct implications for the ways in which organizations – of any type – should be structured: what is sometimes referred to as organizational architecture (James Brickley et al. 2009). An effective organizational architecture must balance three components:

1. The allocation of decision rights: Who has the authority to make what decisions?
2. The reward and incentive systems: How are individuals rewarded for exercising their decision rights?
3. Monitoring and performance evaluation: What key performance indicators are used to evaluate and monitor managers and employees?

---

[16]   For a review of the economics of franchising, see Blair and Lafontaine (2005).

Imbalance in any one of these "three legs of the stool", as Brickley et al. term them, generates a dysfunctional organizational architecture, subject to the risk that the organization will fall prey to the types of behavior that led to major losses at companies such as Enron, J.P. Morgan, Société Général, Sumitomo and Barings Bank.

EMPIRICAL METHODS

The empirical methodologies used in industrial organization research have paralleled the evolution of research questions over the years. In early studies of the structure–conduct–performance paradigm, a common empirical approach entailed inter-industry analysis, regressing measures of performance, such as profitability, on measures of structure, such as industry size. A limitation of such empirical approaches was determining causality (for example, as we noted in the early part of this Introduction, while structure can influence performance, profitability can, in turn, impact market structure). This problem of reverse causality, a form of endogeneity, led to usage of more appropriate methodologies, including instrumental variables and structural equation estimation.

As theoretical research turned to identifying foundations for the theory of the firm and to delineating the nature of strategic interaction among firms, the requirements for empirical research and methods shifted notably towards reflecting optimizing behavior of individual decision-makers within specific industries or markets, such as consumers seeking their highest utility and firms seeking their maximal profits.

Discrete choice models of demand consider the case of a typical consumer selecting one option from among two or more mutually exclusive choices.[17] The econometric analyses, including multinomial probit and logit, nested logit and mixed logit estimation, use consumer demographics, price, and product or choice attributes to estimate demand. The multinomial logit model relies on the assumption of independence of irrelevant alternatives (IIA), which imposes the restriction that the relative probability the consumer chooses one option over another not be influenced by the presence of additional alternatives in the choice set. The IIA assumption can be problematic when the elements of the choice set include close substitutes. Daniel McFadden (1984) and Kenneth Train (2009) provide very useful guides to these models.

In their seminal work, Steven Berry et al. (1995) introduced a demand (and cost) estimation methodology for the automobile industry and,

---

[17]   For a discussion of the theory of discrete choice in the context of industrial organization, see Anderson et al. (1992).

more generally, for industries characterized by product differentiation and imperfect competition. Their methodology allowed the econometrician to use information on product characteristics and on aggregate consumer characteristics as the basis for estimation, rather than relying on consumer-level data. Further, their approach allowed for variation in consumer tastes, as well as for a range of consumer substitution patterns that the IIA assumption in the multinomial logit model precluded.

The empirical requirements of industrial organization research reach beyond supply and demand estimation. For example, differences-in-differences estimation allows the econometrician to measure the impact of a policy over time by comparing outcomes in the group targeted by the policy to outcomes in a group outside of the scope of the policy. If one state adopts tax incentives for firms to invest in alternative energy research, while the neighboring state does not, the rate of adoption of new energy technologies can be compared across the two states (the difference in differences) to determine how effective such tax incentives are relative to a baseline trend. Alternatively, duration analysis methods, which estimate probabilities of "survival", can be used, for example, to estimate the likelihood of a firm continuing to sell one product within a multi-product line, given that the product has survived until time t. For an excellent review of recent developments in empirical industrial organization methodology, see Liran Einav and Jonathan Levin (2010).

REGULATION AND ANTITRUST

The early development of antitrust policy, at least in the United States, predates the formal modeling of imperfectly competitive markets that is the defining characteristic of industrial organization. It is, however, based at least in part on economists' intuitive understanding that the exercise of monopoly power is unlikely to be benign. We noted above that Adam Smith was fully aware of the potential for collusion. He was also aware of the market impact that the exercise of monopoly power, once attained, implies: "The monopolists, by keeping the market constantly understocked, by never fully supplying the effectual demand, sell their commodities much above the natural price" (Smith 1776, Book I, Chapter 7).

The emergence of large firm trusts – such as Standard Oil and American Tobacco – and the ways in which these trusts were created and subsequently behaved led to the enactment of the first-ever US antitrust law, the Sherman Act of 1890. Section 1 prohibits contracts, combinations and conspiracies "in restraint of trade". Section 2 makes any attempt to monopolize a market illegal.

Section 1 remains central to antitrust policy, being an essential statute under which cartels are prosecuted. Section 2 has had a much more checkered history, with the courts' decisions being much less clear on which actions that lead to monopolization should be considered to be illegal. Essentially, the court developed a "rule of reason", requiring that the antitrust authorities not only show that there was monopolization of the relevant market, but also show that this was achieved through explicit intent or exploitation of monopoly power.

The ambiguity introduced by the rule of reason approach to Section 2 of the Sherman Act led to the passage of the Clayton Act of 1914. This Act and the subsequent Celler-Kefauver Act of 1950 were intended to stop monopolization of a market "in its incipiency" by inhibiting the use of rebates, tying practices and exclusive contracts and also by preventing mergers that were considered to be anticompetitive. The Federal Trade Commission Act of 1914 and subsequent amendments to the Clayton Act made illegal "unfair methods of competition" and "unfair and deceptive acts or practices". About the same time, adoption of the rule of reason approach resulted in the judgment in the *US Steel* case of 1920 that "the law does not make mere size an offence or the exercise of unexerted power an offence – it does not compel competition nor require all that is possible".

This decision can be seen as providing the initial intellectual stimulus that led to the emergence of industrial organization as an important field of study. It showed that economists lacked a coherent set of principles upon which the study of imperfectly competitive markets could be based and so lacked the ability to influence the formulation of antitrust policy.

The first step was to provide a consistent and practical way of determining the structure of a market. The second was to draw clear links from market structure to market conduct and market performance. As we saw above, this led to the development of the SCP paradigm and to something of a reversal of the *US Steel* case, with firm size, no matter how attained, becoming an important consideration.

The 1970s brought an important counter-revolution pioneered by the Chicago School of lawyers and economists.[18] Their work reflected a growing sense that there were important failings in the SCP paradigm. Take, for example, the convincing empirical evidence that firms with large market shares earned higher profits. A "traditional" SCP theorist would take this as implying that market share leads to monopoly power and higher profits. On the other hand, it could be argued that the higher profits came from the firm being more efficient or more talented than its rivals,

---

[18]   For a review of the Chicago School's approach to antitrust policy see Posner (1979).

resulting in the firm gaining increased market share while at the same time providing real benefits to its consumers.

More generally, as we noted above, the SCP paradigm ignored important feedback loops from performance and conduct to market structure and paid little attention to strategic interaction. As Joe Bain (1956) noted, for example, firms in a highly concentrated industry might not be able to exploit their market power if they have to take into account the potential for new firms to break into their market. In other words, we cannot look at firms' conduct independent of analyzing the barriers to entry confronting potential rivals. (Of course, we should also recognize that these barriers to entry might be endogenous, determined by the strategic actions of the incumbent firms.)

More generally, the Chicago School argued that many business practices viewed as harmful could, when considered as part of corporate strategy and tactics, actually improve economic efficiency and benefit consumers. Consider the vertical relationships between a firm and its suppliers or its distributors. A negative view of a vertical contract between two firms is that it introduces the possibility of market foreclosure. A more positive view is that it eliminates the inefficiency of double marginalization. More generally, the Chicago School argued that contracts awarding exclusivity or controlling retail prices actually brought benefits to consumers, for example by encouraging retailers to provide support services that they would not otherwise offer.

Similar arguments weakened regulators' ability to prevent horizontal mergers, in this case using the argument that such mergers offered significant cost savings, or the argument that the exercise of market power by the merged firm would be effectively constrained by potential new entrants.

The contributions of the Chicago School to the formulation and implementation of antitrust policy is significant and has been long-lasting. Their analysis was limited, however, by the fact that it lacked an effective framework by which analysts could model strategic interaction. This takes us back to the language of game theory. From the early 1980s, there was a rapid spread of the application of game theory to almost every aspect of imperfect competition. We are now seeing a post-Chicago School view based on the "new" industrial organization, in which antitrust cases are examined using explicitly game-theoretic tools and analyses.[19] For example, the roots of the merger guidelines adopted by the Federal Trade

---

[19] For analysis of recent advances in antitrust policy see, for example, Choi (2007), Motta (2004), Norman (2008) and Whinston (2006). The *Review of Industrial Organization* publishes an annual review of antitrust policy.

Commission in the United States, and many of the simulation analyses of proposed mergers, can be found in the Cournot–Nash game-theoretic model.

The simplest way to conclude this Introduction to the *Dictionary of Industrial Organization* is to note that we have come full circle. Antitrust policy provided the much-needed early stimulus and econometric analysis for the development of industrial organization. Subsequent theoretical developments in industrial organization and more recent advances in econometric techniques have substantially influenced the modern formulation and application of antitrust policy.

REFERENCES

Akerlof, George A. 1970. "The Market for 'Lemons': Quality Uncertainty and the Market Mechanism", *Quarterly Journal of Economics*, Volume 84, pp. 488–500.

Anderson, Simon, de Palma, Andre, and Thisse, Jacques-François. 1992. *Discrete Choice Theory of Product Differentiation*. MIT Press, Cambridge, MA.

Bain, Joe S. 1956. *Barriers to New Competition: Their Character and Consequences in Manufacturing Industries*. Harvard University Press, Cambridge, MA.

Baumol, William J., Panzar, John C., and Willig, Robert D. 1982. *Contestable Markets and the Theory of Industry Structure*. Harcourt Brace Jovanovich, New York.

Berry, Steven, Levinsohn, James, and Pakes, Ariel. 1995. "Automobile Prices in Market Equilibrium", *Econometrica*, Volume 63, pp. 841–890.

Besanko, David, Dranove, David, Shanley, Mark and Schaefer, Scott. 2013. *The Economics of Strategy*, sixth edition. John Wiley and Sons, Hoboken, NJ.

Blair, Roger, and Lafontaine, Francine. 2005. *The Economics of Franchising*. Cambridge University Press, Cambridge.

Bolton, Patrick, and Dewatripont, Mathias. 2005. *Contract Theory*. MIT Press, Cambridge, MA.

Brickley, James, Zimmerman, Jerold, and Smith, Clifford W., Jr. 2009. *Managerial Economics and Organizational Architecture*, fifth edn. McGraw-Hill, New York.

Bulow, Jeremy I. 1982. "Durable Goods Monopolists", *Journal of Political Economy*, Volume 90, pp. 314–332.

Carlton, Dennis, and Perloff, Jeffrey. 2005. *Modern Industrial Organization*, fourth edition, Pearson Addison Wesley, Boston, MA.

Choi, Jay P. 2007. *Recent Developments in Antitrust: Theory and Evidence*, MIT Press, Cambridge, MA.

Coase, Ronald H. 1937. "The Nature of the Firm", *Economica*, Volume 4, pp. 386–405.

Coase, Ronald H. 1972. "Durability and Monopoly", *Journal of Law and Economics*, Volume 15, pp. 143–149.

Demsetz, Harold. 1982. "Barriers to Entry", *American Economic Review*, Volume 72, pp. 47–57.

Einav, Liran, and Levin, Jonathan. 2010. "Empirical Industrial Organization: A Progress Report", *Journal of Economic Perspectives*, Volume 24, pp. 145–162.

Friedman, James W. 1971. "A Non-Cooperative Equilibrium for Supergames", *Review of Economic Studies*, Volume 38, pp. 1–12.

Gabszewicz, Jaskold, and Thisse, Jacques-François. 1980. "Entry (and Exit) in a Differentiated Industry", *Journal of Economic Theory*, Volume 22, pp. 327–338.

Gilbert, Richard, and Shapiro, Carl. 1990. "Optimal Patent Length and Breadth", *RAND Journal of Economics*, Volume 21, pp. 106–112.

Goldberg, Victor. 1976. "Regulation and Administered Contracts", *RAND Journal of Economics*, Volume 7, pp. 426–448.

Gum, Yiquan, and Wenzel, Tobias. 2009. "A Note on the Excess Entry Theorem in Spatial Models with Elastic Demand", *International Journal of Industrial Organization*, Volume 27, pp. 567–571.

Harstad, Ronald M., and Phlips, Louis. 1994. "Informational Requirements of Predation Detection", Mimeo, Department of Economics, European University Institute, Florence, reproduced in Phlips (1995).

Hart, Oliver. 1995. *Firms, Contracts and Financial Structure*, Clarendon Lectures in Economics, Oxford University Press, Oxford.

Hart, Oliver, and Holmström, Bengt. 1987. "The Theory of Contracts", in Bewley, Truman F. (editor), *Advances in Economic Theory, Fifth World Congress*, Cambridge University Press, Cambridge.

Hart, Oliver, and Moore, John. 1990. "Property Rights and the Nature of the Firm", *Journal of Political Economy*, Volume 98, pp. 1119–1158.

Hotelling, Harold. 1929. "Stability in Competition", *Economic Journal*, Volume 39, pp. 41–57.

Jensen, Michael C., and Meckling, William H. 1976. "The Theory of the Firm: Managerial Behavior, Agency Costs and Ownership Structure", *Journal of Financial Economics*, Volume 3, pp. 305–361.

Judd, Kenneth L. 1985. "Credible Spatial Preemption", *RAND Journal of Economics*, Volume 16, pp. 153–166.

Klein, Benjamin. 1996. "Why Hold-Ups Occur: The Self-Enforcing Range of Contractual Relationships", *Economic Inquiry*, Volume 34, pp. 444–463.

Klein, Benjamin, Crawford, Robert, and Alchian, Armen. 1978. "Vertical Integration, Appropriable Rents and the Competitive Contracting Process", *Journal of Law and Economics*, Volume 21, pp. 297–326.

Klemperer, Paul. 1990. "How Broad Should the Scope of Patent Protection Be?" *RAND Journal of Economics*, Volume 21, pp. 113–130.

Laffont, Jean-Jacques, and Martimort, David. 2002. *The Theory of Incentives: The Principal–Agent Model*, Princeton University Press, Princeton, NJ.

Loury, Glenn. 1979. "Market Structure and Innovation", *Quarterly Journal of Economics*, Volume 93, pp. 395–410.

Mason, Edward S. 1939. "Price and Production Policies of Large Scale Enterprise", *American Economic Review*, Volume 29, pp. 61–74.

Mason, Edward S. 1957. *Economic Concentration and the Monopoly Problem*. Harvard University Press, Cambridge, MA.

Matsumara, Toshihiro, and Okamura, Makoto. 2006. "A Note on the Excess Entry Theorem in Spatial Markets", *International Journal of Industrial Organization*, Volume 24, pp. 1071–1076.

McAfee, R. Preston, and Wiseman, Thomas. 2008. "Capacity Choice Counters the Coase Conjecture", *Review of Economic Studies*, Volume 75, pp. 317–331.

McFadden, Daniel L. 1984. "Econometric Analysis of Qualitative Response Models", in Griliches, Zvi, and Intriligator, Michael D. (editors), *Handbook of Econometrics*, Handbooks in Economics series, Volume II, Book 2, North-Holland, Amsterdam.

Milgrom, Paul, and Roberts, John. 1990. "Bargaining Costs, Influence Costs, and the Organization of Economic Activity", in Alt, James E., and Shepsle, Kenneth A. (editors), *Perspectives on Positive Political Economy*, Cambridge University Press, Cambridge.

Milgrom, Paul, and Roberts, John. 1992. *Economics, Organization and Management*, Prentice-Hall, Englewood Cliffs, NJ.

Motta, Massimo. 2004. *Competition Policy: Theory and Practice*. Cambridge University Press, Cambridge.

Motta, Massimo, and Polo, Michele. 2003. "Leniency Programs and Cartel Prosecution", *International Journal of Industrial Organization*, Volume 21, pp. 347–379.

Mussa, Michael, and Rosen, Sherwin. 1978. "Monopoly and Product Quality", *Journal of Economic Theory*, Volume 18, pp. 301–317.

Norman, George. 2008. *Recent Developments in Monopoly and Competition Policy*, Edward Elgar Publishing, Cheltenham, UK and Northampton, MA, USA.

Pepall, Lynne, Richards, Dan, and Norman, George. 2008. *Industrial Organization: Contemporary Theory and Empirical Applications*, fourth edition, Blackwell Publishing, Oxford.

Pepall, Lynne, Richards, Dan, and Norman, George. 2011, *Contemporary Industrial Organization: A Quantitative Approach*. John Wiley & Sons, Hoboken, NJ.

Phlips, Louis. 1983. *The Economics of Price Discrimination*. Cambridge University Press, Cambridge.

Phlips, Louis. 1995. *Competition Policy: A Game-Theoretic Perspective*, Cambridge University Press, Cambridge.

Phlips, Louis. 1996. "On the Detection of Collusion and Predation", *European Economic Review*, Volume 40, pp. 495–510.

Pigou, Arthur C. 1920. *The Economics of Welfare*. Macmillan & Company, London.

Posner, Richard A. 1979. "The Chicago School of Antitrust Analysis", *University of Pennsylvania Law Review*, Volume 127, pp. 925–948.

Reinganum, Jennifer. 1989. "The Timing of Innovation: Research, Development and Diffusion", in Schmalensee, Richard, and Willing, Robert (editors), *Handbook of Industrial Organization*, Elsevier, Amsterdam.

Salop, Steven C. 1979a. "Strategic Entry Deterrence", *American Economic Review, Papers and Proceedings*, Volume 69, pp. 335–338.

Salop, Steven C. 1979b. "Monopolistic Competition with Outside Goods", *Bell Journal of Economics*, Volume 10, pp. 141–156.

Schmalensee, Richard. 1979a. "Market Structure, Durability and Quality: A Selective Survey", *Economic Inquiry*, Volume 17, pp. 177–196.

Schmalensee, Richard. 1979b. "Entry Deterrence in the Ready-To-Eat Breakfast Cereal Industry", *Bell Journal of Economics*, Volume 9, pp. 305–327.

Schmalensee, Richard 1981. "Output and Welfare Implications of Monopolistic Third-Degree Price Discrimination", *American Economic Review*, Volume 71, pp. 242–247.

Schumpeter, Joseph. 1942. *Capitalism, Socialism and Democracy*, Harper Brothers, New York.

Scotchmer, Suzanne. 2004. *Innovation and Incentives*, MIT Press, Cambridge, MA.

Shaked, Avner, and Sutton, John. 1982. "Relaxing Price Competition Through Product Differentiation", *Review of Economic Studies*, Volume 49, pp. 3–13.

Shaked, Avner, and Sutton, John. 1983. "Natural Oligopolies", *Econometrica*, Volume 51, pp. 1469–1483.

Shapiro, Carl, and Varian, Hal R. 1999. *Information Rules*, Harvard Business School Press, Cambridge, MA.

Smith, Adam. 1776, *An Inquiry into the Nature and Causes of the Wealth of Nations*, Cannan, Edwin, (editor) 1904, reprinted 1976, University of Chicago Press, Chicago, IL.

Tirole, Jean. 1988. *The Theory of Industrial Organization*, MIT Press, Cambridge, MA.

Train, Kenneth E. 2009. *Discrete Choice Methods with Simulation*, second edition, Cambridge University Press, Cambridge.

Vickrey, William S. 1964. *Microstatics*, Harcourt, Brace & World, New York.

Waldman, Don E., and Jensen, Elizabeth J. 2013. *Industrial Organization: Theory and Practice*, fourth edition, Prentice Hall, Upper Saddle River, NJ.

Whinston, Michael D. 2006. *Lectures on Antitrust Economics*, The Cairoli Lectures, MIT Press, Cambridge, MA.

Williamson, Oliver E. 1979. "Transaction-Cost Economics: The Governance of Contractual Relations", *Journal of Law and Economics*, Volume 22, pp. 233–261.

Williamson, Oliver E. 1985. *The Economic Institutions of Capitalism*, Free Press, New York.

FURTHER READING

1. There are numerous textbooks and references on the subject of industrial organization and related topics that can be recommended. Some of these have already been referenced but we feel that it is informative to present the list here.

Asteriou, Dimitrios, and Hall, Stephen G. 2011. *Applied Econometrics*, second edition, Palgrave Macmillan, New York.

Cabral, Luis M. 2000. *Introduction to Industrial Organization*. MIT Press, Cambridge, MA.

Carlton, Dennis, and Perloff, Jeffrey. 2005. *Modern Industrial Organization*, fourth edition, Pearson Addison Wesley, Boston, MA.

Church, Jeffrey, and Ware, Roger. 2000. *Industrial Organization: A Strategic Approach*, McGraw-Hill, New York.

Kennedy, Peter. 2008. *A Guide to Econometrics*, sixth edition, Blackwell Publishing, Malden, MA.

Martin, Stephen. 2002. *Advanced Industrial Economics*, second edition, Blackwell Publishing, Malden, MA.

Mas-Colell, Andreu, Whinston, Michael D., and Green, Jerry R. 1995. *Microeconomic Theory*, Oxford University Press, New York.

Milgrom, Paul, and Roberts, John. 1992. *Economics, Organization and Management*, Prentice-Hall, Englewood Cliffs, NJ.

Norman, George, and La Manna, Manfredi. 1992. *The New Industrial Economics: Recent Developments in Industrial Organization, Oligopoly and Game Theory*, Edward Elgar Publishing, Cheltenham, UK and Northampton, MA, USA.

Pepall, Lynne, Richards, Dan, and Norman, George. 2008. *Industrial Organization: Contemporary Theory and Empirical Applications*, fourth edition. Blackwell Publishing, Oxford.

Pepall, Lynne, Richards, Dan, and Norman, George. 2011. *Contemporary Industrial Organization: A Quantitative Approach*, John Wiley & Sons, Hoboken, NJ.

Scherer, Frederic M., and Ross, David R. 1990. *Industrial Market Structure and Economic Performance*, third edition, Houghton Mifflin, Boston, MA.

Shy, Oz. 1995. *Industrial Organization: Theory and Applications*, MIT Press, Cambridge, MA.

Silberberg, Eugene, and Suen, Wing. 2001. *The Structure of Economics: A Mathematical Analysis*, third edition, McGraw-Hill, New York.

Tirole, Jean. 1988. *The Theory of Industrial Organization*, MIT Press, Cambridge, MA.

Waldman, Don E., and Jensen, Elizabeth J. 2013. *Industrial Organization: Theory and Practice*, fourth edition, Prentice Hall, Upper Saddle River, NJ.

Wooldridge, Jeffrey M. 2013. *Introductory Econometrics: A Modern Approach*, fifth edition, Southwestern Cengage Learning, Mason, OH.

2. In addition, there are several books in the "management" literature that are relevant to the study of industrial organization and that are well worth consulting to gain a more applied approach to many of the dictionary entries.

Besanko, David, Dranove, David, Shanley, Mark, and Schaefer, Scott. 2013. *The Economics of Strategy*, sixth edition, John Wiley & Sons, Hoboken, NJ.

Brickley, James, Smith, Clifford, and Zimmerman, Jerold. 2009. *Managerial Economics and Organizational Architecture*, McGraw-Hill, New York.
Saloner, Garth, Shepard, Andrea, and Podolny, Joel. 2001. *Strategic Management*, John Wiley & Sons, Hoboken, NJ.
Spulber, Daniel. 2009. *Economics of Management and Competitive Strategy*, World Scientific Publishing Company, Hackensack, NJ.

3.   In addition to textbooks, there are several journals that specialize in the field of industrial organization.

International Journal of the Economics of Business
International Journal of Industrial Organization
Journal of Economics and Management Strategy
Journal of Industrial Economics
Journal of Law and Economics
Journal of Law, Economics and Organization
RAND Journal of Economics
Review of Industrial Organization

A

Abatement

The process by which emissions of pollution are reduced.

Absolute Advantage

A firm or country has an absolute advantage in the production of a particular product when it is able to produce more of that product than any other firm or country using the identical inputs. Having an absolute advantage in the production of a good or service does not mean, however, that the firm or country will actually specialize in producing that good or service. Specialization and trade are determined by **comparative advantage**. Suppose that the production possibilities of two countries are as described in the following table:

	Country A		Country B	
	Potatoes	Tomatoes	Potatoes	Tomatoes
Produce only potatoes	10 tons	0 tons	25 tons	0 tons
Produce only tomatoes	0 tons	10 tons	0 tons	75 tons

Country B has an absolute advantage in the production of both goods. On the other hand, the **opportunity cost** of producing potatoes in Country A (1 ton of tomatoes per ton of potatoes) is lower than the opportunity cost of producing potatoes in Country B (3 tons of tomatoes per ton of potatoes) with the result that Country A has a comparative advantage in producing potatoes.

Absolute Cost Advantage

A source of competitive advantage arising from the ability of a firm to produce a good at a lower cost than any of its rivals.

Absolute Performance Evaluation

A performance evaluation system that uses predetermined absolute standards to determine an employee's compensation in an **incentive-based compensation** contract. This is to be contrasted with **relative performance evaluation** in which an employee's compensation is determined by that employee's performance relative to performance of some other individual or group.

Absolute Risk Aversion

A measure of risk aversion that stays constant under any monotonic transformation of the **utility function**. Such a measure of risk aversion is needed since a utility function is defined only up to a linear transformation. See **Arrow–Pratt index**.

Absorptive Capacity

The ability of a firm to evaluate, assimilate and apply new knowledge. One motivation that has been claimed for a firm to undertake research and development is to increase its absorptive capacity.

Accommodated Entry

The decision by incumbent firms in a market to accept the entry of a new firm and adapt their behavior post-entry on the assumption that the new entrant will survive, rather than to adopt strategies that are specifically designed to deter entry or induce the exit of a new entrant. Entry is much more likely to be accommodated, and so firm profitability is likely to be low, in markets where there are few natural or **strategic barriers to entry**. Two extreme cases of markets with accommodated entry are **perfect competition** and **monopolistic competition** where in long-run equilibrium firms earn just **normal profit**.

Accounting Rate of Return

The rate of return on an investment over a defined period – quarter or year – calculated by dividing the net income before interest charges over that period by the accounting value of the assets employed by the investment.

Acquisition

The purchase or **takeover** of one company, the "target", by another company, the "acquirer". Such acquisitions can be friendly takeovers, when the acquisition is supported by the management of the target company, or **hostile takeovers**, when management of the target company recommends that the takeover be rejected.

Address Model

A model of **horizontal product differentiation** in which the type of each consumer's most preferred products and of each firm's product offerings are described by their locations in a **characteristics space**. The term arises from the analogy that can be drawn between characteristics space and geographic space. The address of the consumer (firm) in geographic space is the consumer's (firm's) most preferred product (product offering) in characteristics space. A transport cost in geographic space is a loss of **utility** that a consumer incurs in characteristics space from having to consume other than that consumer's most preferred product. Address models typically belong to two classes. The first, based on the work of Hotelling (1929), investigates the location and price (or quantity) choices of oligopolists (typically duopolists). The second, based on the work of Salop (1979), investigates entry and pricing in a monopolistically competitive market characterized by free entry.

Adjustment Costs

The costs that a firm incurs in changing its resource allocation and output choices from a short-run equilibrium to a long-run equilibrium. Adjustment costs increase with the speed of the desired adjustment and with the difference between the short-run and long-run equilibrium resource allocation and output choices.

Administered Prices

Prices that are under the control of firms or that are set by government through regulatory policy without being subject to the forces of demand and supply. Typical examples are agricultural support prices set under both European and United States agricultural policy, defining guaranteed minimum support prices for specific agricultural products. More generally, **price floors** and **price ceilings** are examples of administered prices, which remain unaltered even if there are changes in supply or demand conditions.

Adulteration

Making a product that is designed for one use unfit for other uses. For example, alcohol that is sold at a low price for external, medicinal uses is usually adulterated to make it unfit for drinking, preventing resale of the medicinal alcohol to the higher-priced alcohol drinking market.

Adverse Selection

A situation in a market in which buyers and sellers have asymmetric information prior to entering into a contract. In insurance markets, those seeking insurance have private information with respect to their true behavior; in banking markets, borrowers are privately informed about their true riskiness; in second-hand markets, sellers are privately informed of the true quality of the item that they are offering for sale; in labor markets, potential employees are privately informed of their true abilities. Such asymmetry in information results in inefficient trades being made, or in some value-creating trades failing to be made. In insurance markets raising the premiums, and in banking markets raising the interest rates on lending, will cause low-risk individuals to exit the market, worsening the risk characteristics of those who continue to purchase insurance or seek loans. In markets, such as for automobiles, that offer both new and previously owned goods, the quality of goods on offer in the previously owned market will be lower than the quality in the new market. See also **lemons problem**.

Advertising

A key element in developing and promoting **brand names**, in which the advertiser pays to communicate a message designed by the advertiser and aimed at a target audience. Advertising can be informative, giving truthful information about features such as price and availability; or persuasive, intended to influence the choices of the target audience by changing their attitudes to the item being advertised. Advertising can also be complementary to consumption if consumers derive greater **utility** from purchasing more widely advertised goods.

Advertising Reach

A measure of the effectiveness of an advertising message, defined as the ratio of the number of actual customers created as a result of an advertising message to the number of potential customers who actually received the advertising message. It is usually argued that larger firms, or firms with greater numbers of outlets, have greater advertising reach than smaller firms or firms with fewer outlets. Suppose, for example, that both McDonald's and Wendy's run a national advertising campaign. Since McDonald's has approximately three times as many outlets as Wendy's, a potential consumer influenced by the advertising campaign to try to find a McDonald's is more likely to do so, and so to convert a potential purchase decision into an actual one, than a potential consumer who tries to find a Wendy's. The information gathering activities of websites such as Google and Facebook increase advertising reach by allowing advertisers to target their messages much more effectively.

Aftermarket

A market that is created after an initial sale (in a foremarket), for example to provide support or repair services for the product sold in the foremarket. A foremarket in cars creates an aftermarket in repairs; a foremarket in computer printers creates an aftermarket in ink cartridges. A firm can increase its profitability if it can create a tie between the foremarket and the aftermarket, for example by designing its printers to take only specific types of printer cartridge or invalidating a product warranty if repairs are provided by other than certified mechanics.

Agency Conflicts

Problems that can arise between a **principal** and an **agent** when the two have objectives that are not perfectly aligned and the actions of the agent cannot be perfectly observed by the principal. One important reason for firms to use **incentive-based compensation** systems is to, at least partially, align the interests of principal and agent, ameliorating their agency conflicts.

Agency Costs

The costs incurred inside an organization arising from slack effort by employees, and the resources employed and other administrative costs incurred by the organization in its attempts to detect or deter such slacking. It is suggested that large, more vertically integrated firms suffer proportionately more from agency costs than small, less integrated firms because of the greater difficulty that large firms have in monitoring their employees and in aligning the interests of the employees with those of the firm. As a result, agency costs provide one reason for there being a limit to the degree of **vertical integration** that firms will adopt.

Agency Efficiency

A measure of the extent to which a firm organizes the exchange of goods in the **vertical chain** of production to minimize **coordination, agency, influence** and other **transaction costs**. Suppose that a **transaction** can be conducted by a firm either by using **market** exchange, having the transaction conducted by an external agent, or by **vertical integration**, bringing the transaction inside the firm. Agency efficiency of using the market is likely to be greater than agency efficiency of vertical integration the lower the **asset specificity** of the assets that are necessary to conduct the transaction. The firm's choice of the degree to which the firm will vertically integrate is determined by the balance the firm strikes between agency efficiency and **technical efficiency**.

Agency Relationship

An agreement in which one individual, the principal, employs another individual, the **agent**, to perform a service on the principal's behalf. This relationship can give rise to a **principal–agent problem** if the principal cannot perfectly monitor the actions of the agent and if the interests of the principal and agent are not perfectly aligned.

Agent

An individual to whom decision-making authority has been delegated by a **principal**.

Agglomerated Equilibrium

An equilibrium in which competing firms choose the same locations in geographic or **characteristics space**. In such an equilibrium, no one firm wishes to leave the agglomeration given that no other firm leaves.

Aggregate Profit

The sum of all firms' profits in a particular market.

Aggregate Welfare

The sum of expected **consumer surplus** and **producer surplus** in a market. The **efficiency** of a particular resource allocation is typically judged in terms of the aggregate welfare that the specific resource allocation generates. It should be noted that an implicit assumption in adopting this standard is that consumer and producer surplus are weighted equally.

Airline Deregulation Act

A United States federal law enacted in 1978 eliminating the Civil Aeronautics Board's regulatory oversight of the airline industry, facilitating a more competitive environment, and leading to lower prices for consumers. This act was part of a pattern of **deregulation** in the 1970s and 1980s in industries including transportation, telecommunications and cable television.

Alienable Property Rights

Private property rights that can be transferred by the owner of the property rights through sale or donation to other individuals.

Allocative Efficiency

An allocation of resources such that it is impossible to make any one individual better off without making at least one other individual worse off. With such an allocation, the **marginal benefit** of each good being produced is equal to its **marginal cost** and each consumer is maximizing their **utility** subject to the relevant budget constraint. It should be noted that there is no necessary connection between allocative efficiency and equity. An allocation of resources might be efficient but very inequitable. For example, allocative efficiency is achieved by a monopolist practicing **perfect price discrimination**, however such a pricing policy extracts all **consumer surplus** and converts it into **profit** for the monopolist.

Almost Common Value Auction

(See **common value auction.**) An auction in which the valuation of the item being auctioned is common across the majority of bidders but higher for a (small) subset of bidders.

Amnesty Program

See **leniency program**.

Amortizing

Spreading the fixed cost of an asset over the useful life of the asset.

Ancillary Restraints

Agreements by parties to a joint venture that restrict their actions in areas not affected by the joint venture and that are unnecessary for the effective operation of the joint venture.

Angel Investor

A wealthy individual interested in the opportunities that are offered by investment in new venture creation. Since such investments are high risk, angel investors require high returns, while accepting that many of their investments will fail.

Antidumping Laws

Laws that are intended to prevent firms from selling their products in overseas markets at prices that are lower than the prices these firms set in their domestic markets. These laws are designed to protect firms in the overseas markets from aggressive price-undercutting by outside firms.

Antitrust Authorities

See **Department of Justice** and **Federal Trade Commission**.

Antitrust Laws

Laws that are intended to control the behavior of firms. They make particular actions that are judged to be harmful to consumers illegal, such as the formation of cartels; the abuse of a dominant market position; rigging of bids in **auctions**; market-sharing agreements; **predatory pricing**; and **tying arrangements**. These laws were first formulated in the United States, in response to what was seen as the abuse of market power that characterized the behavior of large firms, or trusts, that emerged in the United States in the late 1800s and early 1900s. See **Sherman Act** and **Clayton Act**.

Applications Barrier to Entry

In computer operating systems a barrier to entry confronted by a new operating system from the property that the majority of applications – word processing, spreadsheet, presentation packages – are written to run on the established operating system. For example, the dominance of the Windows® operating system creates an applications barrier to entry for software companies trying to create programs that will run on Windows® computers.

Applied Research

Research that is aimed at practical and specific usage and that has potentially direct commercial applicability.

Appropriability

The ability of an owner of intellectual property such as proprietary technology to maintain control of the intellectual property without seeing it being lost to competitors through imitation. Appropriability is higher when the intellectual property is difficult to reverse engineer, such as the "secret" formula that Coca-Cola has for its syrup, or where the intellectual property is protected by a **patent** or **copyright** during the life of the patent or copyright.

Arbitrage

The act of exploiting price differentials across markets, buying in a market where price is low and selling in a market where price is high. A seller's ability to prevent arbitrage is necessary for **price discrimination** to be feasible across markets. In financial markets arbitrage opportunities emerge because financial markets are not perfectly connected. As a result, a share of stock may sell for a different price on one exchange than on another. Arbitrage traders buy in the market where the price is low and simultaneously sell in the market where the price is high, thereby earning an almost risk-free profit, but also rapidly eliminating the price differential.

Arbitration

A method of settling a dispute between individuals in which a third party is engaged to provide an external judgment on the conflict. The parties need not agree to be bound by the arbitrator's decision.

Arc Elasticity

A measure of **elasticity** between two points. Suppose that one point is (X_1, Y_1) and the second is (X_2, Y_2). Then the arc elasticity of X with respect to Y between these two points is defined to be the percentage change in X divided by the percentage change in Y or, in absolute terms:

$$\mu_{X,Y} = \left| \frac{X_1 - X_2}{X_1 + X_2} \cdot \frac{Y_1 + Y_2}{Y_1 - Y_2} \right|.$$

Suppose that X and Y are related by a functional relationship $X = f(Y)$. Let $\underline{X}$ be the average of X_1 and X_2 and $\underline{Y}$ be the average of Y_1 and Y_2. Then the arc elasticity between these two points is approximately equal to the **point elasticity**:

$$\frac{dX}{dY} \cdot \frac{Y}{X}\bigg|_{X=\underline{X}; Y=\underline{Y}}.$$

Areeda–Turner Test

A test that has been applied in antitrust cases, which claims that a price below short-run marginal cost should be held to be predatory and unlawful and that short-run marginal cost can be approximated by average variable cost. This approximation is more accurate when **returns to scale** are roughly constant.

Arm's-Length Market Transaction

A market transaction in which independent parties exchange goods or services on agreed terms but with no formal agreement that their relationship will continue in the future. This type of transaction is appropriate when the good or service being exchanged is a **search good** of known and observable quality. It is less appropriate when one or other party to the transaction must make a **relationship-specific investment** to support the transaction, or if the good or service is an **experience good** whose true quality is not observable prior to the exchange.

Arrow–Pratt Index

An index of **absolute risk aversion**. If the **utility function** is U then the Arrow–Pratt index is defined as $-U''/U'$. This measure of risk aversion is unaffected by any monotonic transformation of the utility function. See also **coefficient of absolute risk aversion**.

Ascending Bid Auction

An auction in which price starts low and then is progressively bid higher. The winner of such an auction is the bidder who offers the highest price.

Ask Price

In financial markets, the price at which the seller claims they are willing to sell the financial asset.

Asset Specificity

A situation in which an asset is more valuable in its intended use than in its next-best use. For physical assets this might arise if the asset is designed for a specific purpose or client, or is located geographically to serve a particular client, or is dedicated to serve the needs of a particular client. When these conditions arise, the value of the asset is much higher in its intended use than in its next-best use. For human capital it results from an individual's investment in acquiring or developing specialized knowledge or skills that are imperfectly transferable from their intended use to their next-best use. When assets are specific in any of these ways, this creates **quasi-rents**. As a result, asset specificity and **incomplete contracts** can lead to there being a **hold-up problem** for those who are required to invest in the specific asset in order to support the intended use.

Assignment Problem

A situation in which efficient allocation of resources requires that only one individual or group performs each of a set of tasks that have to be completed. The challenge is to ensure that all the tasks are completed without duplication of effort and that no other allocation of the tasks to the individuals or groups can be found that gives greater output for the same cost, or lower cost for the same output.

Asymmetric Information

A situation in which the parties to a **transaction** have different information with respect to the true worth or quality of the item being traded. In second-hand markets the seller typically is better informed than the buyer regarding the true quality of the item being offered for sale. In labor markets the potential employee is better informed of their true nature and worth than the potential employer. In other markets, for example real estate, the buyer may well be better informed than the seller regarding the true value of the item being offered for sale. In **principal–agent** relationships, asymmetric information arises when the principal cannot perfectly observe the actions or the effort of the agent. Asymmetric information gives rise to **adverse selection** pre-contract and to **moral hazard** post-contract.

Asymmetry Index

A measure of the disparity in firm sizes in a market. If the market contains n firms and the market share of firm i is s_i the asymmetry index is the population variance of market shares,

$$AI = \sum_{i=1}^{n} \left(s_i - \frac{\sum_{i=1}^{n} s_i}{n} \right)^2 \bigg/ n, \text{ where } \sum_{i=1}^{n} s_i = 1.$$

The greater is the asymmetry index, the more likely it is that the market is dominated by a small number of large firms.

Asymmetry Requirement

A condition for there to be **barriers to entry**, stating that incumbents have incurred **sunk costs** of entry that new entrants have not. This places the new entrants at a potential disadvantage relative to the incumbents.

Auction

The process by which the sale or purchase of an item or service is determined through bidding. In the case of an auction to sell a good or service, bids are sought from potential buyers. In the case of an auction for the purchase of a good or service, bids are sought from potential sellers See also **reverse auctions**, **sealed-bid auctions** and **Dutch auctions**.

Authority Relationship

A relationship in which a supervisor has the right to direct the actions of a subordinate, within legal bounds, and to monitor, reward or punish the subordinate, again within legal bounds.

Autocorrelation

See **serial correlation**.

Average Avoidable Cost

Suppose that a firm can avoid or escape a total cost TCA by exiting a market in which it is currently producing a total output X. Then average avoidable cost is $AAC = TCA/X$. A firm will choose not to exit so long as price exceeds average avoidable cost. By contrast, if price is less than average avoidable cost then the firm should exit the market. See also **shutdown price**.

Average Cost Pricing

A price-setting rule according to which a firm charges a price equivalent to **average total cost**. Average cost pricing is of particular importance in the context of regulating a natural monopoly. If the regulation restricts entry, in the absence of additional price regulation, the protected monopolist will charge a price that exceeds **marginal cost**, and will limit the quantity offered for sale. Average cost pricing regulation requires the monopolist to satisfy market demand at a price equivalent to **average total cost**, generally resulting in a lower price and higher quantity sold, thereby improving **social welfare**. See Demsetz (1968) for discussion of **franchise bidding** as an alternative to average cost pricing regulation.

Average Fixed Cost

Fixed cost divided by output. Average fixed cost always decreases as output increases; this can be a major source of **economies of scale**.

Average Incremental Cost

Suppose that it costs a firm a total of TCI to produce added or incremental output of X, including any additional **sunk costs** that the firm needs to incur. Then average incremental cost is $AIC = TCI/X$. Since average incremental cost may include sunk costs, while **average avoidable cost** does not, it must always be the case that average avoidable cost is no greater than average incremental cost.

Average Product

Total output produced by an input divided by the total quantity of the input employed.

Average Revenue

Total revenue from the sale of a given quantity divided by that quantity. If a firm employs a simple linear pricing policy in which it quotes a price per unit and allows consumers to determine how many units to purchase, then average revenue equals price. By contrast, if the firm employs **nonlinear pricing**, as would be the case for example with **second-degree price discrimination**, average revenue need not equal price. Suppose, for example, that the firm charges a **two-part tariff** with a fixed charge F and a price per unit of P. Then average price for a quantity Q is $P + F/Q$.

Average Total Cost

The **total cost** of producing a given quantity divided by that quantity.

Average Variable Cost

The cost that a firm can vary, in producing a given total quantity, divided by that quantity. **Variable costs** are incurred as a result of the firm employing factors of production that vary when the firm changes its output: labor, raw materials, intermediate goods and energy costs are typical factors that generate variable costs.

Averch–Johnson Effect

The incentive for a firm to overinvest in capital under **rate-of-return regulation**, in which regulators use the firm's capital level to determine profit limits, and thus price limits, for the firm. Such rate setting leads regulated firms to overutilize capital at the expense of efficiency in production. See Averch and Johnson (1962).

B

Backloaded Compensation

A compensation scheme in which the wage is set below productivity early in the employee–employer relationship but exceeds productivity with seniority. The intent of such schemes is to retain skilled employees by the promise that they will earn higher future returns on the employees' initial investment in the firm. Such compensation schemes confront employers with a **moral hazard** problem in the event of an economic downturn in that an employer may be tempted to lay off its more senior, but more expensive staff.

Backward Induction

The process of solving a sequential game by starting at the end of the game and working backwards to the beginning of the game. When the game is described in **extensive form**, the solution is found by starting at the final branches and working back to the root of the game tree, eliminating dominated branches of the tree. This solution method for sequential games rests on the property that the resulting equilibrium must be **subgame perfect**.

Backward Integration

The decision by a downstream buying firm to produce some of its own inputs either by establishing a greenfield upstream operation or by merging with or buying some of its upstream suppliers. A firm may adopt backward integration as a means of creating a **barrier to entry**, or as a means of improving its bargaining position with respect to other upstream suppliers of the same product or service. Backward integration can also be adopted when the relationship between buyer and supplier requires that the supplier undertake a **relationship-specific investment**, with the associated fear by the supplier of **hold-up** by the buyer. Integration internalizes the investment, ensuring that it will be undertaken by eliminating the risk of hold-up.

Bain's Hypothesis

The hypothesis that the observed positive correlation between industry concentration and industry profitability was driven by there being a positive relationship between industry concentration and (tacit) collusion. See also **Bain Index** and **cross-industry studies**.

Bain Index

A profitability measure proposed by Bain (1941) designed to reflect monopoly power. The index measures the difference between revenues and explicit input and labor costs, depreciation and foregone interest on the invested capital.

Bandwagon Effect

The observation that an action by one economic agent may trigger similar actions by other economic agents. For example, the decision by one firm to integrate vertically or to merge with a competitor may induce other firms to follow suit; the decision by one group of consumers to adopt a new product or by firms to introduce a new product may induce others to follow suit, leading to a fad. The reason for individuals basing their decisions on this effect is that, when information is imperfect, doing and believing what others do and believe can appear to be rational. As a result, fads can form easily but they also dissipate just as easily as individuals move on to the next fad.

Bankruptcy

The legal provisions that become operative when an individual or firm is unable to pay its creditors.

Bargaining

Direct negotiation between a buyer and seller in which the parties to the negotiation seek to reach agreement on price and other dimensions of the transaction, such as quality, product performance and delivery. The great majority of business-to-business transactions are based on bargaining rather than on a buyer accepting a price posted by a seller.

Bargaining Costs

The **transaction costs** that are incurred during bargaining between individuals. Typical bargaining costs are the time and resources spent while bargaining, the resources expended in an attempt to improve an individual's bargaining position, and any losses that arise as a result of the failure to reach a value-creating agreement or of the delay in reaching such an agreement.

Bargaining Failure

A situation in which **asymmetric information** results in parties to a **bargaining game** failing to reach an agreement even when a mutually beneficial bargain is feasible. The asymmetric information can lead to the seller and buyer misrepresenting their true **reservation prices** to such an extent that they fail to agree on mutually acceptable terms of trade.

Bargaining Game

A **game** in which the players attempt to reach an agreement on how to distribute some aggregate payoff through the offers and counteroffers they make to each other. Typically in such games the players prefer to reach an agreement than not. On the other hand, each player obviously prefers to reach an outcome that is in their favor. The result is that in some cases no successful bargain is reached.

Bargaining Power

The negotiating strength that can be exercised by a player in a **bargaining game**.

Barriers to Entry

Obstacles that firms must overcome in order to enter a market. Entry barriers can be structural, relating to the nature of the market; regulatory, where there are government-imposed controls preventing entry; or strategic, resulting from explicit actions of incumbent firms that are designed specifically to deter entry. The distinguishing feature of strategic barriers to entry is that they are actions that would not be taken if there were no threat of entry. Typical entry barriers are sunk and/or set-up costs of entry; **economies of scale** that are large relative to market size, creating a **natural monopoly**; established reputations of the incumbent firms; patents and copyrights held by incumbent firms; government regulation creating local monopolies in the provision of public utilities such as gas, electricity and water; inability of new entrants to access strategic resources; and the (implicit) threat of **predatory pricing** by incumbents in the event of entry. The existence or creation of barriers to entry allows incumbent firms to earn and to sustain above-**normal profits**.

Barriers to Exit

Costs that a firm must incur in exiting a market. These are typically related to **sunk costs**. High exit barriers can be thought of as **barriers to entry**, in that they increase the implicit costs of entry, but they also imply that there are barriers to exit as a result of there being a reluctance to exit once the entry commitment has been made and the sunk costs have been incurred.

Base Pay

Non-**incentive-based compensation** received by mid-level executives. Base pay is generally determined by the size and breadth of an executive's responsibilities or by the number of people reporting to the executive and so can lead to **empire building** by the executive.

Basic Research

Research whose primary intent is to create new knowledge or develop new theoretical insights, without necessarily having immediate commercial or practical applications.

Basing-Point Pricing

A pricing system in which producers determine the final price that they quote to buyers by setting a mill or factory price at an agreed location, referred to as the basing point, and charging transport costs from that basing point to the buyer's location, even though the seller is not located at the basing point. A well-known basing-point system was the "Pittsburgh plus" system used in pricing US steel, where steel was priced at the mill price plus transport costs from Pittsburgh to the buyer, no matter where the steel was actually produced. The antitrust authorities in the United States have judged this type of pricing to be in violation of **antitrust laws**, primarily because it was felt that such pricing systems facilitated **collusion** by making prices observable and easy to monitor. See also **phantom freight**.

Batch Size

The number of units of one product variant that a manufacturing manager chooses to make before switching to another variant that can be made on the same production line. The increasing use of **flexible manufacturing** systems has allowed firms to reduce batch size significantly without the sacrifice of **economies of scale** or **scope**.

Battle of the Sexes Game

A two-player **coordination game** characterized by the following **payoff matrix**, where in each cell, the **payoff** to the row player is listed first, and the payoff to the column player is listed second:

		George	
		Opera	Ball game
Margaret	Opera	10, 7	6, 5
	Ball game	5, 4	8, 12

The players agree that they would prefer to do the same thing, but do not agree on what that thing should be because they have different relative valuations of the strategies they can choose (in this case, all else being equal, Margaret prefers the opera to the ball game while George prefers the ball game to the opera). There are two **Nash equilibria** in **pure strategies** to this game: (Opera, Opera) and (Ball game, Ball game). There is also an equilibrium in **mixed strategies**. The problem with the mixed-strategy equilibrium, of course, is that it assigns a non-zero probability to an outcome where George and Margaret do different things. See also **coordination game, stag hunt game**.

Bayesian Game

A game in which a player's information regarding the true type of the other players is incomplete. Players have prior beliefs about the other players' types, typically represented by a probability distribution over possible types, and can update their beliefs during the course of the game. Harsanyi proposed treating Nature as another player in the game, where Nature assigns a **random variable** describing the type of each player, with the associated probability distribution for each player being the prior beliefs with respect to types. This converts a game of **incomplete information** to a game of **imperfect information**. These games are termed Bayesian because, as the game progresses, the prior beliefs with respect to players' types are updated using **Bayes's rule**. See Harsanyi (1967, 1968a, 1968b).

Bayes's Rule

A rule that allows us to calculate the posterior probability of a hypothesis A given that we have observed an event B, given that we know the prior probability of A, the prior probability of B and the conditional probability of B given A. If A and B have discrete probability distributions then Bayes's rule states that the conditional probability of A given that we have observed B is

$$P(A|B) = \frac{P(B|A)\,P(A)}{P(B)}$$

where $P(A)$ is the prior probability of A (before observing B); $P(B|A)$ is the conditional probability of B given A; and $P(B)$ is the prior probability of B. Suppose, for example, that a market contains 50 firms, half of which are low-cost and half of which are high-cost. All low-cost firms are believed to set low prices, while high-cost firms are believed to be as likely to set high as low prices. If we observe a firm setting a low price, what is the probability that it is a high-cost firm? In this example, A is that the firm is high-cost, B is that the firm sets a low price. $P(A)$ is the probability that the firm is high-cost no matter what other information is available. This is 0.5 in our example. $P(B)$ is the probability that a firm will set a low price no matter its type. This is 0.75 (all the low-cost firms and half of the high-cost firms). $P(B|A)$ is the probability that a high-cost firm will set a low price, which is 0.5. So the probability that a firm setting a low price is a high-cost firm is:

$$P(A|B) = \frac{P(B|A)P(A)}{P(B)} = \frac{0.5 \times 0.5}{0.75} = 0.333.$$

Becker Model of Regulation

A model of political influence by special-interest groups, proposed by Becker (1983), in which groups expend resources exerting pressure on policy makers to adopt their preferred regulations. Incentives to invest in lobbying depend on the magnitude of harm done, or potential gain, from regulation to each group. The model demonstrates that special-interest groups overinvest in political pressure; all groups could reduce their lobbying efforts while maintaining the current relative pressure and result. This outcome, however, is not sustainable, given the private incentives of each group.

Behavioral Remedies

Constraints imposed by antitrust authorities on firms that are proposing to merge, placing constraints on their property rights and the ways in which those property rights can be employed, with the goal of limiting anticompetitive behavior post-merger. The behavioral remedies must be accepted by the firms if the merger is to be approved by the authorities.

Benchmarking

Identifying the best practices of firms operating in similar market environments. Benchmarking allows firms to develop procedures on how to adopt best practices.

Benefit Advantage

A strategy to achieve a competitive advantage by offering consumers products that give them greater **perceived benefit** while maintaining costs that are comparable to or not significantly greater than those of competitors. A firm that has a benefit advantage can charge a price premium while offering consumers greater **consumer surplus** than its rivals.

Benefit Drivers

The attributes of a product that consumers value or that reduce user and **transaction costs** of the product, increasing its **perceived benefit**. Benefit drivers form the basis on which a firm can differentiate itself from its competitors.

Bertrand Competition

A one-shot, non-cooperative game in which firms compete by setting prices. See **Bertrand equilibrium**.

Bertrand Equilibrium

Consider a market containing n non-cooperative firms playing a one-shot game in which they simultaneously choose the prices they each will set for their products. Define $\mathbf{p} = (p_1, p_2, \ldots, p_i, \ldots p_n)$ and $\mathbf{p}_{-i} = (p_1, \ldots, p_{i-1}, p_{i+1}, \ldots p_n)$ where p_i is the price set by firm i. Denote profit to firm i at the set of prices $\mathbf{p}$ $(i = 1, \ldots, n)$ as $\pi_i(\mathbf{p})$. The Bertrand equilibrium to this game is the set of prices $\mathbf{p}^* = (p_1^*, \ldots, p_i^*, \ldots, p_n^*)$ such that $\pi_i(\mathbf{p}^*) \geq \pi_i(p_i, \mathbf{p}_{-i}^*)$ for all $p_i \geq 0$ and all $i = 1, \ldots n$. This is also referred to as the **Bertrand–Nash equilibrium**. In the case of identical goods and constant marginal costs, the Bertrand equilibrium degenerates to the competitive outcome of marginal-cost pricing, even in the case of small n, resulting in the **Bertrand paradox**.

Bertrand Game

A one-shot, non–cooperative oligopoly game in which firms compete by setting prices simultaneously, leaving the market to determine the quantities that will be bought at the chosen prices. See **Bertrand equilibrium**.

Bertrand–Nash Equilibrium

See **Bertrand equilibrium**.

Bertrand Paradox

Suppose that there are two or more firms producing a homogeneous good with constant returns to scale and identical costs. Then the **Bertrand equilibrium** for this game has the firms price the product at marginal cost, leading to the apparent paradox that the firms are making no more than **normal profit** even though the market contains few firms and so is not **perfectly competitive**. This marginal-cost pricing is in conflict with the expectation that firms in an **oligopoly** setting would exercise at least some degree of market power, leading instead to a mark-up of price over cost.

Best Response Function

A function that maximizes the payoff to a player for any choice of action by its rivals. Suppose that the payoff to player i given that it is playing a_i and its rivals are playing $\mathbf{a}_{-i}$ is $\pi_i(a_i, \mathbf{a}_{-i})$. Then player i's best response to $\mathbf{a}_{-i}$ is defined as $a_i^* = \arg\max_{a_i}(\pi_i(a_i, \mathbf{a}_{-i}))$. This is sometimes referred to as the firm's **reaction function**. The best response function provides insight into how a firm will behave in response to changes in its rivals' strategic choices, and thus serves as a basis for formal comparative statics analysis. Deriving the best response function is an important intermediate step in determining the **Nash equilibrium**, in which all players must be on their best response functions.

Beta Coefficient

A measure of the volatility of a financial asset relative to the **market portfolio**. The beta coefficient is given by

$$\beta_a = \frac{Cov(r_a, r_m)}{Var(r_m)}$$

where r_a is the return of the financial asset, r_m is the return of the market portfolio and $Cov(r_a, r_m)$ is the covariance between the two rates of return. The beta coefficient is an important parameter in the **capital asset pricing model**.

Bidding Game

A game in which potential buyers submit bids to a seller. The bids may be made simultaneously or sequentially. See **auction**.

Bid Price

In financial markets, the price at which the buyer claims they are willing to buy the financial asset.

Bid Rigging

A typically secret and illegal agreement among bidders in an **auction** to cooperate on the bids that they will submit in the auction to ensure that a designated party to the bid rigging agreement will win the auction. This form of **collusion** can be difficult to execute as it requires coordination and agreement on the best bidding price and on how colluding bidders will be compensated for their participation. The arrangement also creates an incentive for each bidder to cheat and choose a price just below the agreed price for winning the auction, as in the **prisoners' dilemma game**.

Bilateral Contracting Principle

If two parties to a contract can contract in isolation, have perfect information about the payoffs to both parties and can make lump-sum transfers between themselves, then the agreement that they reach will maximize their joint payoffs.

Block Pricing

A form of pricing in which the seller **bundles** the quantity offered for sale and charges a lump sum for the bundle, for example offering to sell Q_1 units for a total charge of T_1 dollars. The average price is $AP_1 = Q_1/T_1$ but no such unit price is quoted to the buyer. Block pricing is a method for implementing **second-degree price discrimination** and helps sellers to increase their profits, as compared to **linear pricing**, by converting **consumer surplus** into **revenues**. Such pricing behavior can be used as evidence of monopoly power in the enforcement of **antitrust laws**.

Blockaded Entry

A situation in which entry to a market is not possible even if the incumbent firms are charging the monopoly price and take no strategic actions designed to deter entry. Entry can be blockaded if **economies of scale** or **scope** are large relative to market size or if a potential entrant cannot access essential resources because these are already controlled by the incumbents. See also **barriers to entry**.

Bond

A debt instrument issued by firms and government agencies in order to finance their activities by borrowing. A bond is defined by its face value – the amount that has to be paid by the bond issuer on maturity of the bond; the maturity date – the date on which the face value has to be paid; and the coupon – the interest rate that the issuer pays to bond holders, defined as a percentage related to the face value. The price at which a bond actually sells is determined by the **bond rating**, the years to maturity and the relationship between the coupon and the market interest rate.

Bond Covenants

Restrictions imposed by **bond** holders on the operations of the organization whose bonds they hold, such as the investment projects that the organization can undertake or the methods of financing the organization can adopt. Bond covenants are designed to ensure financial soundness of the organization.

Bond Market

A market in which bonds are bought and sold. In this market, the bond's price reflects the **present value** of the face value of the bond, due at the maturity date, plus the periodic payments received based on the coupon, or effective interest rate, on the bond. Bond prices and market interest rates are inversely related; as the expected rate of return on alternative investments rises with market interest rates, bonds must be sold at lower prices to attract investors. See also **bonds**.

Bond Rating

The assessment of the creditworthiness of the debt instruments issued by a corporation. This rating is a financial indicator of the security offered by the corporation's bonds and typically affects the terms on which the corporation can raise new debt: the lower the bond rating the lower the price at which the corporation's bonds can be sold when first issued.

Bootlegging

The sale of a product by a retailer in one market to retailers in other markets. Bootlegging can undermine a supplier's attempts to **price discriminate** across retailers in different markets.

Bootstrapping

The use by a firm of creative and ingenious methods to obtain resources other than by borrowing or otherwise raising money from traditional sources of capital.

Bootstrap Equilibrium

An equilibrium in which a monopolist credibly commits to producing a product of high quality as a result of the reputational damage that the monopolist will suffer if they renege on this commitment. In a multi-period setting, the longer the period, the stronger the incentive for the monopolist to deviate from choosing high quality, and so the higher the expected rents from high quality must be in order to maintain a bootstrap equilibrium.

Boundary Setting

An organizational arrangement in which managers give subordinates decision-making authority within specified limits.

Bounded Rationality

The limits that rational agents face in processing – acquiring, storing, ordering and transmitting – information. These limits imply that a rational agent has a limited ability to deal with complexity in transactions and to process information, with the result that the agent cannot write complete contracts governing those transactions. The assumption of bounded rationality helps to reconcile deviations between predicted consumer choice based on models of **utility** maximization, and observed market behavior. Bounded rationality also offers an explanation for why contracts are inevitably incomplete.

Brand Extension

A strategy by a firm to extend and exploit brand value and image built in one market to other markets that the firm aims to enter.

Brand Loyalty

A situation in which consumers have a high regard for a firm's product or service, which is exhibited by their committing to repeat purchase the product or service and to advocate the product or service to others. Brand loyalty to an incumbent firm's product can constitute a **barrier to entry** to potential competitors.

Brand Management

The strategic management of the full range of brands that the firm controls.

Brand Name

The identification of a product with a specific name intended to associate the product with particular characteristics that are valued by consumers. This forms part of a firm's **intangible asset** of reputational capital.

Brand Umbrella

See **umbrella branding**.

Break-Even Point

The output at which total revenue just equals total cost. When costs include both explicit monetary costs and implicit **opportunity costs**, including the value of the next-best alternative use of the firm's **capital assets**, then a firm operating at the break-even point is earning zero **economic profit** or **normal profit**. Such a firm has no incentive to exit the current market or enter a new market, since it is doing just as well in the present industry as in the next-best market alternative.

Brick and Click Firm

A firm that sells through real outlets – for example, retail outlets (the "brick" part) – and through virtual or online trading (the "click" part).

Brittleness

A measure of how badly a system's performance will deteriorate when some of the information needed to operate and control the system is missing or inaccurate. For example, suppose that a system can be controlled by the system's operator setting prices or quantities and that marginal benefit and marginal cost of the system are approximately linear. Then the relative brittleness of price and quantity control is given by

$$\frac{\text{loss from price control}}{\text{loss from quantity control}} = \left[\frac{\text{slope of marginal benefit}}{\text{slope of marginal cost}}\right]^2.$$

In such a system, if marginal benefit is steeper (flatter) than marginal cost, then quantity control (price control) is less brittle than price control (quantity control).

Broad Coverage Strategy

A strategy that aims to supply all of the segments in a market by offering a broad range of products, with each product variant being targeted at a specific market segment. Such a strategy can create **barriers to entry** by leaving no market niches for potential entrants. This strategy is related to the more general choice of the extent of **product differentiation** within a market and the degree to which product characteristics overlap in a market.

Broad Task Assignment

An organizational structure in which employees are given responsibility for a relatively large set of tasks.

Budget Constraint

The constraint that a consumer faces because they have a finite income and have to pay non-zero prices for the goods they consume. If the consumer's income is Y, the price of good i is P_i and there are n goods available for purchase, then the budget constraint is

$$Y \geq \sum_{i=1}^{n} P_i Q_i$$

where Q_i is consumption of good i. The basic optimization model in consumer choice theory assumes that a consumer with **utility function** $U(Q_1, \ldots, Q_n)$ chooses $Q_1, Q_2, \ldots Q_n$ to maximize their **utility** subject to their budget constraint.

Bunching

When applied to innovation, the almost simultaneous adoption of a new technology by all firms.

Bundling

A strategy by which a firm selling two or more products offers the products for sale as a package, with the proportions of each product in the package being fixed: for example, a computer with its associated operating system or a set menu in a restaurant consisting of a fixed number of courses. In the context of **antitrust laws**, such a strategy can be deemed a monopolizing practice. In *US v. Microsoft*, the **Department of Justice** alleged that Microsoft engaged in such monopolizing behavior by, in effect, tying the Internet Explorer browser to the Windows® operating system, thereby severely limiting competition in the Internet browser market. See also **tie-in sale**.

Business Environment

The environment within which a business operates, defined by the technology, market structure and regulations that the firm faces.

Business Model

A company's plan for how it will compete, apply its resources, structure its relationships with buyers and suppliers, and create and capture value in order to generate long-term profit.

Business Norms

Expectations in market transactions that are not enforceable by law but that nevertheless determine expected business behavior.

Business Plan

A formal written statement describing all of the aspects of a business venture, usually written to attract investors, state the company's mission and communicate the company's culture to current and potential employees.

Bust-Up

A form of takeover in which the buyer of a company splits up and resells its operating divisions or other assets to other buyers.

Buyer Power

The power that an industry's buyers have to negotiate contract conditions that extract surplus from sellers. Buyer power is one of Michael Porter's **five forces**. The degree of buyer power increases with the number of outside options that are available to buyers, the ease with which buyers can switch to alternative sellers, and decreases with the number of buyers. Increased buyer power diminishes the incentives for firms to operate in the industry due to the adverse impact that buyer power has on the potential profitability of the seller.

C

Capabilities

Activities that a firm does particularly well by comparison to rival firms. Capabilities typically derive from and are embodied in the **resources** that the firm controls. They are usually valuable across multiple products that the firm offers, are embodied in organizational routines and are tacit. A firm's capabilities are the source of its **competitive advantage**. That they are tacit is important in that this makes them difficult to copy by rivals.

Capacity

The level of output at which a firm's average cost begins to rise as output is increased, normally because some of the firm's factors of production, typically capital or land, are in fixed supply.

Capacity Accumulation Game

A game in which non-cooperative firms compete by accumulating **capacity**. If this game is played between an incumbent and a potential entrant then the incumbent can be expected to overinvest in capacity in order to induce the entrant to restrict its choice of capacity and, in the extreme, choose not to enter the market, in which case capacity accumulation becomes a strategic **barrier to entry**.

Capacity Constraint

A constraint that a firm faces when it does not have enough installed capacity, for example capital equipment, to meet the demand for its products at its chosen prices. When a capacity constraint is binding, the firm has to decide which market segments it will supply and how these market segments will be rationed. When demand varies in a roughly predictable manner, either during the day or over some longer period, firms can adopt **peak-load pricing** strategies in order to avoid reaching their capacity constraints, as in the case of electricity provision.

Capacity Expansion

A strategy for deterring entry in which the incumbent firm expands its **capacity** in advance of the anticipated growth of the market and signals that it has done so to actual and potential rivals.

Capacity Utilization

A measure that compares a firm's observed output to its potential output, where the latter is based on the production level that the existing capacity could maximally support.

Capital Asset

An asset that is expected to last for many periods and to provide valuable services over its life. Capital assets can be tangible, such as machinery and buildings; or intangible, such as brand image and reputation. Tangible capital assets tend to depreciate with time and use. See also **physical capital**.

Capital Asset Pricing Model

A model for pricing a financial asset or portfolio of financial assets. Formally the expected return on a capital asset a is given by the equation $E(R_a) = R_f + \beta_a(E(R_m) - R_f)$ where R_f is the risk-free rate of return, β_a is the **beta coefficient** for the asset a, and $E(R_m)$ is the expected return on the **market portfolio**. The capital asset pricing model identifies the asset-appropriate discount rate at which the future cash flows that the asset is expected to generate should be discounted in order to determine whether the asset should be added to the portfolio.

Capital Cost

The cost that a firm would incur if all of its **capital assets** were rented at market rental rates.

Capital Cost Requirement

The required investment for a new firm to enter an industry. High capital costs can constitute **barriers to entry**.

Capital Intensity

A measure of the extent to which an activity uses capital in order to produce goods or services. Capital-intensive industries typically employ a large proportion of capital relative to other inputs such as labor. The degree of capital intensity can be measured as the ratio of the total amount of capital (in monetary terms) relative to the total value of output. Valuing durable capital goods, however, is not entirely straightforward, as they can be valued at **replacement cost**, initial value or some combination; in addition, one must determine how to account for **depreciation** of the capital goods.

Capital–Output Ratio

The ratio of the value of a firm's **capital stock** to the value of its output.

Capital Rationing

An imperfection in capital markets that results in a borrower facing constraints on the amount of capital that it can borrow even when it has profitable uses for the borrowed capital.

Capital Stock

The total value of a firm's **capital assets**.

CAPM

See **capital asset pricing model**.

Capture Theory

A theory that suggests that firms in an industry can "capture" regulatory agencies by lobbying, bribes or other means, in order to ensure that the regulators act in the interests of the industry.

Cartel

A group of firms that have entered into an agreement to coordinate their actions in order to increase their joint profits. The agreement can take many forms such as agreement on prices, market sharing, or bids to be submitted in **auctions**. Cartels are prohibited under **antitrust laws** in most countries, with the result that cartel agreements cannot be enforced by legal means. Rather they must be sustained either by self-interest or by regular meetings of the cartel members to review performance and negotiate prices and market shares; see also **collusion**.

Cartel Instability

The argument that **cartels** are inherently unstable and so can be left to collapse of their own accord without the need for regulatory interference. This is most easily illustrated by the following **payoff matrix**, where in each cell, the **payoff** to the row player is listed first, and the payoff to the column player is listed second. The **Nash equilibrium** is (Defect, Defect) and Defect is a **dominant strategy** for both firms. If this game is played once, a cartel agreement by which the two firms promise to play (Cooperate, Cooperate) is unsustainable in the absence of some enforcement mechanism. By contrast, if the game is repeated indefinitely, then it is possible that the cartel can be sustained if the cartel members are sufficiently patient, that is, provided that the cartel members have sufficiently low **discount rates** at which they value future profits. See also **prisoners' dilemma game**.

		Firm B	
		Cooperate	Defect
Firm A	Cooperate	10, 10	5, 12
	Defect	12, 5	6, 6

Cartel Stability

The suggestion that a **cartel** can be sustained provided that there is repeated interaction by the cartel members and that the cartel members are sufficiently patient. Take the game defined under **cartel instability** and suppose that it is infinitely repeated. Then the cartel may be stable if the two firms use a **trigger strategy** of the form: "I shall Cooperate in the current period so long as we have both Cooperated in every previous period. Otherwise I shall Defect forever." Suppose that both firms have a **discount factor** of d. Then the cartel is stable under the trigger strategy provided that the discount factor is

$$d \geq d* = \frac{12 - 10}{12 - 6} = 1/3.$$

More generally, suppose that the **payoff** to firm i to Defect when firm j plays Cooperate is π_i^D, to Cooperate when firm j plays Cooperate is π_i^C, and to Defect when firm j plays Defect is π_i^N. Then firm i will not defect from the cartel agreement provided that firm i's discount factor is greater than

$$d_i = \frac{\pi_i^D - \pi_i^C}{\pi_i^D - \pi_i^N}.$$

Since it is to be expected that $\pi_i^D > \pi_i^C > \pi_i^N$ it must be that $d_i < 1$ with the result that there is always a discount factor sufficiently close to unity such that the trigger strategy will sustain the cartel.

Cash Cow

A product or division of a company associated with very high levels of profitability. In the **growth share matrix**, cash cows typically have high market share but exhibit slow growth. It is suggested that the high returns from cash cows should be "milked" in order to support other activities. This suggestion should be treated with caution, however, since diverting resources from cash cows runs the risk that the cash cows will decline from lack of investment, cutting off the flow of funds that they generate.

Catchment Area

The geographic area from which a firm draws its customers.

Causal Ambiguity

A situation in which the reasons why a firm is able to create more **perceived benefit** or value than its competitors are complex, obscure and only imperfectly understood, even by individuals within the firm. Causal ambiguity can be a source of **sustainable competitive advantage** since it is difficult for competitors to imitate or improve upon the associated value-creating process.

Cease and Desist Order

An order issued by the **antitrust authorities** prohibiting the firm to which it is issued from undertaking acts specified in the order.

Celler–Kefauver Act

An Act that aimed to close a loophole in the **Clayton** and **Sherman** antitrust **Acts**. The Clayton Act imposed restrictions on proposed mergers and acquisitions that, in the view of the antitrust authorities, substantially reduced competition. However, this act applied solely to mergers and acquisitions that were effected by the purchase of shares of stock in the target company. The provisions of both of these Acts could be circumvented by purchasing the assets of the target company. The Celler–Kefauver Act prohibited such asset acquisition if it led to substantial reduction in competition.

Central Place Theory

A theory that explains the location decisions of firms and individuals based on the presumption that there are benefits to **agglomeration**.

Central Purchasing Agency

An agency that coordinates the purchasing decisions of otherwise independent buyers. Such an agency can undermine the ability of an incumbent supplier to deter entry of another supplier by the incumbent supplier exploiting lack of coordination among buyers, resulting in each buyer committing to an **exclusive dealing** contract with the incumbent supplier.

Centralized Decision System

An **organizational architecture** in which the authority to make most important decisions is assigned to senior managers within the organization. This type of architecture is typical of **U-form organizations**.

Certainty Equivalent

Given a choice between a random income and a certain, nonrandom income, the nonrandom income that would make the chooser indifferent between the two alternatives. If the expected value of the random income is I with variance $Var(I)$ and the individual's **coefficient of absolute risk aversion** is $r(I)$ then the certainty equivalent of the random income is approximated by $I - Var(I)r(I)/2$. Certainty equivalent decreases with the variance of the random income, which can be taken as a measure of the riskiness of the random income, and decreases with the individual's degree of risk aversion.

Certification

An assurance provided by the certifying authority that a good or service has been tested and found to meet or exceed specified standards of performance.

CES Production Function

Suppose that a firm can choose to employ any of n inputs, with the quantity employed of input i being x_i. Then if the production function is CES (**constant elasticity of substitution**), total output is

$$Q = \left(\sum_{i=1}^{n} \alpha_i x_i^\rho \right)^{\frac{1}{\rho}} \text{ where } \sum_{i=1}^{n} \alpha_i = 1$$

and α_i is a share parameter. The **elasticity of substitution** between factors i and j for the CES production function is $\sigma_{ij} = 1/(1 - \rho)$. It can be shown that as $\rho \to 0$, $\sigma_{ij} \to 1$ and the CES production function reduces to the linear homogeneous **Cobb–Douglas production function**

$$Q = \prod_{i=1}^{n} x_i^{\alpha_i}.$$

By contrast, as $\rho \to \infty$, $\sigma_{ij} \to 0$, giving the **Leontief production function** $Q = \min\{\alpha_1 x_1, \ldots, \alpha_n x_n\}$. CES production functions are members of the class of linear homogeneous production functions.

Ceteris Paribus

A Latin term that can be translated as "other things remaining equal". This term is commonly used in **partial equilibrium analysis** when the analyst is interested in tracing the impact of a change in one, or a subset, of the model's parameters while keeping the remaining parameters fixed.

Chain Store Paradox

A game in which a firm faces the threat of sequential entry into a known and finite number of its markets but cannot credibly commit to deterring entry into any of its markets. The paradox, as stated by Reinhard Selten (1978), is that the firm cannot credibly develop a reputation for toughness by adopting strategic entry deterring actions in the "early" markets to make such actions unnecessary in "later" markets. Suppose, for example, that there are ten markets. **Entry deterrence** to create a tough reputation in the tenth and last market is not credible: such a reputation has no value. This makes the ninth market effectively the last market, so entry deterrence is not credible in this market either. This makes the eighth market the last market . . . and so on. The immediate implication of this reasoning is that entry deterrence to create a tough reputation is not credible in any of the ten markets. The paradox is that when this game is played, the player taking the role of the chain store will typically follow a deterrence strategy, choosing to fight to deter entry over some finite number of periods (stores), while reverting to the accommodation strategy in the final number of periods (stores).

Channel-Stuffing

A business practice in which a division of a multi-divisional firm rushes orders from other divisions within the firm or from outside buyers in order to boost their reported end-of-month sales.

Characteristics Markets

See **characteristics space**.

Characteristics Space

A space that is defined by the characteristics of the goods supplied to a market, such as their color, shape, taste and design. The underlying assumption in developing such an approach to consumer choice is that consumers derive utility from consumption of the goods' characteristics rather than from consumption of the goods themselves. **Address models** and the **Hotelling spatial model** are examples of models that use characteristics spaces. See also **discrete choice model of demand**.

Cheap Talk

Speech between players of a game prior to the game actually being played that has no impact on the **payoffs** the players receive from the game. Such speech is non-binding and non-verifiable. For cheap talk to have an impact on the outcome of the game it must affect the beliefs of one or both players regarding the strategy that its rival will adopt in the game. Consider the **battle of the sexes** game described by the following **payoff matrix**, where in each cell, the payoff to the row player is listed first, and the payoff to the column player is listed second:

		George	
		Opera	Ball game
Margaret	Opera	10, 7	6, 5
	Ball game	5, 4	8, 12

Now add a round of cheap talk between the players prior to their actually playing the game. In this round each player declares either "ball game" or "opera" with equal probability, enabling the players to randomize between the pure-strategy Nash equilibria to the game. If both players declare the same strategy, they can solve the coordination problem and avoid the lower-payoff outcomes.

Chicken Game

A game in which players can choose to play Tough or Chicken. The following game matrix illustrates a typical chicken game. If both A and B play Chicken both get zero; if both play Tough both are hurt and lose 2; if one plays Tough and the other Chicken the player who plays Tough gains 1 and the other loses 1. The **payoff matrix** is as follows, where in each cell the payoff to the row player is listed first, and the payoff to the column player is listed second:

		Player B	
		Tough	Chicken
Player A	Tough	−2, −2	1, −1
	Chicken	−1, 1	0, 0

There are two **Nash equilibria** in pure strategies – (Tough, Chicken) and (Chicken, Tough) – and a Nash equilibrium in **mixed strategies**.

Circle Model

A **Hotelling spatial model** in which the market space is assumed to be the circumference of a circle. An advantage of the circle model as compared to the line model that Hotelling specified is that it allows the analyst to make symmetry assumptions in characterizing equilibrium when there are more than two firms in the market. By contrast, in the line model with more than two firms, the two firms nearest to the ends of the line will not be symmetric with the remaining firms since they face competition on only one side of their markets.

Classical Linear Regression Model

A model describing the relationship between a **dependent variable**, y, and a set of k **independent**, or **explanatory variables**, $x_1, \ldots, x_k$, according to the following, $y = \beta_0 + \beta_1 x_1 + \ldots + \beta_k x_k + u$, where u represents the error term, capturing unobserved factors that influence the value of y. The model assumes the explanatory variables are linearly independent; conditional on a set of values for the explanatory variables, the expected value of u is zero, the variance of u is constant across such sets (homoskedasticity);

and u is statistically independent of the x's, with a normal distribution with mean zero and variance σ^2. The additional assumption of no **serial correlation** applies to time-series analysis. This classical linear regression model is the basis for **ordinary least squares (OLS)** regression analysis. Once the β_i coefficients are estimated, the equation can be used to make predictions of the value of y for a given set of values for the explanatory variables.

Clayton Act

A United States **antitrust law** passed in 1914 designed to prevent monopoly "in its incipiency" by outlawing certain business practices such as tying and exclusionary contracts and imposing limits on mergers judged to be anticompetitive.

Club Goods

Goods that some consumers can be excluded from using, but among the consumers using the good, consumption by one individual does not diminish the value of using the product to another, up to some limit determined by whether they become congested. Examples include Internet service and cinemas.

Coalition

An agreement between individuals, for example firms, to form an alliance in order to coordinate their actions. In some cases, coalitions are indistinguishable from **cartels**. In others, for example alliances to coordinate **research and development**, they do not break **antitrust laws**.

Coase Conjecture

Suppose that a monopolist offers an infinitely durable good to infinitely lived consumers who have unit demands. Suppose also that the period between price adjustments by the monopolist is Δ and that resale by consumers is not possible. Coase conjectured that the monopolist's price would tend to marginal cost as Δ tends to zero.

Coase Theorem

If the parties to a negotiation bargain to an efficient agreement for themselves and if their preferences display no **wealth effects** then the activities that they will agree on do not depend upon the bargaining power of the parties or on the allocation of ownership rights to the assets before initiating bargaining. Their choices of activities are determined solely by efficiency: by the total value created. Other factors affect only the distribution of the total value that is created.

Cobb–Douglas Production Function

Suppose that a firm can choose to employ any of n inputs, with the quantity employed of input i being x_i. Then if the production function is Cobb–Douglas, total output is

$$Q = \prod_{i=1}^{n} x_i^{\alpha_i}.$$

The **elasticity of substitution** of the Cobb–Douglas production function is 1. This production function exhibits **constant returns to scale** if

$$\sum_{i=1}^{n} \alpha_i = 1,$$

decreasing returns to scale if

$$\sum_{i=1}^{n} \alpha_i < 1$$

and **increasing returns to scale** if

$$\sum_{i=1}^{n} \alpha_i > 1.$$

Coefficient of Absolute Risk Aversion

Suppose that the **utility** the individual derives from an uncertain monetary outcome x is $U(x)$ and that the **expected value** of x is $\bar{x}$. Then the coefficient of absolute risk aversion is

$$r(\bar{x}) = -U''(\bar{x})/U'(\bar{x}).$$

See also **Arrow–Pratt index**.

Collusion

The agreement by rival entities to coordinate their actions. If the entities are firms then collusion, if it is **explicit**, leads to the formation of a **cartel**. See also **tacit collusion**.

Commitment

In game theory the ability of a player to persuade its rivals about the strategy it will play in the game. See also **credible commitment**.

Commitment Value

The ability of a strategic choice by a firm to influence the actions of potential competitors. Price has low commitment value since price can be easily changed and so it is difficult for an incumbent to persuade a potential entrant that it is committed to maintain the market price post-entry. **Capacity**, by contrast, has higher commitment value because it is expensive to install, difficult to change and a high proportion of the costs incurred in installing capacity are **sunk costs**.

Commodity Bundling

Bundling when it applies to products rather than to services.

Common Agency

The decision by independent manufacturers to sell their products through a common agent, for example, through the same retail outlet.

Common Goods

Non-excludable goods: once such goods are available, consumers cannot be excluded from consuming them, with the result that private firms will be reluctant to produce them. See **tragedy of the commons**.

Common Knowledge

In a game, knowledge that is shared by all players in the game.

Common Resource Problem

A problem that arises when several groups can use a resource for their own benefit and where property rights in the resource are not well defined or well enforced so that individual users of the resource do not bear the full cost of their use or do not receive the full benefits from their use. As a result, private individuals will typically underprovide such resources and will overuse them when they are available, leading to a **free-riding problem**. The resulting inefficiency in the provision and use of the resource is termed the **tragedy of the commons**. For example, a common natural resource such as a lake can be overfished by individuals, relative to the **socially optimal** level, resulting in critical depletions of the stock of fish.

Common Stock

Equity claims held by the residual owners of a publicly traded firm. These stockholders are the last in line to receive any distribution of assets or earnings of the firm.

Common Value Auction

An auction in which the true value of the item being auctioned is common to all of the bidders.

Comparative Advantage

If a firm (or country) has a comparative advantage in producing X the firm (country) has a lower **opportunity cost** of producing X than any rival firm (or country). No firm or country can have a comparative advantage in the production of every good. Alternatively, each firm or country has a comparative advantage in the production of some good. Suppose that the production possibilities of two countries are as described in the following table:

	Country A		Country B	
	Potatoes	Tomatoes	Potatoes	Tomatoes
Produce only Potatoes	10 tons	0 tons	25 tons	0 tons
Produce only Tomatoes	0 tons	10 tons	0 tons	75 tons

Country B has an **absolute advantage** in the production of both goods but Country A has a **comparative advantage** in producing potatoes and Country B has a comparative advantage in producing tomatoes. The **opportunity cost** of producing 1 ton of potatoes by Country A is 1 ton of tomatoes, whereas the opportunity cost of producing 1 ton of potatoes in Country B is 3 tons of tomatoes.

Compatibility of Standards

See **coordination game**.

Compensation

The total remuneration that an employee receives in return for the services that the employee provides to an employer. This typically consists of wage and salary but can also include bonuses, or non-wage perquisites such as subsidized health and dental care, insurance and car allowances.

Compensated Demand Function

The demand function that is obtained when income is adjusted in response to a price change in order to keep the consumer's utility constant. Suppose that **p** is the price vector and u is the consumer's utility. If the **expenditure function** is $E(\mathbf{p}, u)$ then the compensated demand function for good i is, by **Shephard's Lemma**, $x(\mathbf{p}, u) = \partial E(\mathbf{p}, u)/\partial p_i$.

Compensating Variation

The income adjustment that a consumer must receive in order to exactly offset the change in the consumer's utility as a result of a price change. Suppose that **p** is the price vector. Then the **expenditure function** is

$$E(\mathbf{p}, u) = \min_{\mathbf{q}} (\mathbf{p} . \mathbf{q})$$

subject to $U(\mathbf{q}) \geq u$, where $\mathbf{q}$ is the consumption vector, and the **indirect utility function** is

$$V(\mathbf{p}, I) = \max_{\mathbf{q}} U(\mathbf{q})$$

subject to $\mathbf{p} . \mathbf{q} \leq I$, where I is the consumer's income. The compensating variation of a change in the price vector from $\mathbf{p}^0$ to $\mathbf{p}^1$ is

$$CV = I - E(\mathbf{p}^1, V(\mathbf{p}^0, I)).$$

Compensating Wage Differential

The extra wage that has to be paid to encourage an individual to accept less desirable or potentially dangerous employment.

Compensation Principle

The principle that in choosing between competing proposals we need be concerned only with efficiency and not with distribution. If **total surplus** is increased by a shift to proposal A from another proposal B then the winners from A can compensate the losers and all are better off. Under the compensation principle, proposal A is preferred to proposal B even if no compensation will actually be paid after the shift from B to A. This is a weaker principle than **Pareto optimality**. The latter requires that *A* be judged preferable to *B* if and only if the move from *B* to *A* makes at least one person better off while making no one worse off.

Competition

See **imperfect competition, monopolistic competition** and **perfect competition**.

Competitive Advantage

A value-creating activity that a firm is able to perform better than its rivals. Possessing such an advantage allows the firm to earn economic rent: more than **normal profits**. Typically, competitive advantage cannot be sustained in the long term because of imitation by competitors. See also **sustainable competitive advantage**.

Competitive Equilibrium

The equilibrium in a perfectly competitive market, in which each firm prices at **marginal cost** and each consumer maximizes **utility** subject to a standard **budget constraint**. See also **long-run competitive equilibrium**.

Competitive Fringe Firms

The group of competitive firms in a market that prevent a dominant firm in the market from setting the monopoly price.

Competitive Market

A market in which all consumers and producers have perfect information, all agents are price takers (none are large enough that their decisions are expected individually to affect market prices), all firms produce homogeneous products and there is free entry and exit. Demand to each firm in such a market is perfectly elastic at the ruling market price, with the result that each firm produces the output at which its marginal cost equals the market price. In such a market, the process of entry and exit ensures that in the long run, each firm earns only **normal profit**.

Complementarities

A situation in which there are synergies in organizational practices. Activities exhibit complementarities if the marginal product of one activity is increased when more of another activity is performed. Formally, if the **production function** is defined by $q = f(\mathbf{x})$, where $\mathbf{x} = (x_1, \ldots, x_n)$ is the vector of factor inputs, then inputs j and k are complementary if

$$\frac{\partial^2 f(\mathbf{x})}{\partial x_j \partial x_k} > 0.$$

As an example, labor and capital are typically complementary: investing in additional capital increases the marginal productivity of labor that uses the capital.

Complementary Assets

Assets such as brand recognition, **capabilities**, commercial infrastructure, manufacturing facilities and distribution channels that are necessary for transforming a technological innovation into a viable commercial product. The innovating firm may have the technological expertise to pursue the innovation but without the complementary assets the innovation is likely to be a market failure.

Complementary Goods

Goods with the property that the utility that a consumer receives from consuming the goods together is greater than the utility that the consumer receives from consuming them separately. Formally, if a consumer's **utility function** is defined by $u = f(\mathbf{q})$, where $\mathbf{q} = (q_1, \ldots, q_n)$ is a consumption vector, then goods j and k are complementary if

$$\frac{\partial^2 f(\mathbf{q})}{\partial q_j \partial q_k} > 0.$$

As an example, food and wine are typically complementary. If goods 1 and 2 are complementary, then an increase in the price of good 1 (2) will give rise to a reduction in the quantity demanded of good 2 (1).

Complete Contract

A contract in which the contracting parties delineate their individual obligations and rights for every possible contingency: a contract with no unspecified contingencies and no ambiguity in the language of the contract. There are (almost) no examples of such contracts since it is typically the case that the contracting parties have **bounded rationality** and so are unable to identify all possible future states of the worlds and/or agree upon obligations and rights for all such future states. The inability to formulate complete contracts gives rise to the **principal–agent problem, hold-up** and **moral hazard** by allowing for the possibility of **opportunistic behavior** by some or all of the parties to the contract.

Complete Information

In a game, a situation in which every player knows the **strategies** and **payoffs** for every other player in the game and, if "nature" makes a move before the game begins, every player knows what "nature" has done.

Concentration Index

See **dominance index**, **entropy index** and **Herfindahl–Hirschman Index**.

Concentration Ratio

A measure of the relative size of firms in an industry, which gives an indication of the overall industry structure. Industries with high concentration ratios tend to be dominated by a small number of large firms, while industries with low concentration ratios tend to be more competitive. The most commonly used concentration ratio is the **four-firm concentration ratio**, defined as the percentage market share controlled by the four largest firms in the industry. See also **Herfindahl–Hirschman Index**.

Conditional Factor Demand

The input quantity of a factor of production that minimizes the cost of producing a given level of output q at given factor prices w. It is termed a conditional demand because it takes the target level of output as given. If the **production function** is $q = f(x)$ where x is a vector of factor inputs, then the conditional factor demand is the solution to the programming problem $\min_{x} w.x$ subject to $q = f(x)$. Denote the conditional factor demand for input i as $x_i(w, q)$. Then by **Shephard's Lemma**, if the **cost function** is $c(w, q)$, the conditional factor demand for input i is

$$x_i(w, q) = \frac{\partial c(w, q)}{\partial x_i}.$$

Conflicting Out

A situation in which a professional services firm loses potential business from a new client because the firm is already providing services to one or more of the potential client's rivals. Conflicting out imposes a limit on mergers of professional services firms and on the market share that any one such firm can hope to achieve.

Conglomerate

A company that has operating divisions in a series of apparently unrelated activities.

Conglomerate Merger

A merger that brings under common control two or more firms whose products are largely unrelated, being neither complements nor substitutes. Such a merger leads to a **diversified** firm that produces a range of goods with little or nothing in common.

Conjectural Variations

The belief that a player holds with respect to how other players will react to the first player's choice of strategy. Suppose, for example, that in a two-player game firm 1 believes that firm 2 will react to firm 1's choice of output q_1 with its own output choice, q_2, according to the conjectural variation $C_2(q_1)$. Then firm 1 will choose q_1 to maximize its profit

$$\pi_1(q_1, q_2) = \pi_1(q_1, C_2(q_1))$$

giving the first-order condition

$$\frac{\partial \pi_1()}{\partial q_1} + \frac{\partial \pi_1()}{\partial q_2} \cdot \frac{\partial C_2(q_1)}{\partial q_1} = 0.$$

Cournot competition corresponds to zero conjectural variations, or

$$\frac{\partial C_2(q_1)}{\partial q_1} = 0,$$

when firms compete in quantities, and **Bertrand competition** corresponds to zero conjectural variation when firms compete in prices, or

$$\frac{\partial C_2(p_1)}{\partial p_1} = 0.$$

Conjoint Analysis

A set of statistical tools used to estimate the relative benefits of different product attributes. The objective is to identify the combination of product characteristics that consumers will find most attractive.

Conscious Parallelism

A situation in which a group of **oligopolists** behave in an identical manner, for example changing prices by the same amount and at almost the same time, without any evidence that the firms have entered into an explicit price-setting agreement. It is very difficult for the antitrust authorities to successfully prosecute such behavior using the argument that it is evidence of **collusion** since there is no explicit evidence of collusion. Moreover, the firms have a natural defense that, since they are subject to the same market pressures, it is not surprising that they react, for example to changes in costs, in the same manner and at the same time.

Consent Decree

In an antitrust case, a means by which defendants in the antitrust case can settle the case with the **Department of Justice**'s Antitrust Division before the case goes to trial. As part of the consent decree the defendants agree to take specific actions detailed in the decree without necessarily admitting fault in the antitrust case. One of the principal objectives of such consent decrees is to save the time and expense in trial preparation by both the defendant and the Antitrust Division.

Constant Elasticity of Substitution (CES)

See **CES production function**.

Constant Returns to Scale

A **production function** exhibits constant returns to scale when a proportionate increase in all inputs results in a proportionate increase in output. Formally, suppose that the production function is $Q = f(\mathbf{x})$, where f is the production function, Q is output and $\mathbf{x}$ is the vector of factor inputs. If f exhibits constant returns to scale, we have $f(a\mathbf{x}) = af(\mathbf{x})$. Suppose, for example, that the production function is **Cobb–Douglas** such that total output is

$$Q = \prod_{i=1}^{n} x_i^{\alpha_i}.$$

This production function exhibits constant returns to scale if and only if

$$\sum_{i=1}^{n} \alpha_i = 1.$$

If input prices are constant as output increases, constant returns to scale imply that **average total costs** are constant.

Consumer Search

See **search good**.

Consumer Surplus

The difference between what consumers are willing to pay for a good and the amount that they are actually charged. Suppose that the demand function is given by $Q = 0$ for $P > P^{max}$ and $Q = D(P)$ for $0 \le P \le P^{max}$. Suppose further that the good is offered at a unit price of P. Consumer surplus at price P is

$$CS(P) = \int_{P}^{P^{max}} D(p)\,dp.$$

It follows that consumer surplus increases as the price is reduced.

Contestable Market

A market that is characterized by very low **barriers to entry** or **exit**. If the market is **perfectly contestable** there are no barriers to entry or exit.

A contestable market is typically characterized by nearly competitive pricing, even if it contains only one firm, because the incumbent firm is constrained in its price setting by the threat of **hit-and-run entry**.

Contract

A legally binding agreement or exchange of promises between two or more parties that governs some aspect of their relationships as defined in the contract.

Contracting Costs

The costs of negotiating, writing, monitoring and enforcing contracts. They typically include search and information costs, bargaining costs, and monitoring and enforcement costs. See also **transaction costs**.

Contracting Problems

Problems that arise both before and after contracts have been signed because the individuals entering into these contracts have incentives to act opportunistically with the intent of increasing their own well-being at the expense of their contracting partner. Such opportunistic behavior is possible because of **contractual incompleteness**. See also **hold-up problem**.

Contractual Incompleteness

A situation in which some elements of a contract are left unspecified. This can arise because some future states of the world and some contingencies and/or combinations of contingencies cannot be foreseen, or are sufficiently unlikely that they are ignored, or because some actions by the contracting parties are unobservable or cannot be confirmed to an independent third party, for example a court of law, and more generally because of **bounded rationality** of the contracting parties. Almost all contracts are incomplete in at least some dimensions, which can give rise to **hold-up problems** if the contract requires the creation of **relationship-specific assets**, and more generally to **moral hazard** once the contract has been agreed and implemented.

Control

The ability of a particular individual or group within an organization to exercise decision-making rights and rule-making authority within the organization.

Convenience Goods

Consumer goods that are relatively inexpensive, frequently purchased and of reasonably guaranteed quality; examples are detergent, soda, shampoo and socks.

Cooperative Agreement

See **collusion**.

Cooperative Game

A game in which players can form coalitions to enforce cooperation among members of a given coalition. Competition in such games is between coalitions rather than the competition between individuals that is characteristic of **non-cooperative games**.

Cooperative Pricing

Situations in which firms are able to sustain prices in excess of those that would result from a one-shot non-cooperative game. For such pricing to be sustainable it is necessary that the firms are involved in a **repeated game** with their potential rivals.

Coordination

The challenge within an organization of ensuring that the flows of information between subunits within the organization result in the subunits making decisions that are consistent with each other and with the overall objectives of the organization. If the divisions of a firm are established as **cost centers**, **profit centers** or **investment centers**, coordination can be inhibited unless there are clear incentives established to encourage information sharing.

Coordination Costs

The costs of achieving **coordination** across different operating units within an organization and between the organization and its outside suppliers.

Coordination Game

The set of **games** with the property that the only **Nash equilibria** in **pure strategies** are such that all players choose the same strategies. Consider a two-player game with the following **payoff matrix**, where in each cell, the **payoff** to the row player is listed first, and the payoff to the column player is listed second:

		Player Y	
		I	II
Player X	I	A, a	B, b
	II	C, c	D, d

This is a coordination game when $A > C$, $D > B$, $a > b$ and $d > c$. With these restrictions there are two Nash equilibria in pure strategies (I, I) and (II, II) and a **mixed-strategy** Nash equilibrium in which both players randomize between I and II.

In the game above, the mixed strategy equilibrium is for Player X to play I with probability $p = (d - c)/(a + d - b - c)$ and II with probability $1 - p$, and for player Y to play I with probability $q = (D - B)/(A + D - B - C)$ and II with probability $1 - q$.

A typical coordination game arises when there are competing technology standards in a new market, such as with computer operating systems or high-definition televisions. The firms know that they will gain more by adopting a common standard, but they might not agree on what that standard should be. This would arise if, in addition to the constraints above, we have $A > D$ and $d > a$, in which case Player X prefers (I, I) and Player Y prefers (II, II). Other coordination games are the **battle of the sexes game** and the **stag hunt game**.

Copyright

A legal provision granting exclusive rights to the author or artist of an original work for some specified period of time. As with **patents**, copyright is intended to protect the copyright holder from unauthorized copying of the original work, strengthening the incentive to expend resources in creating such works.

Core Competence

An activity or function that a firm performs well compared to its competitors or that is an area of specialized expertise for the firm. It has been suggested that firms should focus on their core competences and **outsource** all non-core activities.

Corporate Control

The authority to exercise control over the decisions of a firm, typically attained by gaining ownership of a significant proportion of the firm's shares of stock or by gaining the senior executive position in the firm, given that there is typically a separation of ownership and control in publicly traded companies. Corporate control can be valuable to senior executives when it allows them to pursue their self-interest rather than the interests of **shareholders**. As a result, we would expect there to be a **market for corporate control**, which inhibits the pursuit of self-interest by senior executives through the threat of their being replaced.

Corporate Culture

The set of shared beliefs, values, precedents, routines and procedures that help define the way in which the firm operates and provides guidance on expected behavior of those who join the firm. Corporate culture can be an important source of **sustainable competitive advantage** since it is typically tacit, embedded in the firm's routines and so difficult to imitate.

Corporate Governance

The organizational architecture at the top of a corporation, focusing on the allocation of decision rights among **shareholders**, the board of directors, top managers and external monitors and the associated incentives of these groups.

Corporate Raider

An individual or group who attempts to undertake a **hostile takeover**.

Corporate Strategy

The choice of the business activities that a firm will pursue.

Correlation Analysis

A measure of the relationship between two items, such as the relationship between the price of a financial security and an indicator, or the relationship between hours of work and productivity. The resulting measure, called the correlation coefficient, indicates how strong the relationship between the two items is. It is important to note that correlation need not imply causation. In some cases causation can be hypothesized: for example, that an increase in the price of corn will increase the price of pork (with some time delay). In other cases, the two items may move together without one "causing" the other. For example, the prices of two competing automobile models may be highly correlated because they are affected by similar outside factors such as the price of gasoline or steel.

Co-Specialization

A situation in which two assets that have unique features are more productive when used together than when operated separately. The assets are **complementary assets**.

Cost Advantage

A strategy to achieve a **competitive advantage** by offering products that give consumers **perceived benefits** that are comparable to those offered by competitors' products but that are produced at much lower costs than the competitors'. A firm can use its cost advantage to undercut its competitors and offer greater **consumer surplus** than its rivals while delivering wider **profit** margins. Alternatively, the firm can maintain price parity with its competitors but again generate wider profit margins.

Cost Center

A business unit whose performance is evaluated on its productive or **technical efficiency**. Such a business unit is usually required to maximize its output while staying within the budget that it is allocated. Establishing business units as cost centers gives these units the incentive never to underspend their allocated budgets and to lobby for increased budgets, leading to a potential loss of efficiency. On the other hand, since cost centers can appear to be a drain on **profit**, since they typically generate no direct **revenues**, they are vulnerable to underfunding and to having their budgets reduced in a downturn. Cost centers can find it difficult to justify investment in new equipment and new technologies since the **perceived benefits** from such investments are indirect rather than direct.

Cost Function

The relationship between a firm's output and its total cost. Suppose that the firm's **production function** is $q = f(\mathbf{x})$ where $\mathbf{x}$ is the vector of factor inputs and q is the firm's output. Suppose further that the vector of factor input prices is $\mathbf{w}$. Then the cost function is the solution $c(\mathbf{x}^*, q)$ to the cost-minimizing program: $\min_{\mathbf{x}} C(\mathbf{x}) = \mathbf{w}.\mathbf{x}$ subject to $q \geq f(\mathbf{x})$. By **Shephard's Lemma**, the partial derivative of the cost function with respect to input x_i is the **conditional factor demand** for input i.

Cost Minimization

The assumption that firms produce output at the lowest cost. Suppose that the production function is $q = f(\mathbf{x})$ where $\mathbf{x}$ is the vector of factor inputs and q is the firm's output. Suppose further that w_i is the unit price of factor input i. Then a necessary condition for cost minimization is that for any pair of factor inputs i and j we have:

$$\frac{\partial f(\mathbf{x})/\partial x_i}{\partial f(\mathbf{x})/\partial x_j} = \frac{w_i}{w_j}.$$

In other words, the ratio of the **marginal product** of factor i to the marginal product of factor j is equal to the ratio of the unit price of factor i to the unit price of factor j.

Cost-Plus Pricing

A pricing scheme in which a firm sets the price of a product or service by adding a margin to the average total costs of production in order to generate an agreed target rate of return. The margin is usually determined by the firm's management's estimation of "what the market will bear", which in turn is related to management's explicit or implicit estimate of the **elasticity of demand** for the product or service. One justification for cost-plus pricing comes from the profit–maximizing condition that

$$p\left(1 - \frac{1}{|\eta_{q,p}|}\right) = mc(q),$$

where p is price, q is output, $mc(q)$ is marginal cost and $\eta_{q,p}$ is the elasticity of demand. This can be rewritten

$$p = \left(\frac{|\eta_{q,p}|}{|\eta_{q,p}| - 1}\right)mc(q).$$

That is, the profit maximizing price is a multiple of marginal cost, with the multiple being determined by the elasticity of demand. Price is lower (higher) the more (less) elastic demand is. The advantages of cost-plus pricing are that it is relatively easy to compute, it economizes on information requirements, and it is simple to understand and administer. Disadvantages are that it may lead to inefficiency (on the belief that cost increases can be passed on in increased prices), it ignores competition from rivals, and it does not take into account **opportunity costs**.

Countervailing Power

A concept that the market power of one group may be balanced by the countervailing market power of another group. The concept was first introduced by John Kenneth Galbraith in his 1952 book *American Capitalism: The Concept of Countervailing Power*. Examples would be the market power of large-scale employers being balanced by the market power of large trade unions, or the market power of large-scale manufacturers being balanced by the market power of large-scale retailers. One controversial implication of this concept is that a downstream merger may actually improve competitive market conditions if it gives the merged downstream firms countervailing power in their negotiations with concentrated upstream suppliers.

Cournot Competition

A one-shot, non-cooperative game in which firms compete by setting outputs. See **Cournot equilibrium**.

Cournot Equilibrium

Consider a market containing n non-cooperative firms playing a one-shot **game** in which they simultaneously choose the outputs they each will set for their products. Define $q = (q_1, q_2, \ldots, q_i, \ldots q_n)$ and $q_{-i} = (q_1, \ldots, q_{i-1}, q_{i+1}, \ldots q_n)$ where q_i is the output of product i set by firm i. Denote **profit** to firm i ($i = 1, \ldots, n$) as $\pi_i(q)$. The Cournot equilibrium to this game is the set of outputs $q^* = (q_1^*, \ldots, q_i^*, \ldots, q_n^*)$ such that

$$\pi_i(q^*) \geq \pi_i(q_i, q_{-i}^*)$$

for all $q_i \geq 0$ and all $i = 1, \ldots, n$. This is also referred to as the **Cournot–Nash equilibrium**.

Cournot Game

A one-shot, non-cooperative **oligopoly** game in which firms compete by setting outputs simultaneously, leaving the market to determine the price(s) that will be paid for the chosen quantities. See **Cournot equilibrium**.

Cournot-Nash Equilibrium

See **Cournot equilibrium**.

Cream-Skimming

A pricing strategy in which a firm when introducing a new, typically high-tech product initially prices it high to sell to those consumers who must always have the latest technology or the latest generation of product, but subsequently reduces the price to sell to a wider range of consumers. This strategy stands in contrast to **penetration pricing**.

Creative Destruction

The theory that market economies progress in technological leaps and bounds that destroy the existing market equilibrium and replace it with a radically different equilibrium, rather than by progressing in incremental or marginal steps. This theory states that dominant companies are undermined and eventually replaced by radical innovations introduced by entrepreneurial newcomers. In the view of Joseph Schumpeter, this process is essential if there is to be sustained economic growth rather than stagnation.

Credence Good

A good whose true quality is rarely learned even after purchase and consumption. Examples are advertising campaigns, fluoride in toothpaste or the timeliness of surgical intervention. For such goods, price can often be taken as an indication of true quality with the result that there can be a positive rather than negative relationship between price and quantity demanded. Reducing the price of a credence good can undermine consumers' assessment of the true quality of the good, leading to less of the good being purchased.

Credible Commitment

A credible promise or threat to adopt a specific action. The player making such a commitment finds it optimal to carry through with the promise or threat even if the outcome that the promise or threat was intended to avoid actually occurs. For a commitment to be credible, it must be irreversible, visible to and comprehensible by those whose actions it is intended to affect.

Cross-Industry Studies

Early empirical work in industrial organization based on the **structure–conduct–performance paradigm**, characterized by estimating the impact of structural measures, such as industry concentration, on performance and **efficiency** measures, such as profits and price–cost margins, using combined data from across industries (for example, Bain, 1951). More recent empirical work has focused instead on industry-specific analysis and firm-level optimization. See also **industry studies**.

Cross-Licensing

A technology agreement in which a group of firms agree to license their patents to each other.

Cross-Price Elasticity

A measure of the sensitivity of quantity demanded of good x to a change in the price of another good y. The cross-price elasticity of x with respect to y is

$$\eta_{x,y} = \frac{\partial Q_x / \partial P_y}{Q_x / P_y}.$$

If the cross-price elasticity is positive, x and y can be thought of as **substitute goods**, while if it is negative x and y can be thought of as **complementary goods**.

Cross-Subsidization

A business practice in which a firm uses profits earned by one group of its business units to subsidize the activities and operations of another loss-making group. For example, revenues from **cash cows** can be used to subsidize the production and marketing of **rising stars**, or charging high prices to one group of consumers or market in order to be able to offer lower prices to another consumer group or market. For example, the high prices charged for prescription drugs in the United States allow the pharmaceutical companies to charge much lower prices for the same drugs in Canada and Europe, while still being able to recoup their **research and development** expenditures in developing these drugs.

Cube-Square Rule

A source of economies of scale when the productive capacity of a **capital asset** is determined by its volume, such as pipelines or oil tankers. The rule is derived from the approximation that while the productive capacity of the asset increases with the volume enclosed, or the cube, the **capital cost** of the asset increases with the surface area, or the square. See also **two-thirds rule**.

Customer Specialization

A business strategy in which a firm targets a set of related products at a particular type of customer.

Cut-Throat Competition

See **ruinous competition**.

D

Darwinian Selection

In an industry that contains firms with different efficiencies, a selection mechanism by which the relatively less efficient firms are forced to exit the market as a result of competition from the relatively more efficient firms, raising the overall efficiency of the market.

Deadweight Loss

A loss of economic efficiency that occurs when equilibrium in the provision of a good or service is not **Pareto efficient**. Interfering in markets by imposing **quotas, taxes, price floors** or **price ceilings** typically leads to a deadweight loss. The deadweight loss of monopoly is the difference between the **total surplus** (**consumer surplus** plus **producer surplus**) that would be generated at the competitive equilibrium, and the total surplus that is generated by the monopolist. A central economic rationale for antitrust laws is that moving a market from a more monopolistic to a more competitive structure will result in diminished deadweight loss and thereby increase total surplus and improve **social welfare**. But see also the **wastefulness postulate** for an alternative definition of the deadweight loss of monopoly.

Debt–Equity Ratio

The ratio of the debt that a firm has issued to finance its assets to the **shareholder** equity in the firm. If a firm has a high debt–equity ratio it is said to be highly geared.

Debt Overhang

A situation in which an organization has profitable investment opportunities that it cannot pursue because its existing debt liabilities result in the organization being unable to finance the new opportunities or in the risk that the profits from the opportunities will be expropriated by the existing creditors.

Debt Workout

Negotiations between an organization and its creditors to reorganize the organization's debt liabilities in order to avoid **bankruptcy**.

Decision Control

Within a firm, the formal approval and monitoring of decisions taken by individuals within the firm.

Decision Management

Within a firm, the formal initiation and implementation of decisions taken by individuals within the firm. It is usually recommended that decision management should be separated from **decision control**. See Fama and Jensen (1983).

Decision Rights

The authority to determine how resources will be used within an organization.

Deconglomeration

A process by which a **conglomerate** company is **busted-up** or spins off individual operating divisions in order to return to its **core competences**.

Decreasing Returns to Scale

A **production function** exhibits decreasing returns to scale when a proportionate increase in all inputs results in a less than proportionate increase in output. Formally, suppose that the production function is $Q = f(\mathbf{x})$, where f is the production function, Q is output and $\mathbf{x}$ is the vector of factor inputs. If f exhibits decreasing returns to scale we have $f(a\mathbf{x}) < af(\mathbf{x})$. Suppose, for example, that the production function is **Cobb–Douglas** such that total output is

$$Q = \prod_{i=1}^{n} x_i^{\alpha_i}.$$

This production function exhibits decreasing returns to scale if and only if

$$\sum_{i=1}^{n} \alpha_i < 1.$$

If input prices are constant as output increases, decreasing returns to scale imply that **average total cost** increases as output is increased.

Dedicated Assets

Assets that are acquired in order to serve the requirements of a specific set of buyers.

Deep Pocket Predation

Predation by a large company that uses its substantial financial resources (deep pockets) to drive out smaller companies with fewer resources (shallow pockets) and so with less ability to sustain losses during the period of predation. Exit of the smaller firms allows the large firm to raise its prices and recover the costs of predation. The extent to which this model applies to a particular market setting depends crucially on the ease with which smaller firms can access financial markets in order to sustain losses during the period of predation.

Delegation

The decision by a superior to assign responsibility for a task or set of tasks to a subordinate, giving the subordinate defined decision-making rights and responsibilities. Delegation is usually associated with a monitoring and assessment system by which the superior assesses the performance of the subordinate.

Delivered Price

The price that a buyer must pay for a product if it is delivered by the seller to the buyer's location rather than collected by the buyer from the seller's location. Adopting a delivered price policy as opposed to **free on board** pricing is one way in which firms can **price discriminate** across geographically distinct markets. In the context of **antitrust laws**, if several sellers employ the same **uniform delivered price** schedules, such behavior can potentially be viewed as collusive and intended to restrain trade.

Demand Complementarities

A situation in which a consumer's utility is increased by consuming goods together rather than separately. These goods are **complementary goods**.

Demand Curve

A curve in (Q, P) space describing the function $Q = D(P; \alpha)$ that gives the relationship between the price of a good and the quantity of the good that consumers are willing to buy, all else, α, remaining equal or constant. The "all else" typically includes variables such as consumer numbers, consumer tastes, consumer income, expected future prices and the prices of other goods. When one of the variables in α changes, the demand curve will shift. For example, when consumer incomes rise, and if the product is a **normal good**, the demand curve will shift rightward, as the quantity demanded at any given price will be higher than prior to the income increase. By convention, price is placed on the vertical axis and quantity demanded on the horizontal axis, despite the fact that the model of demand treats quantity demanded as being dependent upon price, an **exogenous, independent variable**.

Demand Elasticity

A measure of the sensitivity of quantity demanded to a change in price. If the demand function is $Q = D(P, \mathbf{a})$ where $\mathbf{a}$ includes all determinants of demand other than the price, then the absolute value of the demand elasticity is

$$\eta_P = \left| \frac{\partial D(P, \mathbf{a})}{\partial P} \frac{P}{D(P, \mathbf{a})} \right|.$$

If $\eta_P > 1$ demand is said to be **elastic** while if $\eta_P < 1$ demand is said to be **inelastic**. If demand is elastic, a firm can increase its revenue by lowering its price: consumers are sufficiently responsive to price that the loss of revenue resulting from charging a lower price is more than offset by the increased quantity demanded by existing consumers and the attraction of new consumers purchasing the product. If demand is inelastic, an increase in price leads to an increase in revenue. The additional revenues generated by the higher price more than offset the reduction in quantity demanded. Goods for which demand is inelastic, such as cigarettes, are often targets of policy makers for taxation, as a sufficiently large number of customers will continue to buy the product even if its effective price (including the tax) is higher, ensuring a steady source of tax revenues for the government.

Demand Estimation

Econometric methods used to estimate the relationship between the quantity demanded of a product and its own price, the price of related goods, various consumer demographics, and other factors influencing consumer choice. In addition to demand factors, the price of a product will be influenced by supply factors, such as production costs. To achieve proper **identification** of the demand equation, this problem of **simultaneity** can be addressed with **instrumental variables estimation**. For firms operating in markets characterized by **imperfect competition** and **product differentiation**, a system of demand equations can be used to estimate **cross-price elasticities** and the impact of strategic choices of competing firms on demand. See **discrete choice model of demand**.

Demand Function

The solution to the consumer's utility maximizing problem, $\max_{x} U(\mathbf{x})$ subject to $\boldsymbol{p}.\boldsymbol{x} \leq I$, where $\boldsymbol{p}$ is the price vector, $\boldsymbol{x}$ is the set of consumption decisions and I is the consumer's income. Solving this utility maximizing problem generates the consumer's **indirect utility function** $v(\boldsymbol{p},\ I)$, from which the demand function for commodity i is, by **Roy's Identity**,

$$x_i(\mathbf{p}, I) = -\frac{\partial v(\mathbf{p}, I)/\partial p_i}{\partial v(\mathbf{p}, I)/\partial I}.$$

See also **compensated demand function**.

Department of Justice

A department of the executive branch of the US government charged with federal law enforcement. The Antitrust Division oversees enforcement of **antitrust laws**, and does so in conjunction with the **Federal Trade Commission**.

Dependent Variable

In econometrics, the variable that the econometric estimation hopes to explain. If the equation to be estimated is

$$Y = \alpha + \sum \beta_i X_i + \varepsilon,$$

then Y is the dependent variable. See also **independent variable** and **ordinary least squares (OLS)**.

Depreciation

A measure of the extent to which an asset or **durable good** loses value over time, either as a result of physical deterioration or obsolescence. An accounting approach to depreciation uses an allowance of, for example, 10 percent of an asset's value and depreciates the asset by this amount each year for a fixed time period, such as over ten years. An economic approach to depreciation is market-based; depreciation is measured by the difference between the market value of the asset at the start of the year and its market value at the end of the year.

Deregulation

A process by which a government or regulatory agency removes, relaxes or simplifies the rules that it applies to businesses and individuals and that govern their behavior. A common rationale for deregulation is that it will improve the efficiency of the markets that are being deregulated. It is also argued that it is impossible to fine-tune regulations to reflect local market conditions and that regulators run the risk of **regulatory capture**. See, for example, **Airline Deregulation Act**.

Derived Demand

Demand for an upstream product in the vertical production chain that is needed to manufacture a product that is downstream in the **vertical chain**.

Suppose that a firm contains two divisions, Manufacturing and Retailing, and that Retailing faces an **inverse demand** $P_r = 100 - Q_r$ for its product. Suppose further that Retailing sources its product from Manufacturing at unit price P_m, with one unit of Manufacturing's product being needed for each unit of Retailing's sales. Finally, suppose that Retailing has constant **marginal cost** c_r and Manufacturing has constant marginal cost c_m. Given that Manufacturing quotes unit price P_m for its product to Retailing, the latter's profit is $(P_r - c_r - P_m)Q_d = (100 - Q_r - c_r - P_m)Q_r$, giving the profit maximizing output $Q_r = (100 - c_r - P_m)/2$ and downstream price $P_r = (100 + c_r + P_m)/2$. Since $Q_r = Q_m$, the derived demand for Manufacturing is $P_m = (100 - c_r) - 2Q_m$.

Descending Bid Auction

An auction in which the auctioneer starts with a very high price and successively quotes lower prices until a bid is received or a predetermined reserve price is reached. The first bidder wins the auction. See also **Dutch auction** and **reverse auction**.

Design Attributes

A production process has design attributes when there is extensive *a priori* knowledge about the ways in which the activities that make up the process should be related. When there are design attributes, failing to achieve the correct relationships between these activities is generally much more costly than other errors. A motor car assembly line has design attributes. In the sport of crew rowing it is much more important that the rowers are synchronized than that each rower rows as fast as they can. A process that has design attributes has to solve both **assignment** and **coordination** problems.

Deterred Entry

Entry that is prevented as a result of explicit strategic actions of the incumbent firms. An example of such action would be for an incumbent firm to threaten to price below cost if a competitor chooses to enter the market. In order for the incumbent firm to successfully deter entry, it must have a reputation for toughness, otherwise the threat of post-entry price cutting will not be a **credible commitment**. Entry can be deterred if the incumbent controls strategic resources essential for production or has created strong **brand loyalty**. In industries where there are **network externalities** entry can be deterred if the incumbent has a large **installed base** of users.

Development

In the context of **research and development**, the process of taking a product from the concept or prototype stage to the point where there is a product that can be sold to consumers and that is capable of replication.

Difference-in-Differences Estimation

An estimation method used to measure the impact of a policy change over time. For example, an environmental regulation for an industry might apply only to firms operating in a specific region of a state. Average productivity before and after the regulation is adopted is compared for firms within the regulated region (the treated group) and for firms outside of the regulated region (the control group). The difference in these differences provides a measure of the regulatory impact on productivity.

Differentiation Principle

The proposition that when competing firms can choose the characteristics of their products, they will choose not to locate at the same place in **characteristics space** but rather will seek to differentiate their products in order to soften competition. This principle is in contrast to an **agglomerated equilibrium**, in which firms locate close to one another in order to "be where the demand is" (Tirole 1988, p. 286), as agglomerated firms can potentially stimulate additional demand.

Differentiated Goods

Goods that satisfy the same consumer requirements but that are distinct from each other in some characteristic dimensions, such as shape, color, taste or quality. Product differentiation is a central strategic choice in models of product location in **characteristics space**, as with the **differentiation principle** and **agglomerated equilibria**. See **horizontal** or **vertical product differentiation**; see also **discrete choice model of demand**.

Differentiated Products

See **differentiated goods**.

Diffusion of Knowledge

The process by which new knowledge spreads from its original source into more general adoption.

Diminishing Returns

The principle that the **marginal product** of a variable factor of production that is employed in combination with some fixed factors will eventually fall as the variable factor's use increases. For example, if the amount of capital resources, such as the machinery and equipment on a factory assembly line, is fixed, then as labor usage increases, eventually the marginal contribution of an additional worker will decline relative to the previous worker. The effort of the additional worker could be more productive if the company could provide additional machinery for the worker to use; however, with capital fixed, the worker is limited in their productivity contributions once the existing capital is fully utilized.

Discount Factor

The factor by which a future sum M_t is multiplied to convert this sum into its **present value**. If the per-period **discount rate** is r then the discount factor for period t is

$$d_t(r) = \frac{1}{(1 + r)^t}$$

and the present value of M_t is $d_t(r)M_t$. In continuous time models $d(t, r) = e^{-rt}$.

Discount Rate

The rate at which future sums are **discounted** in order to measure their **present values**. The discount rate used by a firm is usually equal to its risk-adjusted cost of capital.

Discounting

The process of finding the **present value** of a sum of money that will be received or has to be paid at some future date. If an amount of money M_t is to be received or paid at time t and the per-period **discount rate** is r, then the discounted, or present value of M_t is

$$PV(M_t, r) = M_t / (1 + r)^t.$$

In continuous time models the discounted or present value of $M(t)$ is $PV(M(t), r) = M(t)e^{-rt}$.

Discrete Choice Model of Demand

A model of consumer choice in which a consumer faces two or more mutually exclusive options and chooses one. Econometric analysis links this choice to consumer demographics, price and attributes of the available choices. For example, a consumer choosing an airline for travel will consider airfare, flight amenities, travel time, number of plane changes and other flight characteristics among all flights. Binary choice models can be estimated with **probit** or **logit models**. Multiple choice, or multinomial choice, models can be estimated with **multinomial probit** and **logit, nested logit** and **mixed logit models**. See McFadden (1984), Berry et al. (1995) and Nevo (2000).

Discriminatory Offers

A situation in which a seller offers the same good to different buyers but at different prices. This is feasible provided that the seller can identify the different types of buyers and is able to prevent **arbitrage** between them. While this type of **price discrimination** can lead to an increase in **total surplus** relative to single **linear pricing**, such pricing can violate **antitrust laws** if it is found to have an anticompetitive impact on the market. See also **first-degree** and **second-degree price discrimination**.

Diseconomies of Scale

The region of the **long-run average cost curve** over which average cost increases as output is increased. Once a **perfectly competitive** market has achieved **long-run competitive equilibrium**, firms will not produce quantities that lie in the region of diseconomies of scale. Similarly, since a firm in long-run equilibrium in a **monopolistically competitive** market operates at an output where its downward-sloping demand function is just tangent to its average **cost function**, such a firm will not operate in the region of diseconomies of scale. A **monopolist**, by contrast, may operate in the region of diseconomies of scale if market size is large relative to the monopolist's **minimum efficient scale**.

Disruptive Technologies

Technologies that create more value than existing technologies and do so by offering consumers slightly lower net benefits but at much lower costs. The owners of such technologies can undercut existing firms to offer greater **consumer surplus** while still enjoying greater **profit** margins than those offered by the existing technologies.

Diversification

In economics, a strategy by a firm to extend its operations into a series of largely unrelated activities. In finance, diversification entails spreading **investments** over several different investment classes.

Divisionalization

The process of splitting a company into a series of more or less independent divisions. This can occur by function, by product or by geography. Divisions can be established as **profit**, cost, **expense**, **revenue** or **investment centers**. Typically, divisions trade with each other at internally agreed **transfer prices**.

Dixit–Stiglitz Model

A monopolistically competitive model in which consumers exhibit a taste for variety. In its simplest form the consumer **utility function** is assumed to be

$$U = \left(\sum_{i=1}^{n} X_i^{\rho} \right)^{1/\rho} X_0^{\alpha}$$

where $0 < \rho < 1$ and $\alpha > 0$. Commodities $1 \dots n$ are **differentiated goods** and commodity 0 is an outside good taken as numeraire. This utility function is maximized subject to the **budget constraint**

$$Y = X_0 + \sum_{i=1}^{n} p_i X_i.$$

The resulting demand functions are

$$X_i = \frac{p_i^{-1/1-\rho}}{P} \hat{Y}; X_0 = \alpha \hat{Y},$$

where P is a price index

$$P = \sum_{j=1}^{n} p_j^{-1/1-\rho} \text{ and } \hat{Y} = Y/(1 + \alpha)$$

is the total amount spent on the differentiated products.

Dominance

A measure of disparity or asymmetry in market shares of the firms or other participants in a market. See **asymmetry index** and **dominance index**.

Dominance Index

Denote the market share of firm i in a market containing n firms as s_i, and index the firms from largest to smallest, so that $s_1 \geq s_2 \geq \dots \geq s_i \geq \dots s_n$. The dominance index for the market is

$$D = \sum_{i=1}^{n} (s_i - s_{i+1})^2.$$

See Kwoka (1977); see also **Herfindahl–Hirschman Index** for a related measure of **market concentration**.

Dominant Firm Model

A model in which the market is supplied by a dominant firm constrained by **competitive fringe firms**. While the dominant firm maximizes its own **profit**, it does so while correctly anticipating the actions of the competitive fringe, with the result that the dominant firm is unable to set the monopoly price.

Dominant Position

Defined by the European Court of Justice as "a position of economic strength enjoyed by an undertaking, which enables it to prevent effective competition being maintained in the relevant market by affording it the power to behave to an appreciable extent independently of its competitors, its customers, and ultimately of the consumers".

Dominant Strategy

A strategy for a player that provides a higher **payoff** than any other strategy the player can adopt no matter what strategies are played by the player's rivals. Suppose that player I has two strategies A and B and player II has two strategies a and b, and denote the payoff to player I from strategy combination X, y as $P(X, y)$. Then A dominates B for player I if $P(A, a) > P(B, a)$ and $P(A, b) > P(B, b)$. A player will always play a dominant strategy if such a strategy exists.

Consider the **Hawk–Dove game**. The **payoff matrix** is as shown, where in each cell, the **payoff** to the row player is listed first, and the payoff to the column player is listed second. If $V > C$ then Hawk is a dominant strategy for both players and the **Nash equilibrium** to this game is (Hawk, Hawk). By contrast, if $V < C$ there is no dominant strategy for either player and the Nash equilibria are (Hawk, Dove) and (Dove, Hawk).

		Player B	
		Hawk	Dove
Player A	Hawk	$(V - C)/2, (V - C)/2$	$V, 0$
	Dove	$0, V$	$V/2, V/2$

See also **weakly dominant strategy**.

Dominated Strategy

A strategy that never provides a best response no matter the strategies that are played by the player's rivals. Suppose that player I has two strategies A and B and player II has two strategies a and b, and denote the **payoff** to player I from strategy combination X, y as $P(X, y)$. Then A is dominated by B for player I if $P(A, a) < P(B, a)$ and $P(A, b) < P(B, b)$. Dominated strategies will never be played and so can be eliminated from a **game** without affecting the outcome of the game.

Consider the **Hawk–Dove game** detailed above. If $V > C$ then Dove is a dominated strategy for both players and the **Nash equilibrium** to this game is (Hawk, Hawk). By contrast, if $V < C$ there is no dominated strategy for either player and the Nash equilibria are (Hawk, Dove) and (Dove, Hawk). See also **weakly dominated strategy**.

Dorfman–Steiner Condition

Suppose that a firm's demand function is $Q = D(P, s)$ where P is the product price, Q is quantity demanded and s is the total expenditures on advertising by the firm. Define

$$-\eta_s = \frac{\partial D(P,s)}{\partial s} \frac{s}{Q} \text{ and } \eta_P = \left| \frac{\partial D(P,s)}{\partial P} \frac{P}{Q} \right|$$

as the elasticities of demand with respect to advertising and price, respectively. The Dorfman–Steiner condition states that the profit maximizing choice of price and advertising expenditure satisfies the condition:

$$\frac{s}{P.Q} = \frac{\eta_s}{\eta_P}.$$

According to this condition, the optimal advertising-to-sales ratio is equal to the ratio of the elasticities of demand with respect to advertising and to price.

Double Marginalization

Suppose that an upstream monopolist supplies a downstream monopolist with a product that is sold at a simple **linear price**. Then the price charged to consumers by the **downstream firm** will be determined by the downstream firm adding a monopoly margin to the input price, which already includes a monopoly margin added by the **upstream firm**. Double marginalization increases the **deadweight loss** of monopoly but can be avoided if the firms adopt **nonlinear pricing** schedules. Suppose that the downstream monopolist faces **inverse demand** $P_d = 100 - Q_d$ for its product. Suppose further that the downstream firm sources its product from the upstream firm at unit price P_u, with one unit of the upstream firm's product being needed for each unit of the downstream firm's product. Finally suppose that the downstream firm has constant **marginal cost** c_d and the upstream firm has constant marginal cost c_u. Given that the upstream firm quotes unit price P_u for its product to the downstream firm, the latter's profit is $(P_d - c_d - P_u)Q_d = (100 - Q_d - c_d - P_u)Q_d$, giving the profit maximizing output $Q_d = (100 - c_d - P_u)/2$ and downstream price $P_d = (100 + c_d + P_u)/2$. Since $Q_d = Q_u$, the inverse demand for the upstream firm is $P_u = (100 - c_d) - 2Q_u$. The upstream firm's profit is $(P_u - c_u)Q_u = (100 - c_d - c_u - 2Q_u)Q_u$, giving the profit maximizing output $(100 - c_u - c_d)/4$ and upstream price $P_u = (100 - c_d + c_u)/2$. Substituting gives the downstream price $P_d = (300 + c_d + c_u)/4$. By contrast, if the upstream firm supplies the downstream firm at **marginal cost**, as it would with a **two-part tariff** the downstream price would be $P_d = (100 + c_d + c_u)/2$. In other words, double marginalization leads to higher downstream prices.

Double marginalization occurs within firms if the upstream and downstream divisions are established as **profit centers**.

Double Mark-Up

See **double marginalization**.

Downstream Firm

In a vertically related market structure, a firm that operates late in the production sequence and is supplied with **intermediate goods** by **upstream firms**.

Downstream Integration

See **forward integration**.

Downstream Process

In manufacturing processes, those processes that arise later in the progression of production stages.

Drastic Innovation

Innovation that reduces a firm's unit cost to such an extent that it can undercut its competitors and drive them out of business even if it sets the monopoly price associated with its new, lower unit cost. Suppose that a market is supplied by **Bertrand competitors** each with **marginal cost** c_h and that **inverse demand** is linear, given by $P = A - B.Q$. Before the innovation, price would be c_h. Now assume that one firm innovates to obtain marginal cost c_l. If it acts as an unconstrained monopolist, it will set price $P_m = (A + c_l)/2$. The innovation is drastic if $P_m < c_h$ or $c_l < 2c_h - A$.

Dual Sourcing

The decision by a buying firm to purchase from more than one supplying firm, as a defense against **hold-up** or to provide the buyer with a **benchmark** by which it can assess the efficiency of its suppliers. Dual sourcing is more likely to be adopted when the production process is characterized by a low degree of **relationship-specific investment**.

Dumping

Selling by a firm in a distant market at a price that is lower than the price being charged by the firm in its domestic or local market, with the result that firms in the distant market are injured by the dumping firm's actions. This type of business practice is constrained in international markets by **antidumping laws** enforced by the World Trade Organization.

Duopoly

An oligopolistic market containing only two firms. The n-firm **Cournot equilibrium** is often illustrated by the case of duopoly to demonstrate that the **Nash equilibrium** to the **Cournot game** results in total output lying between larger output under **perfect competition** on the one hand, and smaller output under **monopoly** on the other hand.

Durable Goods

Goods that provide utility to their consumers over an extended period of time, instead of being used up on first use. Obvious examples are houses, automobiles, home furnishings and capital equipment.

Durable Goods Monopoly

A market controlled by a monopolist that produces a **durable good** and supplies this good to a market containing consumers who "live" for several periods. The challenge that such a monopolist faces is how to price its good over time. If, for example, consumers believe that the monopolist will reduce the price of the good at some later date, they may choose to postpone their purchases. See also **Coase conjecture**.

Duration Analysis

The study of the duration of a survival state, such as a firm continuing to operate in an industry, until a failure state, such as exit from the industry. The survival function is used as a basis for estimating the relationship among time-varying and time-invariant factors expected to influence the likelihood of continued survival, given that the firm survives until time t. If $f(t)$ is the probability distribution of T, then its cumulative distribution is

$$F(t) = \int_0^t f(s)\,ds = \Pr(T \le t).$$

The survivor function, therefore, is

$$S(t) = 1 - F(t) = \Pr(T \ge t),$$

or the probability that a firm continues to operate beyond a specific time, t. The corresponding hazard function is

$$\lambda(t) = f(t)/S(t),$$

which can be interpreted as an exit rate. See Greene (2012, pp. 861–872).

Dutch Auction

An auction in which the auctioneer starts with a very high price and successively quotes lower prices until a bid is received or until the auctioneer quotes a final reserve price if such a reserve price has been agreed in advance between the seller and the auctioneer. The first bidder wins the auction. This type of auction takes its name from its use in auctioning tulip bulbs in the Netherlands. See also **descending bid auction**.

Dynamic Competition

A term that reflects the temporal nature of competition. This can take several forms. First, suppose that there is a large buyer with a series of contracts with different optimal start dates. Each contract will take more than one period to complete and the contracts can be undertaken by a small number of suppliers, each of which has finite capacity. The buyer can affect competition in particular time periods by manipulating the actual start dates, but this imposes costs in that contracts are not started on their optimal dates. Second, suppose that there is **learning-by-doing**. The buyer's trade-off now is that using a single supplier maximizes the cost reductions from learning but gives the favored supplier a **competitive advantage** in bidding against the other suppliers. Third, in many markets competition is based on technological **innovation**. A successful innovator gains temporary **market power**. The main role for competition policy in such markets is to ensure that **entry** to the technology race is sustained.

Dynamic Efficiency

A measure of the extent to which a market operates efficiently over time, introducing new products and new processes.

Dynamic Game

A **game** that extends over several periods, in which players choose their actions sequentially, with those who choose their actions later in the game being able to observe the actions chosen by players who move earlier in the game. These games are usually represented in **extensive form** in order to make the sequence of moves explicit. Any equilibrium to a dynamic game must be **subgame perfect**.

Dynamic Limit Pricing

A pricing strategy in which an incumbent firm sets its prices over time to reduce or eliminate the incentives of potential rival firms to enter the incumbent firm's market. See also **limit pricing model**.

E

Early-Mover Advantage

The competitive advantage that a firm gains from being an early entrant to a new market. This advantage may come from **learning-by-doing** effects, development of **brand name** recognition or the creation of consumer **switching costs**.

Eckbo Test

A test of the likely **welfare** impact of a **merger** by looking at the impact of the merger announcement on the stock market prices of firms in the industry that are affected by the merger but are not part of the merger. If these firms' stock prices decline, this implies that analysts expect the merger to generate **efficiency gains** that are detrimental to outsiders but that will increase total welfare. If the outsiders' share prices increase the implication is that there are few if any efficiency gains from the merger, with the result that total welfare will be reduced. See also **event study**.

Eclectic Paradigm

A theory explaining how firms will choose to supply foreign markets. The theory suggests that this choice is determined by the relative magnitudes of three factors: (1) ownership advantage (O) – the possession by the firm of **intangible assets** such as **reputation**, **brand name**, product and market knowledge; (2) locational advantage (L) – the relative costs of producing domestically and producing in the target market, affected by transport costs, relative wage costs, **tariffs** and other barriers to trade; (3) internalization advantage (I) – the relative cost of exploiting the ownership advantage internally to the firm rather than selling or licensing it to another firm, affected by the nature of the ownership advantage and the ability of the owner of the ownership advantage to receive a market **rate of return** using external markets. This theory gives rise to the OLI Model of **foreign direct investment**. The predictions of the eclectic paradigm can be summarized in the following table (Dunning 1981, p. 32):

		Type of advantage		
		Ownership	Internalization	Locational
Mechanism for market access	Contractual via licensing	Yes	No	No
	Export	Yes	Yes	No
	FDI	Yes	Yes	Yes

E-Commerce

The exchange of goods and services using electronic media such as the Internet. Some companies, such as Amazon, conduct all of their sales activities using e-commerce, but even more traditional companies such as Barnes & Noble are making increasing use of e-commerce, becoming **brick and click** organizations.

Econometrics

The development and application of statistical or quantitative techniques in the study of economic principles. The primary purpose of econometrics is to develop robust statistical techniques that can be used to subject economic theories to empirical testing. See, for example, **classical linear regression model**.

Economic Forbearance

The decision by a firm operating in several markets not to attack its rivals in any one market in order to avoid retaliation by these rivals in other markets.

Economic Model

A framework that captures the essential features of the market and market phenomena that the model is intended to explain.

Economic Good

A good that provides utility to its consumers and that is defined by its characteristics such as its physical properties, its location and the date(s) on which it is available.

Economic Profit

Total revenue minus the **opportunity cost** of the **resources** employed.

Economies of Massed Reserves

Savings in holdings of **inventories** of **intermediate goods** and replacement parts that arise as the scale of operation increases.

Economies of Scale

The region of the **average total cost** curve over which average cost falls as output increases. When economies of scale are extensive relative to market size the market structure is likely to be an **oligopoly**. In the limit, when economies of scale are present over the full range of output that is relevant for the market, the market is a **natural monopoly**. There are several common sources of economies of scale: spreading the costs of **indivisible inputs** or physical assets (for example, when the good or service is transmitted over a grid such as natural gas, electricity, rail service); purchasing economies (buying in bulk on long-term contracts); financial economies (larger firms typically can negotiate lower interest rates on borrowing); marketing (spreading the cost of advertising and having greater **advertising reach**); the **two-thirds rule**; and technological (taking advantage of increased specialization of inputs as operating scale increases).

Economies of Scale Index

A precise measure of the extent of **economies of scale**. Suppose that the firm produces a single product. Denote **marginal cost** at output q by $MC(q)$ and **average total cost** by $AC(q)$. Then the economies of scale index is $S(q) = AC(q)/MC(q)$. If $S(q) > 1$ there are economies of scale, if $S(q) < 1$ there are **diseconomies of scale**, if $S(q) = 1$ there are **constant returns to scale**.

Now consider the case where the firm produces multiple products. Suppose that a firm can produce n products and that its **total cost** function is $C(q_1, \ldots, q_n)$. **Marginal cost** of product i is $MC_i = \partial C(q_1, \ldots, q_n)/\partial q_i$. Define total output q implicitly by the equations $q_i = \lambda_i q$ ($i = 1, \ldots, n$) with

$$\sum_{i=1}^{n} \lambda_i = 1,$$

where the λ_i defines the proportions in which the n products are produced. Then **ray average cost** is total cost divided by q, or

$$RAC(q) = \frac{C(\lambda_1 q, \ldots, \lambda_n q)}{q}.$$

This cost function exhibits multi-product economies of scale if $dRAC(q)/dq < 1$. This allows us to define the multi-product economies of scale index

$$S^M = \frac{C(q_1, q_2, \ldots, q_n)}{\sum_{i=1}^{n} q_i MC_i}.$$

Economies of Scope

A situation in which it is less costly to produce a set of goods in one firm than to produce that set of goods in two or more firms. In the two-good case, economies of scope exist when the **total cost** of producing the two goods, $C(q_1, q_2)$, is such that $C(q_1, q_2) < C(q_1, 0) + C(0, q_2)$. When economies of scope are present we would expect to see extensive multi-product firms. Common sources of economies of scope are: when different products use many common inputs (for example, electronic goods); spreading of promotional and advertising costs over a wide range of related products; cost savings from exploitation of by-products (for example, drilling for oil and also obtaining natural gas); and reduced risk from offering an extensive product range.

Economies of Scope Index

A precise measure of the extent of economies of scope. In the two-good case, the economies of scope index is

$$S_C = \frac{C(q_1,0) + C(0,q_2) - C(q_1,q_2)}{C(q_1,q_2)}.$$

If $S_C > 0$ there are economies of scope.

Edgeworth Cycle

The outcome of **price competition** in which the competing firms make alternate moves in setting their prices. Prices fall until they approach **marginal costs**, after which there is a **war of attrition** as each firm waits for its rival to increase its price. When one firm eventually raises price the other firms quickly follow, but then the cycle starts again.

Efficiency

A market outcome is efficient when there is no reallocation of the resources in the market that will improve the well-being of one individual in the market without making at least one other individual worse off. A **perfectly competitive** market is efficient, while **monopolistic competition, oligopoly** and **monopoly** typically are inefficient. See also **Pareto efficient** and **Pareto optimality**.

Efficiency Effect

The hypothesis that an incumbent monopolist values a cost-reducing **innovation** more than a potential entrant with the result that the monopolist attempts to protect its monopoly position by innovation. Suppose that innovation reduces **marginal cost** from c_h to c_l and that **entry** is feasible only if the entrant has innovated to attain marginal cost c_l. Assume also that if entry occurs the incumbent has marginal cost c_i and the entrant has marginal cost c_e. Define monopoly **profit** with marginal cost c as $\pi^m(c)$, post-entry incumbent's **duopoly** profit as $\pi_i^d(c_i, c_e)$ and post-entry entrant's duopoly profit as $\pi_e^d(c_i, c_e)$. The efficiency effect states that the incumbent monopolist values the innovation more than the entrant if

$$\pi^m(c_l) - \pi_i^d(c_h, c_l) > \pi_e^d(c_h, c_l).$$

The left-hand side is the value that the monopolist places on the innovation: the additional profit that the monopolist makes by innovating rather than accommodating entry of a low-cost entrant. The right-hand side is the value that the entrant places on the innovation. This inequality is likely to be satisfied – a low-cost monopoly is likely to be more profitable than a combination of a high-cost and low-cost duopoly. As a result, the efficiency effect implies that we are likely to see the persistence of monopoly resulting from the monopolist's continuing innovative efforts.

Efficiency Gains

An argument that is often used to support a proposed **horizontal merger** by arguing that the merger will allow the merged firms to reduce their costs, with resulting benefits to consumers in lower prices as a result of the merger.

Efficiency Principle

A principle that states that if individuals can successfully bargain and can execute and monitor their agreements, then the outcome will be efficient for the bargaining parties. When applied to organizations, one implication of the efficiency principle is that the organizational and institutional arrangements that persist are likely to be efficient, otherwise they would have been replaced by superior arrangements. See Milgrom and Roberts (1992, p. 24).

Efficiency Wages

Wages that are set above the market wage rate in order to discourage employees from shirking, to reduce labor turnover and to mitigate **moral hazard**. These wages are used when it is difficult to monitor employees' actions or measure their abilities and where **incentive-based compensation** schemes are difficult to devise or implement. Suppose that an employee's wage is w, let w_0 be the outside wage that the employee could get after being fired from the current job after being caught shirking or cheating (adjusted for search costs and any period of unemployment); let v be the marginal value to the employee from shirking or cheating on the current job; let p be the probability that shirking or cheating is detected and the employee fired; and let Y be the discounted value of future earnings from the current job. Then the efficiency wage – the minimum wage necessary to ensure that the employee does not shirk – is $w = w_0 + v/Y.p$. Efficiency wages tend to be lower in long-term relations (for example, "lifetime contracts" such as those that used to be prevalent in Japan) and when monitoring and detection of shirking or cheating are easy. Efficiency wages tend to be higher when employees can extract considerable gains by cheating or shirking and when shirking or cheating is difficult to detect.

Efficiency Wage Hypothesis

The hypothesis that workers inside a firm are given a **rent** relative to the unemployed as a means of providing them with incentives not to shirk when shirking is difficult to detect and there are limited opportunities for punishing shirking. From the example of **efficiency wages** the rent is $w - w_0$.

Efficient Market Hypothesis

The hypothesis that financial markets are efficient in that they respond rapidly and rationally to current and new information and so are unbiased by reflecting the collective beliefs of all market participants. If the efficient market hypothesis is valid then it is not possible to outperform the market using only information that is available in the market. See also: **weak**, **semi-strong** and **strong forms** of this hypothesis, which are distinguished by the information that is assumed to be embodied in prices.

Elastic Demand

Demand for which the absolute value of the **price elasticity of demand** is greater than unity.

Elastic Supply

Supply for which the **price elasticity of supply** is greater than unity.

Elasticity

A measure of sensitivity. Suppose that a change in x changes y. Then the elasticity, or **point elasticity**, of y with respect to x, denoted $\eta_{y:x}$, is defined as the percentage change in y divided by the percentage change in x. More formally

$$\eta_{y:x} = \frac{dy}{dx} \cdot \frac{x}{y}.$$

Elasticity of Demand

The sensitivity of quantity demanded with respect to a change in price. If quantity demanded is $q(p)$ then

$$\eta_{q:p} = \frac{dq(p)}{dp} \cdot \frac{p}{q(p)}.$$

Demand is **elastic (inelastic)** if $|\eta_{q:p}| > (<) 1$. Demand is more likely to be elastic: if there are many close substitutes; in the long run; for luxuries rather than necessities; if the good or service takes a large share of the consumer's budget; and for individual brands rather than product classes (for example, for Coca-Cola rather than carbonated drinks).

Elasticity of Substitution

For a **production (utility) function** $f(x)$ the elasticity of substitution between inputs (goods) i and j at the point $\mathbf{x}$ is defined as

$$\sigma_{ij} = \frac{d\ln(x_i/x_j)}{d\ln(f_i(\mathbf{x})/f_j(\mathbf{x}))}.$$

As σ_{ij} approaches infinity, i and j are more nearly perfect substitutes and the **isoquants (indifference curves)** approach straight lines. By contrast, as σ_{ij} approaches zero, i and j become less and less substitutable and the isoquants (indifference curves) become approximately L-shaped.

Elasticity of Supply

The sensitivity of quantity supplied with respect to a change in price. If quantity supplied is $q(p)$ then

$$\eta_{q:p} = \frac{dq(p)}{dp} \cdot \frac{p}{q(p)}.$$

Supply is **elastic (inelastic)** if $\eta_{q:p} > (<) 1$.

Emerging Markets

A term used to describe economic activity in newly industrializing markets that are transitioning from being developing markets to being developed markets.

Empire Building

(1) The desire on the part of senior management to expand the size and scope of the enterprise they are managing, often suggested as a managerial motive for **mergers** that are not necessarily in the interests of **shareholders**. (2) The attempt by mid-level management to increase **base pay** by expanding the size and scope of the units that they manage.

Employee-Owned Firm

A firm in which the employees hold a controlling interest.

End-Game Problem

The problem that can arise when an **agent** is in a relationship that is about to end. The agent has incentives that are different from those in an ongoing relationship and may be tempted to act inefficiently, dishonestly or more generally in the interests of the agent rather than the **principal**. When the end-game problem is present, mechanisms intended to encourage efficient behavior based on concern with **reputation** are less likely to be effective. One solution is to increase the use of **incentive-based compensation** for managers approaching retirement. Alternatively, a business founder may decide to sell the business at retirement: the founder then has an incentive to act in ways that maintain and grow the value of the business.

Endogeneity

In **regression analysis**, when one or more **independent variables** are correlated with the error term. For example, with profitability of firms across industries as the **dependent variable**, including the number of firms within each industry as an independent variable would introduce endogeneity, since, in addition to the number of firms impacting profits, profitability will impact entry and exit decisions and thus the number of firms. In this case, the number of firms would be correlated with the error term. Potential sources of endogeneity include **simultaneity**, error in measuring independent variables, omitted independent variables, bias in sample selection, and **serial correlation** when lagged dependent variables are used as **explanatory variables**. Endogeneity can be corrected using **instrumental variables estimation**.

Endogenous Mergers

Modeling **mergers** in a dynamic framework in which firms make explicit, strategic choices regarding whether and with whom they will merge.

Endogenous Variable

A variable in an economic model whose value is determined by the model. See also **endogeneity**.

Enforcement Costs

The costs of ensuring that a party to a contract is abiding by the terms of the contract and the costs of ensuring contract compliance when it is felt that there is non-compliance. See **contracting costs** and **transaction costs**.

English Auction

Another name for an **ascending bid auction**.

Entrepreneur

An individual who seeks to develop and make returns from new ventures or businesses, usually where successful development of the venture entails considerable **innovation** and risk.

Entropy index

A measure of **market concentration**. If there are n firms in a market and the **market share** of firm i is s_i then the entropy index is

$$E = \sum_{i=1}^{n} s_i \ln s_i.$$

See also **concentration ratio** and **Herfindahl–Hirschman Index (HHI)**.

Entry

The decision by a firm to open up operations in a market.

Entry Barriers

See **barriers to entry**.

Entry Condition

Firms will choose to enter a market if expected **profit** is positive, and will choose to **exit** the market if expected profit is negative. The decision to enter requires that the firm expects the price post-entry to exceed the firm's minimum **average total cost**. By contrast, the decision to exit is determined by the relationship between price and **average variable cost**.

Entry Deterrence

Deliberate and strategic actions by incumbent firms in order to prevent new firms from entering their market. These can take many forms, such as installing **excess capacity**, **bundling**, gaining control of strategic resources, **tying arrangements** and **vertical integration**. The intent of these actions is to make **entry** difficult, unattractive or more costly for the **potential entrant**. For them to be effective they must be credible, in other words they must be actions that the incumbent will take even if entry takes place.

Envelope Theorem

A theorem that is useful in solving problems of optimization in the theory of industrial organization. Consider the constrained maximization problem

$$\max_{x} f(x,a)$$

subject to the constraint $g(x, a) \geq 0$ where a is some parameter. The Lagrangian for this problem is: $L(x, a, \lambda) = f(x, a) + \lambda g(x, a)$ where λ is the Lagrange multiplier. Let $x(a)$ and $\lambda(a)$ be the values of x and λ that solve this maximization problem given the parameter a and denote $V(a) = f(x(a), a)$: $V(a)$ is the value function for this maximizing problem. The envelope theorem describes how $V(a)$ changes with the parameter a:

$$\frac{dV(a)}{da} = \frac{\partial L(x,a,\lambda)}{\partial a}\bigg|_{x(a),\lambda(a)}.$$

Applications include the problem of a consumer maximizing **utility** subject to a **budget constraint** or a firm maximizing profit subject to a technology constraint defined by the firm's **production function**.

Equal Compensation Principle

The principle that if an **agent** is expected to allocate effort across a series of different activities then the agent's incentive payments should equalize the marginal return to effort applied to each activity. If this principle is violated then the agent will concentrate effort on the activities with the highest marginal returns to effort. For example, if a taxi driver is expected to maintain his car then his incentive contract should take into account the condition of the car.

Equilibrium

A situation in which no participant in a market wants to change their actions given that no other participant in the market changes their actions. See also **equilibrium prices**, **competitive equilibrium** and **Nash equilibrium**.

Equilibrium Existence Theorem

If players' strategy sets S_i are compact and convex for all $i = 1, \ldots,$ n and if the players' **payoff** functions $\pi_i(s_i)$ are continuous and quasi-concave in s_i for all $i = 1, \ldots, n$, then there exists a **pure strategy Nash equilibrium**.

Equilibrium Outcome

The **payoffs** that players receive in a **Nash equilibrium**.

Equilibrium Prices

Prices in a market that result in equality between the quantities that consumers demand from the market and the quantities that suppliers are willing supply to the market. The market clears at these prices. If prices are not equilibrium prices, market forces are expected to restore equilibrium. Thus, if there is **excess supply** in a market, price in that market should fall; whereas if there is **excess demand**, price should rise.

Equivalent Variation

The income adjustment that a consumer would accept in order to avoid a price change. Suppose that $\mathbf{p}$ is the price vector. Then the **expenditure function** is

$$E(\mathbf{p}, u) = \min_{\mathbf{q}} (\mathbf{p}.\mathbf{q})$$

subject to $U(\mathbf{q}) \geq u$, where $\mathbf{q}$ is the consumption vector, and the **indirect utility function** is

$$V(\mathbf{p}, I) = \max_{\mathbf{q}} U(\mathbf{q})$$

subject to $\mathbf{p}.\mathbf{q} \leq I$, where I is the consumer's income. The equivalent variation to avoid a change in the price vector from $\mathbf{p}^0$ to $\mathbf{p}^1$ is

$$EV = E(\mathbf{p}^0, V(\mathbf{p}^1, I)) - I.$$

Essential Facilities

Facilities or resources that are considered to be necessary for a firm to be able to operate in a particular industry or market and that are not easily duplicated or substituted.

Event Study

An **econometric** method designed to measure the influence that an event, or the dissemination of new information, has on a variable of interest. The method is widely applicable to the area of industrial organization, including assessing the impact of **regulations** on firm performance, and is commonly used in finance applications to measure the effect of announcements, such as **mergers** or monetary policy shifts, on stock prices. See also **Eckbo test**.

Evolutionary Game

The application of genetics-based models of change to **game theory**. These **games** are concerned more with the dynamics of changes in strategy than in the properties of strategic **equilibrium**.

Excess Capacity

Capacity that a firm installs in excess of the capacity needed to satisfy expected demand. Firms in **monopolistically competitive** markets typically have excess capacity in that, in **long-run equilibrium**, they operate on the downward sloping part of their **average total cost** functions. In **oligopolistic** markets excess capacity can be used as a strategic **entry-deterring** device provided that **potential entrants** must incur some **sunk costs** of **entry**. Suppose, for example, that the incumbent firm and the potential entrant are **Cournot competitors**. If the entrant must incur sunk costs to enter, then there is a minimum output level q_e below which the entrant will not be able to recover its sunk costs. The incumbent can then choose between **accommodating entry** or installing sufficient capacity such that the **Cournot equilibrium** gives the potential entrant an output less than q_e.

Excess Demand

A situation in which the quantity demanded is greater than the quantity supplied at the ruling market price. If there is excess demand in a market then price should be expected to rise to clear the market, unless price is regulated by the imposition of a **price ceiling**.

Excess Profit

Profit in excess of **normal profits**. In **perfectly** or **monopolistically competitive** markets such profits will induce new firm **entry**, competing the excess profits away. If, by contrast, there are **barriers to entry**, excess profit can persist into the long run.

Excess Return on Sales

The ratio of **economic profit** to total **sales revenue**.

Excess Supply

A situation in which the quantity supplied is greater than the quantity demanded at the ruling market price. If there is excess supply in a market then price should be expected to fall to clear the market, unless price is regulated by the imposition of a **price floor**.

Exchange Rate

The price of one country's currency in terms of another's. Countries can typically choose between one of two exchange rate regimes. With fixed exchange rates, a country attempts to fix the rate at which its currency is traded with respect to some major currency, usually the US dollar or the euro. With floating exchange rates the exchange rate is left free to vary in response to market conditions.

Exclusionary Practices

Strategic actions that are taken by incumbent firms in order to **deter entry** by new firms or force the **exit** of rival firms.

Exclusive Dealing

An agreement between a retailer or wholesaler and a manufacturer that the retailer or wholesaler will not sell any brand that competes with the manufacturer's product. Such agreements can viewed as anticompetitive under **antitrust laws**. See also **refusal to deal**.

Exclusive Territory

An agreement between a manufacturer and a retailer that guarantees to the retailer the sole rights to sell the manufacturer's product in a well-defined geographic area. In **franchise** agreements, a contract offered by the franchisor to the franchisee guaranteeing that no additional franchises will be awarded within the agreed territory. Offering such exclusive territories is a means of mitigating the **moral hazard** problem to which a franchisor can be subject, when a franchisee builds an unexpectedly successful franchise in an area in which the franchisor had not previously been active.

Executive Compensation

The compensation paid to senior executives in a company. This will typically be a combination of a fixed salary, an **incentive-based compensation** package and **stock options**.

Exit

The decision by a firm to close down its operations in a market. Such an exit decision is more likely if the market price is less than the firm's minimum **average variable costs**.

Exit Barriers

See **barriers to exit**.

Exit Costs

The costs that are incurred in exiting a market, usually because **entry** requires that the firm incurs **sunk costs**. Exit costs can constitute a **barrier to entry** but they also can constitute a **barrier to exit**.

Exogenous Variable

A parameter in an economic model whose value is determined independently of or outside the model. See also **explanatory variable**.

Expansion Path

Suppose that w is the vector of **factor prices** and $q = f(\mathbf{x})$ is the firm's **production function**, where $\mathbf{x}$ is the vector of factor inputs. The firm's expansion path is the path traced out by the tangency points between the firm's **isocost lines** at factor prices w and the firm's **isoquants**.

Expected Utility

Suppose that the **utility function** for a consumer is $U(x)$ where x is a **random variable** with probability density function $f(x)$. Then expected utility is

$$\int_{-\infty}^{\infty} U(x)f(x)\,dx.$$

Expected Value

Suppose that x is a **random variable** with probability density function $f(x)$. Then the expected value of x is

$$E(x) = \int_{-\infty}^{\infty} xf(x)\,dx.$$

Expenditure Function

Suppose that $\mathbf{x}$ is a vector of consumer goods, $\mathbf{p}$ is its associated price vector and $U(\mathbf{x})$ is the consumer's **utility function**. Then the expenditure function $E(\mathbf{p}, u)$ is the solution to the programming problem: $\min_{\mathbf{x}} \mathbf{p} \cdot \mathbf{x}$ subject to $\mathbf{x} \geq 0$ and $U(\mathbf{x}) \geq u$. The **compensated demand function** can be derived from the expenditure function according to **Shephard's Lemma**. The Lagrangian of the constrained optimization problem is

$$L = \sum_{i=1}^{n} p_i x_i + \lambda(u - U(x_1, \ldots, x_n))$$

and the minimand is the expenditure function $E(\mathbf{p}, u)$. By the **envelope theorem**

$$\frac{\partial E}{\partial p_i} = \frac{\partial L}{\partial p_i} = x_i(\mathbf{p}, u).$$

Expense Center

A business unit that is allocated a fixed budget and asked to maximize a service or output that is difficult to measure objectively. Examples are accounting, patenting and public relations business units.

Experience Good

A good or service whose true quality and other characteristics cannot be observed before purchase, but are observable only following consumption of the good or service. Examples are (high-class) restaurant meals, surgeons, hi-tech stereo systems, advertising campaigns and consultancy reports. Experience goods are to be contrasted with **search goods**. Experience goods are challenging for consumers as they seek to make accurate consumption decisions, leading consumers to expend resources in gathering information on such goods pre-purchase. They can also encourage consumers to take price as a signal of unobservable quality, implying that demand for experience goods tends to be **inelastic**.

Experimental Economics

A method of analyzing individuals' responses to economic incentives using experiments designed to mimic real-world market and choice settings. The methodology allows the researcher to identify empirical patterns of strategic choice that might otherwise be difficult to identify using industry data. For example, an experimenter might instruct subjects to make pricing decisions, under a variety of simulated market conditions, and compensate subjects based on the total profitability of their choices over several periods of play. Such an experiment can provide evidence on factors likely to influence the sustainability of tacitly collusive price arrangements in industries.

Explanatory Variable

A variable that is on the right-hand side of a **regression equation**. The known values of explanatory or **independent variables** are used to predict the value of a **dependent variable**. If the equation to be estimated is

$$Y = \alpha + \sum_{i=1}^{n} \beta_i X_i + \varepsilon_i,$$

then the X_i are the explanatory variables. **Ordinary least squares (OLS)** regression techniques implicitly assume that all explanatory variables are also **exogenous**. If there is a possibility that some of these variables are **endogenous**, then **instrumental variables estimation** will typically be needed.

Explicit Collusion

Collusion that is sustained though explicit communication and information sharing by the parties to the collusive agreement.

Explicit Contract

A formal **contract** between a firm and an individual related to the firm, such as an employee, a buyer, a supplier or a provider of capital to the firm.

Extensive Form Game

The representation of a **dynamic game** in the form of a **game tree**, detailing the players, the players' **strategies**, the order of moves, the information available to the players at each stage of the game and the **payoffs** at each terminal node of the game. Play begins in such a game at an initial node, and flows through the decision nodes of the game until the terminal nodes are reached. An extensive form game is solved by **backward induction** based upon Selten's concept of **subgame perfection**: any **equilibrium** to the entire game must also be an equilibrium for every **subgame** of the entire game.

Externality

The cost or benefit that results from an economic transaction but that falls on third parties who are not parties to the transaction. In the case of an external **benefit**, the third parties do not have to pay the full value of the benefit they receive. In the case of an external **cost**, the third parties do not receive full compensation for the harm that they suffer. The immediate implication is that the market, when left unregulated, will tend to under-provide goods or services that confer external benefits and to overprovide goods or services that impose external costs.

F

Facilitating Practice

A business practice that facilitates tacit or explicit coordination between firms by softening inter-firm competition without violating **antitrust laws**. Typical such practices are price leadership, advance notice of price changes, **meet-the-competition clauses** and **most-favored-customer clauses**.

Factor Demand Function

The relationship between the price of a **factor of production** and the amount of the factor that the firm wishes to employ. If p is the output price, $\mathbf{w}$ is the vector of prices of the factors of production and $\pi(p, \mathbf{w})$ is the **profit function**, then the factor demand function for factor i is $x_i(p,\mathbf{w}) = -\partial\pi(p,\mathbf{w})/\partial w_i$ (**Hotelling's Lemma**).

Factor of Production

An **input** that is necessary for production. Typical factors of production are labor, land and capital. **Factor demand functions** are derived from solving the firm's profit-maximization optimization problem using **Hotelling's Lemma**.

Factor Price

The price of a **factor of production**.

Factor Substitutability

A measure of the ease with which a firm can change the combination of **factors of production** it uses in response to changes in factor prices. The most commonly used measure of factor substitutability is the **elasticity of substitution**. This characteristic of the firm's technology is of interest when analyzing a firm's responsiveness to **factor price** changes in the long run, when all of the firm's factors of production are variable.

Failing-Firm Defense

The defense of a proposed **merger** in which the firms argue that if the merger is not allowed to proceed, one of the firms will go out of business, thus the merger will not have detrimental **welfare** effects for consumers.

Fair Rate of Return

See **rate-of-return regulation**.

False Advertising

The use of deliberately deceptive or false statements in advertising that are designed to give the advertiser a commercial advantage.

Fast-Second Innovators

Firms that are rapidly able to imitate innovative activities of their rivals and so reduce or eliminate the **first-mover advantages** of their rivals. In some circumstances a fast-second can come to dominate the market.

Fat-Cat Effect

Assume that a **strategic commitment** makes a firm soft and so potentially softens competition in the market. The firm has an incentive to **overinvest** in this type of commitment, become a "fat cat", if the choice variables are **strategic complements**. For example, consider the following two-period model. In the first period, the incumbent monopolist chooses a level of advertisement to generate customer awareness and "goodwill". In the second period, the monopolist faces **potential entry**. The monopolist might choose to overinvest in advertising in the first period, to increase its customer base, and avoid matching the entrant's low price in the second period, thereby softening competition and **accommodating entry**. See Fudenberg and Tirole (1984), **lean-and-hungry look**, **puppy dog strategy** and **top dog strategy**.

Federal Trade Commission (FTC)

An independent federal agency whose principal charge is to enforce the **antitrust laws** of the United States particularly with respect to **mergers** and anticompetitive business practices. See also **Department of Justice**.

Fidelity Rebate

A discount offered by a seller to a buyer that rewards the buyer for sourcing most or all of its requirements for a given good from the seller.

Fighting Brand

A brand that is created specifically in order to meet a competitive threat. The fighting brand is typically priced low and supplied only in those markets where a rival has emerged and is potentially successful.

Finitely Repeated Games

Games that are repeated a finite number of times, where the number of repetitions is known to the players in advance of the game being played. When a **prisoners' dilemma game** is formulated as a finitely repeated game, lasting for N periods, players will choose to defect in the final (Nth) period, since there are no future gains from investing in a cooperative reputation. By **backward induction**, this logic will apply to period $N-1$, and then to period $N-2$, and so on, leading players to choose to defect in all periods, beginning with the first. More generally, if a game has a unique **Nash equilibrium** and the game is played finitely many times, its equilibrium is the Nash equilibrium in each period: **Selten's theorem**. This is in contrast to the case of **infinitely repeated games**, in which cooperation can be sustained under certain **discount factors**.

By contrast, consider the following game, where in each cell, the **payoff** to the row player is listed first, and the payoff to the column player is listed second:

		Firm 2		
		Low	Medium	High
Firm 1	Low	70, 70	80, 65	90, 60
	Medium	65, 80	85, 85	100, 70
	High	60, 95	70, 100	90, 90

There are two **Nash equilibria** to this game, (Low, Low) and (Medium, Medium), while both firms prefer (High, High). Suppose that this game is played twice. Then cooperation on (High, High) can be sustained in the first period by the following strategy for each firm:

- First period: Play High
- Second period: If the history from the first period is (High, High), play Medium otherwise play Low.

Note that the strategy combination in the second period is a Nash equilibrium. If one firm is expected to play Medium (Low) then the other firm should play Medium (Low). The payoff to each player from cooperating in the first period is $90 + 85D$, while cheating in the first period gives a payoff of $100 + 70D$ where D is the **discount factor**. Cooperation on (High, High) is sustainable for the first period if $D > 0.67$. More generally, for cooperation in a finitely repeated game to be sustainable over the early periods of play, it is necessary that the game have more than one Nash equilibrium.

Finiteness Property

In a market characterized by **vertical product differentiation**, assume that firms play a three-stage **game**: in the first stage they choose whether or not to enter; in the second stage they each choose the quality of the good they will produce; and in the third stage they compete in prices. Then if the distribution of consumer **marginal willingness to pay** for quality is finite, only a finite number of firms can have positive demand with positive prices, even if there are zero costs of production and no fixed entry costs. This stands in sharp contrast to markets characterized by **horizontal product differentiation**, where if there are no fixed entry costs and consumers are continuously distributed over the **characteristics space** the market will contain an infinite number of firms.

Finking

The decision by a player of a **game** to cheat upon an agreed-upon strategy or to reveal the existence of **explicit collusion**. The antitrust authorities can encourage finking by introducing **leniency programs** offering reduced sentences to **cartel** members who fink on their partners.

Firm-Specific Capital

Physical and **human capital** that is less productive when used outside the firm that has created it or outside the firm in which the employee has invested to acquire the human capital. The latter case can lead to there being a **hold-up problem** for the employee who has acquired the knowledge and skill set specific to the firm. See also **asset specificity**.

First-Best

An allocation of scarce resources that maximizes **total surplus**. A **perfectly competitive** market achieves this first-best outcome, as does **monopoly** under **first-degree price discrimination**. While both of these market outcomes achieve the first-best allocation of resources, total surplus under perfect competition comprises both **consumer** and **producer surplus**, whereas under monopoly with first-degree price discrimination, the entirety of total surplus goes to the monopolist; total surplus in this case is equivalent to producer surplus.

First-Degree Price Discrimination

A form of **price discrimination** in which the seller is able to extract the maximum **willingness to pay** of each consumer for every unit of the product that is sold, transforming all **consumer surplus** into **producer surplus**. One method for implementing this type of price discrimination is by means of a **two-part tariff** in which the seller sets the unit price equal to **marginal cost** and then applies a consumer-specific fixed charge equal to the consumer surplus that the consumer would receive at this unit price. An alternative method is to offer a consumer a package of quantity Q_i at a total charge W_i where W_i is the consumer's willingness to pay for the quantity Q_i. If a monopolist employs first-degree price discrimination there is no **deadweight loss** of monopoly: the monopolist will offer the **efficient** quantity, converting all consumer surplus into revenues to the firm.

First-Mover Advantage

The advantage to a firm from being the first to move into a new market segment. This advantage can stem from the firm being able to preempt essential resources, register **patents** or **trademarks**, exploit learning economies, **economies of scale** or **economies of scope**, or build a **reputation**. In **sequential games**, the first-mover advantage derives from the first mover's ability to anticipate the strategic choices of later players, according to these players' **best response functions**. This leadership position can yield profit advantages, as in the **Stackelberg model** of quantity competition relative to the **Cournot equilibrium**. Depending on the nature of the game and strategic choices, such as with sequential pricing, the advantage can instead accrue to the second mover.

First-Price Auction

A sealed-bid auction in which the winning bidder pays the amount submitted by that bidder. See **sealed-bid first-price auction**.

First-to-File Rule

In a **patent system**, the rule that a patent for an innovation is awarded to the first individual to file an application for patent protection, no matter the actual date of the innovation.

First-to-Invent Rule

In a **patent system**, the rule that a patent for an innovation is awarded to the first individual to invent. Invention is defined as consisting of: actually developing the original idea for the invention; and reducing the invention to practice. The latter requirement is fulfilled either when the invention has been produced in physical form or when the inventor has filed for a patent for the invention.

Fisher Separation Theorem

Suppose that there are **perfect capital markets** so that a decision maker can borrow on the same terms as he/she can lend. Then the decision maker's choice of investment projects depends solely upon the returns that are forecast from the investment and on the interest rate. This choice is unaffected by the decision maker's preferences with respect to personal consumption and the timing of such personal consumption. In other words, the decision maker can separate investment decisions from consumption decisions.

Five-Forces Analysis

See **industry analysis**.

Fixed Costs

Costs that are invariant with output over some range of output. If fixed costs are F_i over the output range (q_i, q_{i+1}) then the **total cost** function can be written as $TC(q) = F_i + V(q)$ for $q \in (q_i, q_{i+1})$ where $V(q)$ is **variable cost**. Fixed costs can be an important source of **economies of scale**. A firm maximizes its profit by choosing the output at which its **marginal revenue** equals its **marginal cost**; fixed costs do not factor into this computation.

Fixed-Proportions Production (Utility) Function

A **production (utility) function** for which the **elasticity of substitution** is zero. The functional form of this function is $y = \min\{a_1x_1, a_2x_2, \ldots, a_nx_n\}$ ($u = \min\{a_1q_1, a_2q_2, \ldots, a_nq_n\}$), where x_i (q_i) is input (consumption) of factor (good) i. Also known as the **Leontief production (utility) function**. The shape of the **isoquants (indifference curves)** is L-shaped, reflecting the perfect **complementarity** of the inputs (goods), based on a constant factor of proportional usage (consumption).

Flexibility Analysis

When a **strategic commitment** involves uncertainty, the calculation of the **option value** of delaying the commitment in order to reduce the uncertainty associated with the commitment; if there is no uncertainty then the option value of delay is zero.

Flexible Manufacturing

A manufacturing process by which the producer can produce a wide range of customized products at little or no cost penalty.

Flow Analysis

Examining data on consumer travel patterns and consumer geographic purchase decisions.

FOB Pricing

See **free on board pricing**.

Focal Point

In a game with multiple potential equilibria, the solution that players will tend to choose in the absence of explicit communication between the players because of noteworthy or obvious features of this solution besides its **payoffs**. Focal points can be especially useful in determining the outcome of a **coordination game**.

Focus Strategy

The decision by a firm to offer only a narrow range of products or services, or supply only a narrow subset of consumer markets, or both.

Fold-Back Method

Identifying the **subgame perfect Nash equilibrium** of an **extensive form game** by starting at the end of the game and working back to the initial node of the game. See also **backward induction**.

Folk Theorem

The theorem that in an **infinitely repeated game** any set of feasible outcomes can be supported as a **subgame perfect Nash equilibrium** for that game by some **discount factor** that is sufficiently close to unity. One simple method of proving the folk theorem is to assume that all players are following a **grim trigger strategy**. The folk theorem implies that infinitely repeated games have multiple equilibria provided that the players do not discount future **payoffs** "too heavily". To see why, suppose that there are n

firms, that the payoff to player i in a proposed equilibrium is π_i^e, the payoff to player i if that player plays its best response to the strategies of the other players in the proposed equilibrium is π_i^d, and the payoff to player i when all firms revert to the **Nash equilibrium** is π_i^n. The folk theorem states that this proposed equilibrium is subgame perfect provided that the **discount factor** for firm i, denoted d_i, satisfies

$$d_i > d_i^* = \frac{\pi_i^d - \pi_i^e}{\pi_i^d - \pi_i^n}.$$

Clearly, we have $\pi_i^d > \pi_i^e > \pi_i^n$ as a result of which $d_i^* < 1$.

Followers

See **Stackelberg followers**.

Forced Distribution

An employee assessment system in which the distribution of ratings assigned by supervisors is forced to follow a pre-set curve.

Foreclosure

The refusal by an **upstream firm** with market power to supply its product or service to particular **downstream firms**.

Foreign Direct Investment

Investment undertaken to acquire a controlling interest in enterprises operating outside of the home country of the investor. The organization so created involves a parent company and a foreign affiliate that comprise a **multinational corporation**. Control is defined as ownership of at least 10 percent of the voting power of the enterprise being acquired.

Forward Integration

The decision by an **upstream firm** to merge with or purchase at least one of its **downstream-firm** customers or to open a greenfield operation in the downstream market. Such action can lead to **foreclosure** in the downstream market, with the upstream division of the integrated firm refusing to supply other than the downstream division of the same firm.

Four-Firm Concentration Ratio

The market share controlled by the largest four firms in an industry. See **concentration ratio**.

Franchise

A business unit that is established using a **franchising** business model. Typical franchises are McDonald's and Subway.

Franchise Bidding

Government **privatization** of a monopoly by selling the right to operate the monopoly to the highest bidder.

Franchising

A business model in which a franchisor licenses a franchisee to operate a franchise in exchange for a regular payment. The franchisor typically controls the method of doing business and the trademark and may provide training, advertising and other support services. The payment usually consists of a fixed fee plus an agreed percentage of gross **sales revenues** or gross **profits**. The size of the percentage share will influence the franchisee's incentives to manage costs and invest in maintaining the value of the franchisor's brand. Provided this percentage is not too large, franchising makes the franchisee the **residual claimant**, aligning the interests of the franchisee and the franchisor.

Free Cash Flow

The amount of a firm's cash flow in excess of the amount that can be profitably invested in new projects.

Free Cash Flow Problem

Conflicts between owners and managers of a firm with respect to how the firm's **free cash flow** should be allocated. Managers will typically wish to use these resources to expand the size of the firm while owners would prefer to see them distributed as dividends.

Free Entry

The absence of any **barriers to entry** to a market or industry. When this condition is met it is to be expected that **entry** will constrain **profits** in the industry to near-normal levels. See **perfect competition** and **monopolistic competition**.

Free on Board (FOB) Pricing

A geographic pricing system in which the seller quotes a price at the factory or warehouse and the buyer pays this price plus transport costs from the seller's to the buyer's location. Transportation can be arranged by the buyer or the seller.

Free-Riding

The decision by an economic agent to consume more of a shared good or resource or to incur less than the agent's fair share of the effort required to produce a good or service. Free-riding typically leads to inefficiency either by causing value-creating activities not to be pursued or as a result of the overuse of shared resources. Organizations that rely on extensive teamwork must be careful in how they construct teams and assess the performance of the teams and the individuals within the teams. See **common resource problem** and **free-riding problem**.

Free-Riding Problem

The problem of how to prevent or limit **free-riding**. With **public goods** the free-riding problem is normally resolved by having the production of the good financed through taxes. (See **common resource problem**.) If production requires teamwork then free riding by team members can be

controlled by having each team member assessed by other team members
and making the assessment part of the individual's record.

Free Trade

The absence of artificial barriers to trade between nations such as tariffs,
licensing restrictions or quota restrictions. For example, the North
American Free Trade Agreement (NAFTA), involving the United
States, Canada and Mexico, significantly reduced barriers to trade
among these countries; and the European Union removed barriers to
the movement of goods, services and individuals between the member
states.

Freight Absorption

In **geographic markets** the decision by a seller to charge buyers only a
fraction of the freight costs from the seller's to the buyer's location.
Suppose that a seller supplies consumers in a number of different cities,
with transport cost per unit to city i being t_i. Further suppose that **marginal costs** for the seller are constant at c per unit and that demand in city
i is given by:

$$D(p) \quad \begin{aligned} &= \left(\frac{x}{b}(a - p) \right)^{1/x} \quad (x > -1; x \neq 0) \\ &= ae^{-bp} \quad\quad\quad (x = 0) \end{aligned}$$

The price charged in city i equates **marginal revenue** with **marginal cost** and
so satisfies

$$p_i \left(1 - \frac{1}{\eta_i} \right) = c + t_i$$

where η_i is the absolute value of the **price elasticity of demand** in city i.
From the demand function we have that the elasticity of demand is:

$$\eta \quad \begin{aligned} &= p/x(a - p) \text{ if } x \neq 0 \\ &= bp \quad\quad\quad \text{ if } x = 0 \end{aligned}$$

Substituting into the pricing equation gives:

$$p_i \begin{cases} = \dfrac{ax + c}{1 + x} + \dfrac{t_i}{1 + x} & \text{if } x \neq 0 \\[3mm] = \dfrac{1}{b} + c + t_i & \text{if } x = 0 \end{cases}.$$

So if $x > 0$ a fraction $1/(1 + x)$ of freight costs are charged to consumers and a fraction $x/(1 + x)$ of freight costs are absorbed by the seller. If $x = 0$ there is no freight absorption and if $x < 0$ the seller charges more than the full transport cost to buyers.

Fringe Benefit

Employee compensation other than salary or **incentive-based compensation**. Fringe benefits are usually received either in kind or are deferred (such as pension entitlements).

Full Price

In **geographic markets** the **free on board price** plus transport costs. In **characteristics markets** the product price plus the consumer's valuation of the utility lost by buying a product that is not the consumer's most preferred product.

Fulfilled Expectations Equilibrium

In a **network industry**, an **equilibrium** in which firms' quantities constitute a **Nash equilibrium** and in which consumers' expectations with respect to the size of the network are also fulfilled.

Full-Line Forcing

A constraint imposed by a multi-product seller on a buyer forcing the buyer to purchase the full range of the seller's products or services. A full-line forcing contract between a manufacturer and a distributor would stipulate that the distributor must carry all of the manufacturer's products. However, the distributor may stock the products by purchasing them from both the multi-product manufacturer and competing manufacturers.

The latter feature of this arrangement distinguishes it from tie-in sales in the context of **antitrust laws**; full-line forcing contracts do not necessarily result in anticompetitive outcomes.

Fully Distributed Cost Pricing

A price-setting rule for firms that serve two or more markets, based on allocating common fixed costs across markets by assigning pre-determined proportions to each market. This approach to cost distribution is used by regulators to determine rates for public utilities, whose cost structures can be characterized by such sub-additive costs. Customers in different usage classes, such as residential versus commercial, are assigned different proportions of the common fixed costs in the rate determination process.

Functional Myopia

A situation in which employees concentrate on their own assigned activities rather than on the broader array of activities that have to be performed if overall value created is to be maximized.

Functional Organization

An organization in which the separate functions, such as accounting, human resource management, sales and manufacturing are each controlled by a single department.

Fundamental Transformation

Suppose that a bilateral business relationship requires that one or other or both of the parties invest in **relationship-specific assets**. Once the investment is made, the negotiating relationship between the two parties changes from large-numbers bargaining to bilateral bargaining and so is fundamentally transformed. One important risk that arises from this fundamental transformation is that of the **hold-up problem**.

Futures Market

A market in which buyers and sellers can enter into contracts to buy and sell agreed quantities of commodities or financial assets at a price agreed at the date of the contract but with delivery and payment at an agreed date in the future. Typical futures markets are in commodities such as wheat, rubber and oil, and in financial instruments such as foreign currencies and shares of stock.

G

Gains from Trade

The increase in total surplus that results from the process of exchange between individuals. If all the parties involved enter voluntarily into the exchange then all will enjoy gains from trade. Intuitively, a potential seller will not agree to sell unless the price received is greater than the seller's **reservation price** and a buyer will not agree to buy unless the price paid is less than the buyer's reservation price. For a successful trade to take place a necessary condition is that the seller's reservation price is less than the buyer's reservation price. Suppose that the seller's reservation price is P_s and the buyer's reservation price is P_b, with $P_s < P_b$. Then if the seller and buyer agree to trade at a price P such that $P_s < P < P_b$ both gain from this trade.

Gain-Sharing Plan

A **group incentive compensation** system in which, if the group exceeds its predetermined targets, the members of the group receive bonuses determined by the extent to which the targets were exceeded.

Game

Strategic interaction described by the players, the **strategies** that they have available, the information that each player has at each point in the game, the **payoffs** that arise from each possible strategy combination, the timing of moves by each player and the time horizon over which the game is to be played. Games can be **simultaneous** or **sequential**, **static** or **dynamic**, finite-horizon or infinite-horizon, perfect information or **incomplete information**.

Game Theory

The set of techniques that can be applied to study decision making by economic agents who are interdependent and interact through **games**.

Game Tree

The representation of an **extensive form game** as a tree with decision nodes and branches. Each decision **node** defines the player to whom the decision at that node belongs and the information that the player has at that node. Each branch identifies the decision that has been taken along that branch.

Gaming a System

Opportunistic actions taken by an individual to exploit the rules of the system for the personal benefit of the individual. For example, a **principal** in designing an **incentive-based compensation** package should anticipate that the **agent** will attempt to game the incentive package. An essential element of good design is that the package aligns the interests of the principal and the agent.

General Equilibrium Model

An economic model that seeks to explain production, consumption and the determination of prices by aggregating the maximization decisions of the individuals and firms in the economy. This type of model takes explicit account of the property that all markets are interconnected. A change in any one market will have knock-on effects on a series of other markets. For example, a change in the demand for corn will affect the costs of restaurants that specialize in steak or pork dishes as a result of the increased corn price leading to increased feed prices for cows and pigs. When these interconnections are important, **partial equilibrium analysis** that analyses individual or small groups of markets in isolation can give misleading results.

General Human Capital

Training, education and other investment in human capital that is useful and productive across a wide range of different firms. Since such human capital is mobile, the cost of its acquisition is typically paid for by the individual making the investment rather than by the firm that employs the individual.

General Knowledge

Knowledge that has general applicability and is easy to transfer in contrast to specific knowledge. See also **specific human capital**.

Generalized Method of Moments

A more general approach to **method of moments estimation** in which parameter estimates are derived by minimizing deviations from moment conditions according to a weighted sum of squared errors criterion. **Ordinary least squares** is one example. In addition, this method provides parameter estimates for cases in which the number of moment conditions exceeds the number of parameters. This generalized method of moments approach is central to Berry et al.'s (1995) method of estimating **discrete choice models of demand** with **random coefficients**.

Genetically Altered Products

Products that are manufactured by modifying the genetic structure of some base product.

Geographic Market

A market defined by its geographic extent, the locations of individuals and firms in the market and the ways in which goods and services can be transported in the market. Geographic markets are often used as analogies for more general **characteristics markets**.

Geographic Specialization

A **targeting strategy** in which a firm sells a specifically selected or designed set of related products within the boundaries of a narrowly defined **geographic market**. Such a strategy is appropriate when there are sharp differences in consumer tastes across geographic markets.

Geographic Subunit

A unit of a firm that has responsibility for operations within a defined geographic area.

Gibrat's Law

The proposition that the growth rate of a firm and firm size are unrelated; however, within an industry, in the limit, firm size follows a power law or log-normal distribution. Let x_t denote the size of a firm at time t and let the **random variable** ε_t be the proportionate rate of growth of the firm from time $t-1$ to t, so that $x_t - x_{t-1} = \varepsilon_t x_{t-1}$. Then $x_t = (1 + \varepsilon_t)x_{t-1} = x_0(1 + \varepsilon_1)$ $(1 + \varepsilon_2) \ldots (1 + \varepsilon_t)$. Assuming that the time period is short we can use the approximation $\log(1 + \varepsilon_t) \cong \varepsilon_t$. Taking logs then gives $\log x_t \cong \log x_0 + \varepsilon_1 + \varepsilon_2 + \ldots + \varepsilon_t$. Assuming that the random variables are independent with mean m and variance σ^2 we have that as $t \to \infty$ the term $\log x_0$ is "small" so that $\log x_t$ is approximately a normal distribution with mean mt and variance $\sigma^2 t$. As a result, the limiting distribution of x_t is log-normal, implying that over time, the industry will become heavily concentrated and in the limit, dominated by a single firm.

Giffen Good

An **inferior good** for which the negative **income effect** of a price decrease offsets the positive **substitution effect** with the result that quantity demanded decreases (rises) as price decreases (rises). The **price elasticity of demand** for a Giffen good is positive. Giffen goods are rare and difficult to find. Typically, they are necessities such as rice or, as in Giffen's initial discussion, potatoes, on which households living at near subsistence levels spend a substantial proportion of their incomes. In such circumstances an increase in the price of rice makes it difficult for the household to purchase non-rice foodstuffs, forcing them to purchase more rice in order to maintain at least a subsistence level of calorie intake.

Gini Coefficient

A proportionate measure of inequality, often applied to the income levels of a population, based on the statistical distribution of the measure (income) under study. Values closer to zero imply more equality, while values closer to 1 imply a larger degree of inequality. In a **Lorenz curve** diagram, suppose that the area under the 45 degree line, the baseline for uniformly distributed income, is A, and the area under the Lorenz curve is

$$B = \int_0^1 L(X)dx$$

then the Gini coefficient is defined as $G = A/(A + B)$.

Giveaways

Products that are offered at no charge as a strategy to attract and develop a strong customer base. The intention is to make **profit** subsequently by selling products to the customer base or by charging advertisers for access to the customer base. For example, Google and Facebook offer their primary services – search and access to a wide personal network – at no charge. They earn considerable revenues from advertisers by monitoring their users' search and network activity, generating information that allows advertisers to target their marketing messages much more effectively.

Globalization

The increased global connectivity, interdependence and integration of worldwide economic activity. Proponents of globalization argue that it will lead to the convergence of prices, products, wages, interest rates and **profits** across world markets. Critics, by contrast, suggest that it leads to increased inequality and exploitation and to environmental degradation as companies relocate to regions that offer low wage rates and in which environmental protections are weak.

Goal-Based Systems

Incentive systems in which each employee is given a defined set of goals for the next period of appraisal. For such systems to be effective it is important that the goals be objective, easy to monitor and measure, and capable of being achieved by the employee. Subjective goals are undesirable because it is possible for the employer to claim that such a goal has not actually been achieved. Raising goals when the agent exceeds the set goals creates a ratchet effect that undermines the effectiveness of goal-based systems.

Goal Congruence

The ability of an **incentive contract** to align the interests of the individual to whom the contract is offered with those of the individual offering the contract. In **principal–agent** cases, the ability of an incentive contract to align the interests of the agent with those of the principal.

Golden Handcuffs

Compensation schemes that promise employees substantial deferred compensation that will be lost if the employees leave the firm. This can take the form of **stock options** with delayed vesting periods or bonuses that have to be refunded if the employee leaves the firm within a defined period. The primary objective of these schemes is to reduce turnover, particularly of skilled employees.

Golden Parachute

An agreement between a company and an executive guaranteeing that the executive will receive (generally large) benefits if the contract is terminated. These clauses typically apply if termination is the result of **acquisition** of the company and so can act as a form of **takeover** defense by increasing the cost of acquisition. Supporters of golden parachutes argue that they help maintain executive objectivity during takeover negotiations, aid recruitment and retention of executives and discourage **hostile takeover** attempts. Critics suggest that the threat of dismissal is a necessary discipline for senior executives, that executive incentive packages should be sufficient motivation, and that takeover defenses of this type are not necessarily in the interests of shareholders.

Good-Citizen Model

A model that assumes that employees have a strong personal desire to do a good job, perhaps because they take pride in their work or are altruistic. In such a model the role of management is threefold: to communicate the goals and objectives of the organization; to help employees achieve these goals and objectives; and to provide feedback on performance in order to enable employees to improve their performance. An important implication of this model is that there is no need for

incentive-based compensation since individuals are already self-motivated to perform well.

Goods

Products and services that people value.

Goodwill

An intangible asset that a firm has, based upon the trust that it establishes in the market that it will perform all of its transactions in a correct and ethical manner.

Government Intervention

The deliberate decision by government to intervene in the operations of a market. This may take the form of imposition of commodity **taxes** or enactment of regulations that market participants must observe. In some markets governments impose **price floors** and in others they impose **price ceilings**. In yet other markets governments intervene by setting **quotas**.

Government Regulation

The formal rules that government sets determining how particular aspects of a market should operate.

Granger Causality

In econometrics, a method of determining causality between two time series variables. Suppose the econometrician seeks to identify factors influencing the time series variable X_t. If the econometrician finds that lagged values of another time series variable, Y_t, have a strong predictive relationship to X_t, then Granger causality may be established. The possibility remains, however, that both time series variables are, in fact, caused by a third time series variable.

Greenmail

A **takeover** defense in which the management of a firm offers to buy back, at a premium, the shares in the firm that are owned by an individual who is trying to take over the firm.

Gray Markets

The flow of new goods and services using distribution channels other than those intended or authorized by the manufacturer or producer. When applied to trade across national boundaries, grey markets give rise to **parallel imports** by which a good exported from country A to country B is subsequently re-exported from B to A. Gray markets tend to arise in such cases if the price at which the good can be bought in country B is much lower than the price at which it can be sold in country A, perhaps because of price restrictions in country B.

Grim Trigger Strategy

A strategy in *n*-person **repeated games** defined as follows: "I shall cooperate in the current period so long as we have all cooperated in all previous periods. However, if any player has deviated in any previous period, I shall revert to the **Nash equilibrium** for the current and all future periods." This strategy can be shown to sustain **cooperative agreements** so long as each player's **discount factor** is sufficiently close to unity – see the **folk theorem**. As an example, suppose that we have the following **payoff matrix**, where in each cell, the **payoff** to the row player is listed first, and the payoff to the column player is listed second. The one-shot Nash equilibrium is (Defect, Defect). If this game is played once, (Cooperate, Cooperate) is unsustainable. By contrast, if the game is infinitely repeated, the grim trigger strategy sustains (Cooperate, Cooperate) as a **subgame perfect Nash equilibrium** provided that the discount factor is

$$d \geq d^* = \frac{12 - 10}{12 - 6} = 1/3.$$

		Firm B	
		Cooperate	Defect
Firm A	Cooperate	10, 10	5, 12
	Defect	12, 5	6, 6

More generally, suppose that the payoff to firm i to Defect when firm j plays Cooperate is π_i^D, to Cooperate when firm j plays Cooperate is π_i^C, and to Defect when firm j plays Defect is π_i^N. Then the grim trigger strategy sustains cooperation provided that firm i's discount factor is greater than

$$d_i = \frac{\pi_i^D - \pi_i^C}{\pi_i^D - \pi_i^N}.$$

Since it is to be expected that $\pi_i^D > \pi_i^C > \pi_i^N$ it must be that $d_i < 1$, with the result that there is always a discount factor sufficiently close to unity such that the grim trigger strategy sustains cooperation.

Group Incentive Compensation

A compensation scheme that rewards individuals based upon their performance in the group to which they have been assigned. There are numerous reasons why organizations may prefer group incentive schemes to individual schemes: (1) group performance, such as performance of an individual business unit, is often easier to measure than individual performance; (2) group schemes encourage cooperation and teamwork by those in the group; (3) group schemes encourage members of the group to monitor each other's contribution to the group, which can be particularly effective in that the group members have specific knowledge about individual performance. On the other hand, group incentives suffer from potential **free-riding problems**, particularly when the group is large or when the group is formed to work on a short-term assignment.

Group Pricing

See **third-degree price discrimination**.

Growth Share Matrix

A management technique that categorizes products according to their growth potential and relative **market share**. This technique is used to aid the firm in taking a strategic view of how its product range should be managed. A typical growth share matrix has the following form:

		Relative market share	
		High	Low
Relative market	High	Rising Star	Problem Child
growth	Low	Cash Cow	Dog

The suggestion is that the firm should eliminate Dogs since these products at best break even and more generally constitute a drain on the firm's resources, lowering the firm's return on capital. Problem Children have the potential to develop into Stars if they can gain sufficient market share. Cash Cows generate surplus cash relative to their operations costs. This technique suggests that a company should take a strategic approach to the product mix that it brings to market. For example, the technique recommends that the company use revenues from its Cash Cow products to correct Problem Children and assist Rising Stars and that it should seek to eliminate Dogs.

Guild

An association of individuals skilled in the same trade or craft.

H

Happy-is-Productive Model

A model in which it is assumed that happy workers are more productive, with the result that management's goal should be to create work environments that keep their employees happy.

Hawk–Dove Game

A game in which players can choose between an aggressive "hawk" strategy and a passive "dove" strategy. If both players play Hawk they stand to gain V but risk a loss of C. Each player has an equal probability of winning. If both play Dove they share V equally. If one plays Hawk and the other Dove the Hawk player gets the full gains V at no cost. The **payoff matrix** is as follows, where in each cell, the **payoff** to the row player is listed first, and the **payoff** to the column player is listed second:

		Player B	
		Hawk	Dove
Player A	Hawk	$(V - C)/2, (V - C)/2$	$V, 0$
	Dove	$0, V$	$V/2, V/2$

If $V > C$ this is a **prisoners' dilemma game**, with (Hawk, Hawk) as the **Nash equilibrium**. If $V < C$ it is a **chicken game** with (Hawk, Dove) and (Dove, Hawk) as the Nash equilibria. A feature of this second case is that the players must try to anticipate which of the two equilibria the other player expects. This is especially important when C is significantly greater than V, such that the consequences of both parties' choosing Hawk are extreme, resulting in significant losses, perhaps to the point of forcing exit by one or both firms. In such games, both players might choose a **focal point**. In a **repeated game** setting, firm A might invest in a "hawkish" reputation over time, resulting in firm B's expectation that firm A will always play Hawk, leaving Dove as firm B's best response.

Hedonic Prices

The implicit product characteristics prices that are estimated using a **hedonic regression** technique.

Hedonic regression

A technique for estimating product characteristics prices. The product being investigated is treated as a whole, comprising a set of characteristics; the regression measures the implicit prices of the characteristics. The technique is widely used in real estate markets where houses are defined in terms of characteristics such as location, numbers of rooms, numbers of bedrooms and so on. It has also been applied to automobile markets.

Herfindahl–Hirschman Index (HHI)

An index of market concentration. Suppose that there are N firms in the industry and that the market share of firm i, as a percentage, is s_i. Then

$$HHI = \sum_{i=1}^{N} s_i^2.$$

When determining whether or not a proposed **horizontal merger** will have harmful effects on competition in a given market, the **Federal Trade Commission (FTC)** will consider the HHI expected to result from the merger as well as the expected change in the HHI. According to the 2010 **Horizontal Merger Guidelines**, an industry HHI lower than 1500 reflects an unconcentrated market; an industry HHI above 2500 reflects a highly concentrated market; and values in between reflect moderate concentration.

Heterogeneous Consumer Demand

Markets in which consumers vary in their **willingness to pay** for the products on offer. In such markets a firm with market power can make higher profits if it is able to implement discriminatory pricing policies that exploit the consumers' heterogeneity.

Heterogeneous Goods

Goods that are characterized by either **horizontal** or **vertical product differentiation**, or both.

Heuristics

Principles or guidelines that senior management establish to reduce the time that is spent in solving complex and unusual problems. See, for example, **rule-of-thumb pricing**.

Hicksian Demand Function

The demand function that is obtained when the consumer's income is adjusted to keep the consumer's utility constant. See also **compensated demand function**.

Hidden Action

In a **principal–agent model**, actions that can be taken by the agent but that are not perfectly observable by the principal. Any contract between the principal and the agent that requires the agent not to take hidden actions is unenforceable since the principal cannot verify whether the agent's actions actually fulfill the terms of the contract. For example, the goal of a manager is to maximize **profits**, which are determined, in part, by the effort level of a worker. The worker, however, is motivated by maximizing **utility**, which is determined by the worker's wealth and effort level. If the worker experiences disutility from effort, if it is costly for the manager to observe effort, and there is uncertainty in the relationship between the agent's effort and the resulting profit, then the worker will have an incentive to shirk. This problem can be mitigated by tying the payment of the worker to the profits generated by the agent's effort, but only if there is not a significant amount of noise in the relationship between the agent's effort and the resulting profit. Moreover, this solution can be complicated by the fact that the worker might, in addition, be **risk averse**. See also **incentive compatibility constraint** and **moral hazard**.

Hidden-Action Model

See **hidden action** and **moral hazard**.

Hidden Information

In a **principal–agent model**, information that is available to the **agent** but that cannot be observed or confirmed by the **principal**. A seller of a good or service or an individual applying for employment, for example, have hidden information regarding the true quality of the good or service or the true abilities of the potential employee. Hidden information is particularly troubling in insurance markets where the individuals seeking insurance have hidden information about their true risk classes or behaviors. See **adverse selection** and the **lemons problem**.

Hidden-Knowledge Model

An economic model in which an economic agent has superior knowledge about some exogenous variable whose true value will affect the outcome of the model.

Hierarchy

Within a firm, the formal separation of **decision management** from **decision control**.

Historic Cost

Valuing an economic item at its original monetary cost of acquisition, used in the determination of accounting **profit**. By contrast, **economic profit** includes all **opportunity costs**, both monetary and non-monetary, with negative economic profits signaling to a firm the value of shifting resources to the next-best alternative activity or investment.

Hit-and-Run Entry

In **perfectly contestable markets** where there are no costs of **entry** or **exit**, the ability to enter a market if price rises above **marginal cost**, and exit when competition drives prices back down to marginal cost. If a market is characterized by hit-and-run entry then price will be close to marginal cost even if the market is monopolized. In the enforcement of **antitrust laws**, contestability plays an important role in determining whether or not monopoly conditions are anticompetitive.

Holding Company

A company with an ownership interest in another company through its stock holdings. A holding company may provide strategic and other guidance to the companies whose shares it controls but is typically not directly involved in production activities.

Hold-Out Problem

In an **acquisition**, if a potential acquiree expects that an acquirer is going to purchase other firms, thereby gaining substantial market power, the potential acquiree may demand such a high price that the acquisition is rendered unprofitable.

Hold-Up Problem

Suppose that a value-creating exchange between two economic agents requires that one or the other of them invests in a **relationship-specific asset**. Such an investment creates **quasi-rents**. Because the contract governing the exchange is inevitably incomplete, there is the risk that, post-investment, the agent not making the relationship-specific investment will attempt opportunistically to renegotiate the contract, exploiting the vulnerable position of the agent who has made the investment in order to expropriate some or all of the quasi-rents. Fear of hold-up may lead to the value-creating exchange not taking place, or to the agents incurring additional costly investment to protect against hold-up, or to the parties to the exchange agreeing to integrate their activities, putting them under common ownership.

Home Country

The country in which a **multinational corporation** has its headquarters operations.

Homogeneous Products

Products that are identical in quality and in their product characteristics. In **perfect competition**, firms are assumed to produce homogeneous products.

Horse Race

A model used by some companies to determine promotion to senior management positions by requiring that the internal candidates compete against each other.

Horizon Problem

An incentive conflict that can arise between owners and employees because the two have different time horizons within the firm. The employee's horizon is their anticipated tenure within the firm while the firm's horizon is typically much longer.

Horizontal Agreements

Agreements between competing firms governing some aspect(s) of competition between them, usually intended to restrict their competition.

Horizontal Boundaries

The boundaries of a firm determining the volume or scale of production, and breadth or scope of goods and services that it produces.

Horizontal Externalities

Externalities that arise between competing firms. For example, a retailer may gain an external benefit by **free-riding** on brand advertising undertaken by a competing retailer.

Horizontal Integration

See **horizontal merger**.

Horizontal Merger

The merger of competing firms that produce products that, in the eyes of buyers, are close substitutes with considerable overlap in the firms' product lines. An example would be the merger between two US domestic airlines. See also **Horizontal Merger Guidelines**.

Horizontal Merger Guidelines

The guidelines published by the **Department of Justice** and the **Federal Trade Commission (FTC)** in the United States detailing the principles that the government applies in its enforcement of antitrust laws relating to **horizontal merger** activity. The guidelines provide specific criteria for determining whether a merger can be potentially harmful to competition based on **market concentration** measures, including comparisons of pre- and post-merger **Herfindahl–Hirschman Indexes (HHI)**. In addition, the Guidelines provide guidance on the appropriate market definition, including the **hypothetical monopolist test**; on post-merger **entry conditions**; and on potential **efficiency gains** resulting from the firms combining their production activities.

Horizontal Product Differentiation

Product differentiation in which products are viewed by consumers to be identical in quality but differentiated in terms of their product characteristics: typical characteristics are color, style, taste and location.

Host Country

A country in which a **multinational corporation** undertakes **foreign direct investment**.

Hostile Takeover

A **takeover** bid is considered to be hostile if the board of the target company recommends rejection of the takeover bid but the bidder continues with the offer, or if the bidder makes an offer without prior notification to the board of the target company.

Hotelling Line Market

See **Hotelling spatial model**.

Hotelling Spatial Model

A model of **horizontal product differentiation** that relies on a spatial analogy. The market is typically assumed to be a one-dimensional line market that can be either a geographic or characteristics line. Consumers are distributed according to some density function with the "address" of a consumer being that consumer's most preferred product. Firms choose location(s) on the characteristics line, with the "address(es)" of a firm being the product characteristic(s) that the firm actually offers. Transport costs in **characteristics space** are the psychic costs that a consumer incurs from buying a product that is not their most preferred type. Depending on the assumptions on transport cost functions, firms will choose either **minimum differentiation** (agglomeration) or **maximum differentiation**.

Hotelling's Lemma

Let the firm's **profit function** be $\pi(p, \mathbf{w})$ where p is the output price and $\mathbf{w}$ is the vector of input prices. Then Hotelling's Lemma states that the firm's **supply function** is $y(p,\mathbf{w}) = \partial\pi(p,\mathbf{w})/\partial p$ and the firm's **input demand function** for input i is $x_i(p,\mathbf{w}) = -\partial\pi(p,\mathbf{w})/\partial w_i$.

Hub-and-Spoke Network

A method of organizing passenger airline travel in which the carrier flies its passengers from a set of "spoke" airports through a central "hub" where passengers change planes in order to fly to their final destination.

Human Asset Specificity

Situations in which individuals have acquired skills, knowledge and information that are more valuable within a particular relationship or employment contract than outside it. Such **relationship-specific investment** gives rise to potential **hold-up problems**.

Human Capital

Investment by individuals in the acquisition of skills and knowledge, for example through education.

Human Resource Management

The management systems by which a firm attracts and retains employees, develops their potential, skills and knowledge, and informs, motivates and rewards them.

Hypothetical Monopolist Test

See **SSNIP criterion**.

I

Identification

In econometric modeling, the case in which parameters of interest can be estimated, or identified. For example, in a structural model of supply and demand, both supply and demand can be represented by equations with quantity as a function of price, among other relevant variables. Industry data on prices and quantities will reflect equilibrium values, but the separate effect of price changes on quantity supplied and quantity demanded cannot be isolated if the model includes only quantity as a function of price. With the additional information on factors that influence only one side of the market, such as production costs for firms, variation in such supply shifters will allow us to identify the price coefficient for the other structural equation, in this case for the demand equation.

Imperfect Commitment

The limited ability of an economic agent to bind themself to avoid **opportunistic behavior**. This is particularly troublesome and gives rise to **moral hazard** when the agent can take **hidden actions** or where there is **asymmetric information** regarding the true actions of the agent. If a transaction requires one or other party to the transaction to invest in a **relationship-specific asset**, imperfect commitment can give rise to a **hold-up problem**.

Imperfect Competition

A market structure in which firms have some degree of **monopoly** power perhaps because they produce **differentiated products** or because there are **barriers to entry** to the market. Where there are no barriers to entry and **economies of scale** are not too strong, an imperfectly competitive market tends to become **monopolistically competitive**. Where there are barriers to entry or where economies of scale are strong the market tends to **oligopoly** or **monopoly**.

Imperfect Information

A situation in which economic agents are not perfectly informed about important aspects of the economic system, such as, for example, demand or costs or the true nature of their rivals.

Implicit Contracts

Contracts that are not written down formally but are set implicitly by a handshake or other informal means. Parties to such contracts are willing to abide by the contract terms if breach of contract undermines their reputations, preventing them from entering into future contracts. Floor traders in stock and commodities exchanges, for example, enter into implicit contracts when they make verbal agreements to buy and sell shares of stock or bundles of commodities. They honor such contracts, even when the contracts turn out to be bad ones, since failure to do so means that the trader will no longer be able to operate on the exchange.

Import Substitution

The decision to switch from consumption of imported goods or services to consumption of domestically produced goods or services. Policies designed to encourage import substitution, such as tariff and non-tariff barriers to trade or "buy domestic" advertising efforts, are founded on the proposition that countries should reduce their reliance on foreign-produced goods and services by encouraging the growth of domestic substitutes. Critics suggest that these policies encourage the growth and subsequent protection of industries that have no **comparative advantage**.

Incentive-Based Compensation

A method of compensation in which some or all of the compensation is based on agreed **performance measures**. Typical examples are basing chief executive officer (CEO) compensation on stock-market performance and paying sales staff commission based on sales. This type of compensation is intended, in **principal–agent problems**, to align the interests of the agent with those of the principal. To be effective, such compensation packages must satisfy two constraints: (1) a **participation constraint**: the agent prefers to accept the incentive compensation contract than not; and (2) an

incentive compatibility constraint: the agent prefers to act in a manner that is "good" for the principal than not.

Incentive Compatibility Constraint

A constraint that any set of offers made to buyers of different types, where each buyer's type is unobservable by the seller, that induces each buyer to make a choice that reveals that buyer's true type. For example, in **second-degree price discrimination** when difference in **willingness to pay** is unobservable, any price–quantity pair intended to attract a high-demand consumer must offer that consumer at least as much **consumer surplus** as they would obtain from purchasing a price–quantity pair intended to attract lower-demand consumers. Suppose that the utility a consumer of type i enjoys from consuming a quantity q at a total charge T is $U_i(q,T) = \theta_i V(q) - T$. Suppose further that the seller knows that there are two types of buyer, types 1 and 2 with $\theta_1 < \theta_2$. So type 1 consumers are low demand and type 2 consumers are high demand. However, the seller has no way of telling each consumer's true type. The seller then wishes to offer two bundles (q_1,T_1) designed for type 1 consumers and (q_2,T_2) designed for type 2 consumers. The incentive compatibility constraints are: (1) $U_i(q_i,T_i) \geq 0$ ($i = 1, 2$): each consumer type is willing to purchase the package designed for their type; (2) $U_1(q_1,T_1) > U_1(q_2,T_2)$: type 1 consumers prefer the bundle designed for them to the other bundle; and (2) $U_2(q_2,T_2) > U_2(q_1,T_1)$: type 2 consumers prefer the bundle designed for them to the other bundle. When these constraints are satisfied the consumers self-select according to their true types. (See Tirole 1988, pp. 143–144.)

In **principal–agent** relationships the effort expended by the agent is unobservable. An **incentive-based compensation** contract is incentive compatible when the agent finds it to be in their self-interest to exert a high level of effort. Suppose that an agent has utility of $u(w - e)$ from exerting effort e and receiving a return w. The agent can exert a "high" level of effort e_h or a "low" level of effort e_l, neither of which is observable by the principal, creating a **hidden action** problem. When the agent's effort is high, profit is Π_h with probability x and Π_l with probability $1 - x$ (with $\Pi_h > \Pi_l$). If the agent's effort is low, profit is Π_h with probability y and Π_l with probability $1 - y$, with $y < x$. In other words, high effort increases the probability of high profit. The principal offers the agent an incentive contract that pays w_h when profits are high and w_l when profits are low, with $w_h > w_l$. For this contract to result in the agent exerting the high level of effort it must satisfy the agent's incentive compatibility constraint

$$xu(w_h - e_h) + (1 - x)u(w_l - e_h) \geq yu(w_h - e_l) + (1 - y)u(w_l - e_l):$$

the agent's expected return from exerting high effort is greater than expected return from exerting low effort. (See Tirole 1988, pp. 36–38.)

Incentive Contract

See **incentive-based compensation**.

Incentive Intensity Principle

The principle that the intensity of incentives offered to an **agent** should increase with the agent's marginal productivity of effort and with the agent's ability to respond to incentives, but should decrease with the agent's risk aversion and the noise with which the agent's performance can be measured.

Incentive System

See **incentive-based compensation**.

Incipiency Precedent

The argument that a proposed **merger** should be prevented in order to prevent future increases in **market concentration**.

Income Effect

The impact on quantity demanded of an increase in income. If the **demand function** is written $Q = D(p, y, a)$ where p is a vector of goods prices, a includes all determinants of demand other than the price and income, and y is income, then the income effect is $\partial D()/\partial y$. For **normal goods** the income effect is positive while for **inferior goods** it is negative. See also **Slutsky equation**.

Income Elasticity

A measure of the sensitivity of demand to a change in income. If the demand function is $Q = D(P, y, \mathbf{a})$ where $\mathbf{a}$ includes all determinants of demand other than the price and income, and y is income, then the income elasticity is

$$\eta_y = \frac{\partial D(P,y,\mathbf{a})}{\partial y} \frac{y}{D(P,y,\mathbf{a})}.$$

Income elasticity is positive for **normal goods** and negative for **inferior goods**. Within the class of normal goods, if income elasticity is less than unity the good is considered a necessity, while if income elasticity is greater than unity it is considered a luxury good.

Incomplete Contract

A **contract** that leaves some contingencies unspecified either because the contingencies cannot be foreseen or because there are too many to make it efficient to include all of them in the contract. On this definition, all contracts are necessarily incomplete because the individuals who enter into contracts suffer from **bounded rationality**. If the contract in question requires some or all of the parties to the contract to make a **relationship-specific investment** then the fact that the contract is necessarily incomplete can give rise to a **hold-up problem**.

Incomplete Information

A situation in which there are gaps in the knowledge of the parties to an exchange with respect to some aspects that will affect the outcome of the exchange. For example, employers have incomplete information regarding the true nature of potential employees and consumers have incomplete information regarding the true **quality** of **experience** or **credence goods**. This can lead to inefficiency as sellers seek to misrepresent the true quality of the item being offered for sale and buyers expend resources in an effort to improve their information regarding that true quality.

Increasing Returns to Scale

A **production function** exhibits increasing returns to scale when a proportionate increase in all **inputs** results in a more than proportionate increase in **output**. Formally, suppose that the production function is $Q = f(\mathbf{x})$, where f is the production function, Q is output and $\mathbf{x}$ is the vector of inputs. If f exhibits increasing returns to scale we have $f(a\mathbf{x}) > af(\mathbf{x})$. Suppose, for example, that the production function is **Cobb–Douglas** such that total output is

$$Q = \prod_{i=1}^{n} x_i^{\alpha_i}.$$

This production function exhibits increasing returns to scale if and only if

$$\sum_{i=1}^{n} \alpha_i > 1.$$

If input prices are constant as output increases, increasing returns to scale imply that **average total cost** decreases as output is increased.

Incremental Cost

For a multi-product firm, the additional cost of increasing the output of product i given that the output of all other goods is kept constant. If the **total cost** function is $TC = f(\mathbf{q})$, where $\mathbf{q} = (q_1, q_2, \dots q_n)$, then the incremental cost of product i is $IC_i = \partial f / \partial q_i$.

Incumbent Firms

Firms who are already active in a market when a **potential entrant** considers whether or not to enter the market.

Independent Variable

See **explanatory variable**.

Indifference Curve

A hypersurface in goods space for which all combinations of goods on the hypersurface give the consumer the same utility. If the **utility function** is $u = f(q)$ where q is a consumption vector, then an indifference curve is all consumption vectors q that satisfy $f(q) = $ constant. Indifference curves are level functions of the utility function. A consumer offered the choice between two consumption bundles q_1 and q_2 that lie on the same indifference curve would rank the two bundles as being equally preferred. Indifference curves cannot cross – otherwise this leads to a contradiction. Suppose the opposite: that an indifference curve of consumption bundles that give utility u_1 crosses an indifference curve of consumption bundles that give utility u_2, with $u_1 > u_2$. Denote the consumption bundle at which the two indifference curves cross as q_0. Then we have $u(q_0) = u_1 > u(q_0) = u_2$, which cannot hold.

Indirect Competitor

One firm is an indirect competitor with a second firm when actions taken by the first firm impact the second firm indirectly by influencing the behavior of another firm in the market.

Indirect Utility Function

The function that gives a consumer's maximal utility when faced with a budget constraint defined by a vector of prices **p** and income y. Formally this function is defined as $v(\mathbf{p}, y) = \max_{\mathbf{x}} u(\mathbf{x})$ subject to $\mathbf{p}.\mathbf{x} \leq y$. The indirect utility function is continuous, homogeneous of degree zero in $(\mathbf{p}, y)$, strictly increasing in y and decreasing in **p**. It also satisfies **Roy's identity**. The **Marshallian demand function** for good i is

$$x_i(\mathbf{p}, y) = -\frac{\partial v(\mathbf{p}, y)/\partial p_i}{\partial v(\mathbf{p}, y)/\partial y}.$$

Indistinguishability Theorem

The suggestion that parties to a collusive agreement can make detection of **collusion** by the **antitrust authorities** difficult by selectively misrepresenting **private information**, for example regarding their production costs, in such a way that the agreement can be made to appear competitive. This theorem suggests that the regulatory authorities face potentially insurmountable problems in successfully detecting and prosecuting **cartels** using purely market-based information. Rather, they have to rely on information provided by insiders, such as disgruntled employees, or by firms seeking to take advantage of **leniency programs**.

Individual-Rationality Constraint

The constraint that a necessary condition for an economic agent to make a decision is that the decision gives the agent positive **surplus**. In consumer markets, for example, a consumer will buy a good only if it provides positive **consumer surplus**. In labor markets, a potential employee will accept an employment contract only if it offers the employee positive **utility**.

Indivisibility

An **input** that cannot be scaled down below some minimum limit even when the **output** level is very small. A typical example is the rail track that is necessary if passenger train service is to be provided between two cities or the distribution grid for providing products such as gas, electricity and water to consumers. Indivisibilities can give rise to **fixed costs** and **economies of scale**.

Industrial Organization

The branch of economics that extends the analysis of firm behavior to **imperfectly competitive** and, in particular, **oligopolistic** markets. Subfields range from the internal organization of the firm, through the strategic decision-making by firms, to the study of regulation and the formulation of antitrust policy. Non-cooperative **game theory** and applied **econometrics** have become the standard methods of analysis.

Industry

The set of firms in an economy that produce a specific good or service. Industries are defined in North America by the **North American Industry Classification System (NAICS)**.

Industry Analysis

Structural analysis of an industry by considering the forces that can affect industry and firm performance. This typically takes the form of Michael Porter's **five-forces analysis** – **internal rivalry**, **entry**, **substitute** and **complementary goods**, **buyer power**, **supplier power** – supplemented by an analysis of the potential for cooperation between market participants.

Industry Demand Function

The function that is obtained by aggregating the individual demand functions of all firms in the industry, with each firm's individual demand function being derived by aggregating the consumers' **demand functions** for each firm's product. Industry demand functions are typically less **elastic** than individual firm demand functions.

Industry Standard

A product design or technology that is accepted by all firms in an industry. Establishing industry standards is particularly important in new product markets as a way to encourage consumers to adopt the new products and to encourage producers of **complementary goods** to invest in producing these goods. Failure to agree on industry standards as, for example, occurred in the early years of the development of video recorders (VHS versus Betamax) tends to slow the adoption of the new products. Consumers delay their purchases, and complementary product producers delay their investment, until the dominant standard has emerged. See **coordination game**.

Industry Structure

A measure of the size distribution of firms in an industry, usually represented by a summary measure such as a **concentration ratio** or the **Herfindahl–Hirschman Index**.

Industry Studies

Analysis of empirical patterns of competition and strategic choice within a particular industry. Focusing on one industry allows the researcher to identify factors influencing such choices as pricing, product attributes and strategic investment within a fixed institutional setting, redressing a central limitation of early empirical work on **cross-industry studies**.

Inelastic Demand

Demand for which the absolute value of the **price elasticity of demand** is less than unity.

Inelastic Supply

Supply for which the **price elasticity of supply** is less than unity.

Inferior Good

A good for which the **income effect** is negative with the result that quantity demanded falls as income rises. Inferior goods are typically low-quality goods that satisfy specific consumer needs. In the case of a price decrease, which effectively frees up income for the consumer, so long as the negative income effect for an inferior good is less than the **substitution effect** into the now cheaper good, the quantity demanded of an inferior good is inversely related to the good's price, such that the **law of demand** holds. If the negative income effect offsets the substitution effect we have a **Giffen good**. See also **Slutsky equation**.

Infinite-Horizon Model

An economic model in which, at each period, there is a positive probability that the market will continue to operate into the next period. When a **prisoners' dilemma game** is placed in an infinite-horizon model, cooperation can be sustained as a **subgame perfect Nash equilibrium** provided that players are sufficiently patient; that is, have **discount factors** "close to" unity.

Infinitely Repeated Game

A game in which, at each period, there is a finite probability that the game will continue into the next period. When a **prisoners' dilemma game** is formulated as an infinitely repeated game, cooperation can be sustained as a **subgame perfect Nash equilibrium** provided that players are sufficiently patient (that is, have **discount factors** "close to" unity) and the probability of the game continuing in each period is sufficiently large.

Inflexibility

The outcome of an organization or individual making a **strategic commitment** that is long term and expensive to reverse.

Influence Activities

Activities that are undertaken with the aim of redistributing resources within an organization, typically by political activity, lobbying, or distorting or misrepresenting information. These activities impose **influence costs** on the organization, since their primary objective is to change the internal distribution of the organization's resources rather than to increase the overall resource base of the organization. See Milgrom (1988).

Influence Costs

Costs that arise inside an organization from **influence activities**. These can be direct costs, such as lobbying, time-wasting and efforts aimed at countering the influence activities of others. Or they can be indirect costs, the costs that result from the wrong decisions that can be made as a result of these influence activities. It is argued that influence costs tend to be proportionately greater in large, vertically integrated firms than in small, independent, entrepreneurial firms, providing one reason for there being limits on the degree to which firms will become vertically integrated. See Milgrom (1988).

Information Failures

Situations in which **incomplete information** leads to the breakdown of markets in which there is the potential for value-creating exchange.

Informational Advertising

Advertising that provides truthful and objective information, for example with respect to prices, locations or qualities of goods on offer.

Informational Asymmetry

Differences in the information that is available to economic agents and that affects their ability to enter into efficient exchanges. When there is such asymmetry, exchanges that have the potential to be mutually beneficial for the agents involved may fail to take place because the agents have the incentive to misrepresent their true valuations. See also **asymmetric information**.

Informational Rent

The additional return that an economic agent receives as a result of the agent having precontractual **private information**. Payment of this rent provides the agent with the incentive not to take advantage of the **informational asymmetry**.

Informativeness Principle

The principle that in an **incentive-based compensation** contract an agent's payment should be made dependent upon an observable variable only if including that variable reduces the error with which the agent's performance can be measured. For example, if each agent's performance is subject to similar external influences, it is reasonable to include relative **performance measures** in the design of the incentive contract. (See also **relative performance evaluation**.)

Innovation

A process that increases **total surplus** by introducing a new product or process.

Inputs

Resources such as raw materials, labor and capital, used in the production of **outputs**, or final goods and services.

Input Demand Function

The relationship between the price of an input and the quantity of that input that a profit maximizing firm will employ. By **Hotelling's Lemma**, if the firm's **profit function** is $\pi(p, \mathbf{w})$ where p is the output price and $\mathbf{w}$ is the vector of input prices then the firm's input demand function for input i is $x_i(p, \mathbf{w}) = -\partial \pi(p, \mathbf{w})/\partial w_i$. See also **conditional factor demand**.

Inside Prices

In financial markets, the lowest **ask price** and the highest **bid price**.

Inside Spread

The difference between the **inside prices**.

Installed Base Opportunism

The case in which a seller takes advantage of a customer who purchases one product, the purchase of which locks the consumer into buying a secondary product or service from that same seller, resulting in potentially anticompetitive pricing in the secondary market. For example, the purchase of an electronic reader can limit the consumer to purchasing electronic books only from the company selling the reading platform, creating the potential for such opportunism.

Instrumental Variables Estimation

An estimation method designed to address the problem of **endogeneity**. The method requires identification of one or more variables that are correlated with the endogenous regressor, but that are uncorrelated with the error term in the main estimation equation. For example, consider a model of retail sales within a given market, such as home improvement products, within a fixed radius of the center of a metropolitan area. Sales will be impacted by a number of factors, including the distance of the retail outlet from the metropolitan center. However, the initial choice of retail location, and thus distance from the center, is likely to be correlated with unobserved factors that themselves are correlated with expected sales, thus rendering the distance variable endogenous. Variables such as local construction costs, or local commercial real estate taxes, at the time of the location choice, could serve as good instruments for the original location choice, as long as these variables are correlated with distance from metropolitan center, and uncorrelated with unobserved factors that influence sales volume.

Intangible Asset

An asset of a firm that is created through the expenditure of time and effort by the firm but that cannot be touched or physically measured. Typical intangible assets are **reputation, patents,** brand image, **corporate culture** and know-how. Intangible assets can be a source of **sustainable competitive advantage** since they are often tacit and generally difficult to imitate.

Integration

The transfer of **residual rights of control** from one party to another. See **backward integration, forward integration** and **horizontal integration.**

Intellectual Property Rights

The legal rights to innovations resulting from new ideas, including inventions, product designs, and production processes. Intellectual property is protected by **patent, trademark** and **copyright** laws.

Intensity of Incentives

A measure of the extent to which expected compensation under an **incentive contract** changes with improved or worsened performance. Suppose, for example, that an individual is offered a profit-sharing incentive contract of the form $w = w_0 + \beta\Pi$, where w_0 is the base wage and Π is profit. Then β measures the intensity of the incentive contract.

Interbrand Competition

Competition between different brands of the same basic product or service.

Interest-Group Theory

The theory that interest groups such as firms, consumers or other groups seek to influence the legislation that a regulatory body passes. See **Becker model of regulation**.

Intermediate Goods

Goods or services that are used as **inputs** in the production of other goods or services. Vertically integrated firms will typically both make and consume a range of intermediate goods. More specialized firms may buy intermediate goods from other firms **upstream** in the production chain and use these goods as inputs to their production process or make such goods for sale to other firms **downstream** in the production chain.

Internal Capital Markets

The methods by which firms allocate human and financial resources to internal divisions and departments of the firm. It is suggested that internal capital markets tend to be "soft" in that they become subject to wasteful **influence activities** of individuals within the firm.

Internal Labor Markets

The methods by which firms fill non-entry-level jobs from within the firm. Internal labor markets tend to be used when employees are required to invest in the acquisition of firm-specific skills, in order to reassure the employees that they will receive a return on their investment.

Internal Rate of Return

The **discount rate** that reduces the **net present value** of a set of intertemporal cash flows to zero. Suppose that an investment project has a projected life of T periods and that the net cash flows in each period t are C_t, then the internal rate of return i is such that

$$\sum_{t=0}^{T} \frac{C_t}{(1 + i)^t} = 0.$$

The internal rate of return is used to assess the desirability of an investment: the higher the internal rate of return, the potentially more desirable the investment can be considered to be. This must be treated with care, however, for several reasons. First, since the internal rate of return is the solution to a polynomial of degree T, there is no reason to believe that it is unique. Second, an implicit assumption in the use of internal rate of return is that any positive cash flows that result from the investment in any period can be reinvested in another project at the internal rate of return. Third, it can be that for two competing investment opportunities, one may yield a higher internal rate of return than the other but have a lower net present value. The project with the higher net present value should be chosen, subject to the availability of capital.

Internal Rivalry

The ways in which firms in an industry compete for market share. Internal rivalry tends to be fiercer when: there are many firms in the market; the industry is slow growing or declining; firms have **excess capacity**; products are relatively undifferentiated and consumers have low **switching costs**; prices or conditions of sale are unobservable; orders are large or infrequent; demand is highly elastic; and there is no history of **facilitating practices**. This is one of Porter's **five forces**.

Internalization

The decision by a firm to exploit an **ownership advantage** by bringing it inside the firm rather than selling or licensing the ownership advantage to another firm. One reason to internalize an ownership advantage is if the market in the ownership advantage is either imperfect or missing, for example when the ownership advantage is intangible or is knowledge based. See also **eclectic paradigm**.

Interstate Commerce Commission

A regulatory agency established in 1887 with the mandate to regulate surface transportation and subsequently telephone companies to ensure that the rates being charged were fair and non-discriminatory. The ICC was terminated in 1995. A year later, the Surface Transportation Board was established and assigned responsibility for some of the ICC's previous oversight authority.

Intertemporal Substitution

The choice to delay consumption or production to a later date.

Intertemporal Price Discrimination

In multi-period settings, charging different prices for the same good in different periods. The firm's ability to price discriminate in this manner is determined by the ability of consumers to anticipate or delay their purchase decisions.

Intertemporal Pricing

In multi-period settings, the prices that are set by a seller in each period.

Intrabrand Competition

Competition between firms offering the same brand of product or service.

Inventory

The stock of **intermediate** or finished goods that a firm holds, typically to avoid problems caused by unanticipated fluctuations in demand.

Inverse Demand Function

The function that is obtained by inverting the **demand function** to write price as a function of quantity demanded. If the demand function is $Q = D(p, y, \mathbf{a})$, where p is price, y is income and $\mathbf{a}$ is all other determinants of demand, then the inverse demand function is $p = D^{-1}(Q, y, \mathbf{a})$.

Inverse Elasticity Rule

The proposition that **profit maximization** for a monopolist requires that the ratio between the profit margin and the price – the **Lerner index** – be equal to the inverse of the **demand elasticity**. The profit-maximizing condition for a monopolist is that

$$p\left(1 - \frac{1}{|\eta_{q,p}|}\right) = mc(q),$$

where p is price, q is output, $mc(q)$ is marginal cost and $\eta_{q,p}$ is the **elasticity of demand**. This can be rewritten as

$$p - mc(p) = \frac{p}{|\eta_{q,p}|}$$

which gives

$$\frac{p - mc(p)}{p} = \frac{1}{|\eta_{q,p}|}$$

as required.

Investment

The production of goods that are not consumed but are used for future production.

Investment Center

A business unit that has all of the **decision rights** of a **profit center** as well as the right to make capital investment decisions, at least up to some limit. They are appropriate when local managers have specific knowledge regarding potential investment opportunities and have local knowledge regarding the center's operating decisions. They can be susceptible to **opportunistic behavior** by the center managers, for example with respect to the criteria by which investment opportunities are assessed.

Invisible Hand

A theory propounded by Adam Smith (1776). The theory states that if each consumer aims to maximize their utility in their choice of goods and services to purchase, and each firm aims to maximize profits in determining which goods and services to produce, and markets are **competitive**, then the resulting resource allocation will be **efficient**. The market will determine the goods and services being produced and the prices at which they are traded, being those that benefit society as a whole without the need for government intervention.

Isocost Line

A hypersurface in **input** space such that the **total cost** of each input bundle on the hypersurface is constant. If w is the vector of input prices and x is the vector of inputs then an isocost line is all vectors x that satisfy $w.x =$ constant. The points of tangency between isocost lines and **isoquants** trace out the **expansion path** for the firm.

Isolating Mechanisms

Strategic actions that a firm can take to protect a **competitive advantage** from imitation or duplication.

Isoquant

A hypersurface in **input** space such that all input bundles on the hypersurface produce the same **output**. If the **production function** is $q = f(x)$ where x is the vector of inputs, then an isoquant is all vectors x that satisfy $f(x)$ = constant. Isoquants are level functions of the firm's production function. Suppose, for example, that the production function is **Cobb–Douglas** of the form $Q = AK^\alpha L^\beta$, where Q is output, K is capital input, L is labor input and A is a technological constant. Then in (K, L) space the isoquant for output Q_0 is

$$K = \left(\frac{Q_0}{AL^\beta}\right)^{\frac{1}{\alpha}}.$$

Iterated Dominance

Simplifying a **game** and, in the limit, identifying the **Nash equilibrium** to a game by the sequential elimination of **dominated strategies**. Consider the following game, where in each cell, the **payoff** to the row player is listed first, and the payoff to the column player is listed second.

		Firm 2		
		Left	Middle	Right
Firm 1	Low	10, 10	20, 5	20, 20
	Medium	5, 30	10, 50	40, 40
	High	25, 40	30, 60	30, 5

Neither player has a **dominant strategy** but Low is a **dominated strategy** for Firm 1 (High always does better for Firm 1 than Low). So Low can be eliminated from the game giving the simplified game:

		Firm 2		
		Left	Middle	Right
Firm 1	Medium	5, 30	10, 50	40, 40
	High	25, 40	30, 60	30, 5

Now Left is dominated for Firm 2 by Middle and Right is dominated for Firm 2 by Middle. So Left and Right can be eliminated, giving the simplified game:

		Firm 2
		Middle
Firm 1	Medium	10, 50
	High	30, 60

Now Medium is dominated for Firm 1 by High, leading to the **Nash equilibrium** (High, Middle). In applying iterated dominance the order of elimination does not affect the final result.

The same technique can be applied when a player has a **weakly dominated strategy** but in this case the order of elimination of weakly dominated strategies can affect the final result.

J

Job Design

The determination of which projects individuals should work on, the tasks that should be allocated to them, and the teams with which the individuals should be expected to work.

Job Ladder

A sequence of jobs of increasing seniority and rank through which employees attempt to climb by competing for promotions.

Joint Dominance

A situation in which a proposed **merger** has the potential to create structural market conditions that facilitate **tacit** or **explicit collusion** by the post-merger firms, potentially resulting in an anticompetitive environment.

Joint Payoff

The combined payoff to economic agents involved in a contract or in a strategic interaction. This measure is useful for comparing the market outcomes, under identical demand and cost conditions, but under different competitive or strategic assumptions. For example, in the **duopoly Cournot game**, with quantity competition, and equal and constant marginal costs across firms, the total **profits** across the two firms are less than those that would have been earned if the two firms had instead **colluded** and chosen the monopoly quantity.

Joint Predation

The combined decision of **incumbent firms** to react aggressively to new **entry**, not necessarily as a result of explicit coordination by the predators.

Joint-Profit Maximization

Profit maximization in which the firms act to maximize their combined profits rather than their individual profits, perhaps as a result of a collusive agreement between the firms. See also **joint payoff**.

Joint Venture

A strategic agreement among a group of firms to establish and jointly own a new independent organization. Joint ventures are often formed to fund projects that require more financing than one firm alone is able to provide or to allow the firms to exploit synergies in their research or market knowledge.

Judgment Analysis

In analyzing a **strategic commitment**, reviewing the qualitative organizational and management factors that might distort a firm's choice of optimal strategy.

Judo Economics

A strategy used by a **potential entrant** to credibly limit capacity such that a larger **incumbent firm** will **accommodate** rather than attempt to **deter entry**.

Junk Bonds

A **bond** that offers a high yield but that is not investment grade (with below BBB-rating) and so is considered a risky investment since there is a high risk that the bond issuer will default. However, the high yield relative to that of less risky assets can provide an investment incentive.

Just-in-Time

An inventory management system in which inventories of parts and **intermediate goods** in process are minimized by requiring that **inputs** to each stage in a manufacturing process are delivered to the relevant work station just as they are needed, resulting in potentially significant cost savings.

K

Keiretsu

A business grouping comprising a set of Japanese firms that have inter-related business and financial interests. Most keiretsus are centered on a bank that lends money to the members of the keiretsu and has sharehold-ings in these companies. Keiretsus typically also contain a large trading company, a series of satellite companies and other financial institutions.

Key Performance Indicators

Measures that are used by an organization to assess the performance of individuals and groups within the organization. These will vary from individual to individual and from group to group since what is a relevant measure of performance varies across individuals and groups. The usual process in identifying key performance indicators is: (1) identify the relevant business unit; (2) identify the performance measures that are relevant for that unit; (3) set quantitative and qualitative targets for these performance measures; (4) regularly review performance with respect to the targets set and the relevance of the targets themselves.

Key Success Factors

The **human capital** knowledge and other asset requirements that are neces-sary, but not sufficient, for a firm to succeed in a market. Success requires that these factors are also aligned with the firm's **resources** and **capabilities**.

Kinked Demand Curve

A **demand curve** that has a convex kink at the ruling market price. This results in a jump discontinuity in the **marginal revenue** curve with the result that prices will remain unchanged for any **marginal cost** curves that pass through the discontinuity. The underlying assumption for this demand curve is that demand is more **price elastic** to a price increase than a price decrease – because competitors are more likely to react to a reduction in price, by matching their competitors' price cuts, than to an increase in price. Proponents of kinked-demand theory formulated the theory in order to provide an explanation for why many prices seemed to be sticky, rather than to change rapidly and smoothly in response to changes in economic conditions. Critics of kinked-demand theory argue that it is descriptive rather than prescriptive. In particular, it does not explain how the ruling market price is established, or how the kink reacts to significant changes in market conditions. Critics further suggest that there are other more convincing explanations of sticky prices such as contractual rigidities, **regulation**, collusive behavior and **menu costs**.

Knowledge Advantage

The **competitive advantage** that a firm gains as a result of its superior knowledge regarding how to produce a particular product or how to operate a particular production process. Since such knowledge is typically embodied in the firm's skilled labor, the firm has to be concerned with ensuring that it retains such skilled labor.

Knowledge Capital

The expertise that a firm or organization develops from sharing and developing the expertise, information, knowledge and skills of the individuals within the firm or organization. Knowledge capital can be a source of **sustainable competitive advantage** since it is largely tacit rather than explicit and so can be difficult to copy. Since knowledge capital largely resides within the **human capital** of the firm, however, it can be dissipated by labor turnover.

Kreps–Scheinkman Model

Suppose that oligopolistic firms are involved in a two-stage **game** in which in the first stage they choose capacity and in the second stage they compete in prices. Suppose further that capacity, once installed, is prohibitively expensive to change. The Kreps–Scheinkman model predicts that under some circumstances, the first-stage equilibrium to this two-stage capacity–price game is identical to the Cournot quantities, with the result that the equilibrium to the capacity–price game is the **Cournot equilibrium**. An important advantage of this model is that it can allow us to use a Cournot model, which is relatively easy to analyze, as an analogy for a capacity-constrained price model, which is typically very difficult to analyze.

L

Labor Intensity

The extent to which **output** is produced by labor **inputs** rather than by other **factors of production**.

Labor–Leisure Trade-Off

A theory suggesting that the number of hours that an individual chooses to work is determined by the individual comparing the additional **welfare** that is derived from additional leisure against the loss of income that additional leisure implies. For unskilled workers, at the lower end of the wage scale, wage increases tend to lead to more hours worked and thus less leisure. However, once wages reach a sufficiently high level, a worker might choose to cut back on hours worked as wages increase, resulting in a backward-bending labor **supply curve** at high wage levels.

Labor Union

A formal organization of labor with the aim of negotiating working conditions such as **contracts**, hours of work and compensation.

Latent Variable Model

An econometric model in which the **dependent variable**, y^*, is unobserved, or latent, and is determined by $y^* = \beta_0 + \beta_1 x_1 + \ldots + \beta_k x_k + u$, with **explanatory variables**, $x_1, \ldots, x_k$, and error term u. The researcher observes only an outcome variable, y, which is related to y^*, according to an index function. In the case of the **probit** or **logit model**, $y = 0$ if $y^* \leq 0$, and $y = 1$ if $y^* > 0$. For the **tobit model**, $y = 0$ if $y^* \leq 0$, and $y = y^*$ if $y^* > 0$. For example, suppose firms within a given industry expand into a new product line if the expected economic profit, y^*, from doing so is positive; however, the researcher observes only whether or not a firm expands, but does not directly observe the firm's expected profits. A logit or probit model would be an appropriate econometric specification in this context.

Law of Demand

The prediction that for most goods and services the quantity demanded will fall as the price increases, all else equal. A notable exception to this law includes a **Giffen good**, for which quantity demanded rises with price increases.

Law of Diminishing Returns

The prediction that as more and more variable **factors of production** are used in combination with a set of fixed factors, the **marginal product** of the variable factors will eventually decrease and may, in the limit, be negative. For example, consider a small factory with a fixed number of machines used in a production process. Initially, as each additional worker is hired, their marginal product is likely to exceed that of the worker hired previously. This may result from workers interacting optimally with the available capital, in addition to gains from specialization as additional workers realize efficiencies from coordinated effort. Eventually, however, the machines will be fully utilized by the workers, such that an additional worker will contribute less to output than the previously hired worker, leading to the onset of diminishing returns. As more workers are hired beyond this point, each worker's marginal product declines further, until workers begin actually to interfere with the production process, resulting in negative marginal productivity.

Law of Proportionate Effect

See **Gibrat's Law**.

Law of Supply

The prediction that for most goods and services the quantity supplied will increase as the price increases, all else equal.

LBO

See **leveraged buyout**.

Leader–Follower Model

See **Stackelberg model**.

Leaders

See **Stackelberg leaders**.

Lean-and-Hungry Look

Assume that a **strategic commitment** makes a firm soft and so potentially softens competition in the market. The firm has an incentive to **underinvest** in or reject this type of commitment, stay "lean and hungry", if the choice variables are **strategic substitutes**. For example, consider the following model. An incumbent firm that is a **Cournot competitor** in its current market A has the opportunity to make a commitment to invest in opening another, spatially distinct market B in which it will have a local monopoly. However, in order to open and operate in market B, scarce management and other resources will have to be diverted from market A, raising marginal costs in market A. The incumbent firm may choose to underinvest in the commitment to market B, and in the limit reject such an investment altogether in order to maintain its competitiveness in market A. See Fudenberg and Tirole (1984), **fat-cat effect**, **puppy dog strategy** and **top dog strategy**.

Learning-by-Doing

The ability of workers to increase productivity as a result of the experience that they gain from performing the same functions over an extended period of time. The increased productivity derives from repeated and focused effort, skill development, and the ability to identify efficiency improvements through experience. The benefits from learning-by-doing can be represented by a two-period model of costs. In the first period, **total cost** is a function of the output produced in that period; in the second period, total cost is a function of both first- and second-period production, such that second-period costs decline with an increase in first-period levels of production. A firm seeking to maximize profits over the two periods will take account of the second-period benefits of increasing first-period production, and thus of moving up the **learning curve** faster.

Learning Curve

The relationship between the **average total cost** curve and the firm's cumulative experience. When there is **learning-by-doing** it is to be expected that average total cost will fall with cumulative experience.

Learn-to-Burn Ratio

The ratio of the rate at which a firm learns, by gaining new information relevant to its strategic choices, to the burn rate, the rate at which the firm has to expend resources in order to generate the new information. See Ghemawat (1993).

Leasing

Granting the right to use a good or service for a defined period of time in return for a defined payment and under defined usage conditions. **Ownership** of the good or service is retained by the individual granting the lease.

Lemons

Poor-quality second-hand goods. See also **lemons problem**.

Lemons Problem

The equilibrium of an economic model that predicts that there will be a higher proportion of **lemons** in the second-hand market for a particular good than in the new market for that good, such as in the market for used automobiles. The model, proposed by Nobel Laureate George Akerlof (1970), is based on the assumption that the owner of a used good is better informed of its true **quality** – whether or not it is a lemon – than is a potential buyer. In the face of this uncertainty about quality, the buyer would choose to pay the average product value. Since the seller knows the true value of the used product, the seller would choose not to sell a high-quality product, since its known value exceeds the expected average but would choose to offer a low-quality product for sale since its known value is less than the expected average. This logic implies that low-quality products will be disproportionately represented in the used-good market. Thus **asymmetric information** on product quality leads to this problem of **adverse selection**.

Leniency Program

A program developed by the **antitrust authorities** to offer reduced fines and other penalties to members of **cartels** who provide evidence of the operations of the cartel that is sufficient to lead to successful prosecution of the cartel. These programs are used extensively in Australia, the European Union and the United States and have been credited with enabling the antitrust authorities in these regions to detect cartels much more effectively. On first sight, leniency programs appear to reduce the incentive to form cartels since the programs confront cartel members with a **prisoners' dilemma**: if the cartel suspects that it is under investigation, there is the temptation for each member of the cartel to seek leniency in order to escape with a reduced fine. However, the effects of these programs are actually more complex. On the one hand, they make cartels easier to detect. On the other hand, they may actually lead to more cartels being formed, since each cartel member calculates that its cost of being discovered is low – potentially zero – provided that it is the first to confess.

Leontief Production (Utility) Function

See **fixed-proportions production (utility) function**.

Lerner Index

A measure of market performance defined as the ratio of the profit margin to the market price, or

$$LI = \frac{P - MC}{P},$$

where P is the market price and MC is **marginal cost**. In **antitrust law** enforcement, the Lerner index provides a baseline measure for assessing the extent to which a monopolist can mark up their price above cost and thus the extent of the potential loss of **consumer surplus** resulting from monopolization. See also **market power**.

Leverage

The ratio of a firm's debt to the firm's equity. See **debt–equity ratio**.

Leveraged Buyout

The managers of a publicly traded company taking the company private by using debt to purchase the outstanding shares of the company.

Licensing

A **patent** holder or **trademark** holder granting the right to use the patent or trademark to another firm for a defined period of time, under defined conditions and in return for an agreed payment.

Life Cycle – Business

The suggestion that a business or company goes through various stages during its life. There is no settled opinion on what these stages are. One suggestion is that the cycle consists of five stages: birth, growth, maturity, decline and death. Another suggests that the life cycle is seed, start-up, growth, established, expansion, maturity and exit.

Life Cycle – Product

The stages through which a good or service progresses from its initial introduction to eventual decline. There are four stages: (1) introduction – the initial launch of the good or service; (2) growth – the acceptance of the good or service in the market and growth in its sales; (3) maturity – the end of the growth stage when sales growth begins to slow and the good or service has been fully accepted by the market; and (4) decline – reduction in sales and the eventual replacement of the product or service by a new generation of products and services.

Limit Output

The level of **output** that is just great enough to deter the **entry** of a rival firm.

Limit Price

The price that is just low enough to deter the **entry** of a rival firm.

Limit Pricing Model

A multi-period strategic model in which an **incumbent firm** attempts to **deter entry** of a rival by setting a low price – the **limit price** – in early periods, expecting to raise price in later periods as a result of the entry deterrence derived from the limit price. The implications of both limit pricing and **limit output** models rest on strong assumptions about the **potential entrant's** expectations of future demand conditions and of the incumbent's production costs and, in particular, on whether the incumbent firm's threat to, for example, maintain a high post-entry level of output is credible.

Limited Information

See **imperfect information**.

Limited Liability

A form of corporation such that if the corporation fails, the **stockholders** cannot be held responsible for the corporation's debts. The stockholders' losses are limited to the value of the shares that they purchased in the corporation. This is in contrast to the **unlimited liability** facing proprietorships, where the owner's personal assets are available to creditors in case the firm fails.

Linear Price

A simple pricing arrangement according to which consumers pay a price, p, for each unit of the good purchased, irrespective of the total quantity bought. This is in contrast to more complex pricing mechanisms, including **first-**, **second-** and **third-degree price discrimination**.

List Price

The price at which a good or service is listed for sale, or the price that a manufacturer recommends the retailer charge consumers for the good or service for sale. This is not necessarily the price at which the good or service will actually be sold.

Local-Content Rule

A rule that constrains the proportion by value of a product that is assembled in country A that must come from parts and components produced in country A if the assembled product is to be marketed as having been made in country A.

Location Advantage

The **competitive advantage** that a firm gains by **internalizing** an **ownership advantage** and by exploiting that advantage by locating production abroad rather than in the home country.

Location Game

A game of strategic interaction in which one of the decision variables is the location that a player will choose. See **location models**.

Location Models

Economic models that predict the locations that firms and, in some cases, consumers will choose in either geographic or more generally **characteristics space**. Firms will choose either **minimum differentiation** or **maximum differentiation**, depending on the functional form for consumer transportation costs. Specifically, if transport costs are linear in distance, firms will choose minimum differentiation (subject to an existence constraint), whereas if transport costs are quadratic in distance they will choose maximum differentiation. See **Hotelling spatial model**.

Lock-In Effect

The act of making it difficult and expensive for consumers to substitute from one firm's product or service to a rival's as a result of artificial **switching costs** created by the former firm.

Logit Model

A **latent variable model** in which the **dependent variable**, y, takes on the value zero or one, depending on the value of an underlying latent variable, y^*. The logit estimation assumes that the probability that y equals one, conditional on the values of the **independent variables**, follows the logistic distribution, according to $(e^{X'\beta})/(1 + e^{X'\beta})$, where X is the vector of independent variables and β is the vector of coefficients in the model. This specification is useful when the researcher observes an outcome variable, such as whether or not a firm serves a particular market, when the choice is determined by an unobserved variable, such as the firm's expected profits from doing so. The **probit model** assumes a standard normal distribution instead.

"Long Purse" Story

The idea that an **incumbent firm** can successfully prey on a **potential entrant** because the incumbent has substantial resources that can be used to finance the predation. A rationale for threatening to engage in, for example, **predatory pricing**, is that the firm can **deter entry** by threatening to charge a price lower than cost to force eventual **exit** by the competitor, then raise price in a later period. However, maintaining those higher prices might not be sustainable, particularly in **contestable markets** characterized by low **barriers to entry**.

Long Run

The period of time that is sufficiently long that all **factors of production** can be varied and all **contracts** renegotiated. Since all costs are variable in the long run, and thus **fixed costs** are zero, **total variable costs** are equivalent to **total costs** in the long run.

Long-Run Average Cost Curve

The lower envelope of the **short-run average total cost** curves. A typical long-run average cost curve is U-shaped. For lower levels of output, as output increases, the lowest attainable per-unit cost of production falls, as a firm experiences **economies of scale**. Once the firm reaches its **minimum efficient scale**, the long-run average cost curve may become horizontal for a range of output corresponding to **constant returns to scale**. As output increases beyond this range, the firm will experience **diseconomies of scale** and thus rising long-run average cost.

Long-Run Competitive Equilibrium

Equilibrium in a **competitive market** such that no **incumbent firm** wishes to **exit** and no **potential entrant** wishes to **enter**.

Lorenz Curve

A graph representing the cumulative distribution of a probability distribution, where the members of the distribution are ordered in increasing size. For example, if the Lorenz curve measures the distribution of wealth and we have a population of size n we begin by ordering this population by income y_i such that $y_n \leq y_{n+1}$. The Lorenz curve is then derived from linear interpolation at each point (F_i, L_i), $i = 0, \ldots, n$. For $i = 0$, we initialize $F_0 = 0$, $L_0 = 0$, and for $i = 1, \ldots, n$ we have

$$F_i = i/n; \ S_i = \sum_{j=1}^{n} y_j; \ L_i = S_i/S_n.$$

For a cumulative distribution function $F(y)$ where y is ordered by increasing magnitude, the Lorenz curve is

$$L(y) = \frac{\int_0^y x \, dF(x)}{\mu}$$

where μ is the average. The Lorenz curve provides a visual representation of the relationship between the percentage of the population comprising the lowest income earners and the total percentage of income earned in the population. For example, the graph indicates whether the 25 percent of the population that earns the lowest income earns 25 percent or less of the society's income. The extent to which this curve lies below the 45 degree line is the measure of the society's income inequality. See Lorenz (1905) and Gastwirth (1972, p. 306); see also **Gini coefficient**.

Loss

A situation in which a firm's revenues are less than the firm's costs. When the firm's costs include opportunity costs, and thus **economic profit** is negative, such a loss will provide a signal to the firm to **exit** the industry, since the net benefits from the best alternative use of the firm's resources are greater than those deriving from their current use.

Loss-Leader Pricing

A business strategy by which a firm offers a product at a low price – perhaps even below its cost – in order to attract consumers to purchase other products that have much higher profit margins. The objective of the loss leader in retail markets is to attract customers to the retail outlet, at which point they might be encouraged to purchase other items that give the retailer higher returns than the loss-leader.

Low-Price Guarantee

A guarantee offered by a seller to a buyer that the seller will match or beat any competitor's price. These guarantees are common in retailing, particularly in markets for consumer electronic goods. They are usually justified by companies who offer them on the basis that they save consumers **search costs** and ensure that consumers are offered the best possible prices. By contrast, it is argued that such clauses actually result in higher prices. See **meet-the-competition clause**.

Loyalty Business Model

A business model in which a firm strategically deploys its resources to increase the loyalty of its customers, its suppliers and its other **stakeholders** with the intention that these strategies will increase the profitability of the firm.

Lumpy Orders

Orders are lumpy when they arise infrequently and in large, indivisible batches. In markets characterized by lumpy orders tacit or explicit cooperation between sellers is difficult to sustain. Each firm is tempted to cheat on the cooperation, knowing that the time before the rival can retaliate is lengthy. There is, for example, no evidence of cooperation between Boeing and Airbus for lumpy orders for new airplanes by the major airlines.

M

Make-or-Buy Decision

The decision by a firm regarding whether to perform an upstream, down-stream or support activity by **internalizing** it to the firm or by contracting it from an independent supplier. This decision determines the extent to which the firm is **vertically integrated**. It requires that the firm balance the market and **transaction costs** of using external providers against the same costs when performing the activity inside the firm, otherwise referred to as achieving a balance between **agency efficiency** and **technical efficiency**. "Buy" is more likely to be preferred when market providers can exploit **economies of scale** and **scope** not available to internal divisions. "Make" is more likely to be preferred if the activity requires the creation of highly **relationship-specific assets** since "buy" opens the contracting parties to the risk of **hold-up**.

Managerial Objectives

The objectives that management pursues in the operation of the companies that management controls. These may include objectives other than **profit maximization**, such as growth or **sales revenue maximization**.

Management Buyout

The purchase of a firm by its managers. When the purchase is financed by debt this is referred to as a **leveraged buyout**.

Management by Objectives

A system in which the **performance standards** that employees are required to meet are established by negotiation between the employees and management.

Margin Strategy

A strategy in which a firm exploits a **cost advantage** by maintaining price parity with its rivals, or exploits a **benefit advantage** by charging a premium price, delivering superior profits through the higher price-cost margin that the benefit or cost advantage creates, while still offering **consumer surplus** comparable to that offered by its rivals. A firm is more likely to pursue a margin strategy the less elastic the demand for its products or services is.

Marginal Benefit

The additional benefit of consuming an additional unit of a product or service. If the total benefit function is denoted $B(Q)$ then marginal benefit is $MB = dB(Q)/dQ$. When marginal benefit is measured in monetary terms then an individual's marginal benefit function with respect to a good or service is also that individual's **demand function** for that good or service.

Marginal Cost

The additional cost of producing an additional unit of **output** of a product or service. If the **total cost** function is denoted $C(Q)$ then marginal cost is $MC = dC(Q)/dQ$. A firm maximizes its profit by choosing the output at which its marginal cost equals its **marginal revenue**.

Marginal Effects

In econometrics, the estimated marginal impact of a unit increase in an **explanatory variable** on the **dependent variable** of interest. In **ordinary least squares (OLS)**, this impact is measured by the estimated coefficient, β_i, for the **independent variable** X_i. For example, if the dependent variable is sales volume, and the independent variable of interest is advertising expenditure, the estimated coefficient provides a measure of the change in sales volume that will result from a dollar increase in advertising spending. In the **logit** and **probit models**, the marginal effect of interest is the impact of a unit increase in an independent variable on the probability of the outcome of interest, such as the probability of a firm expanding its product line. The estimated coefficients in these models do not provide this direct interpretation; further computation is required to obtain the marginal effects.

Marginal Outlay

The additional cost to a **monopsonist** of buying an additional unit of **input**. If total expenditure on L units of a **factor of production** is $E(L)$ then marginal outlay is $MO = dE(L)/dL$. A monopsonist maximizes **profit** by employing factors of production up to the point where marginal outlay on a factor equals the **marginal revenue product** of that factor.

Marginal Product

The additional **output** that is produced by employing an additional unit of a variable factor. If the firm's **production function** is $Q = f(x)$, where x is a vector of factor **inputs**, then the marginal product of factor i is $MP_i = \partial Q/\partial x_i$. Suppose that the vector of factor prices is w. Then the firm minimizes cost of producing a given level of output by employing its factor inputs in quantities such that

$$\frac{MP_i}{MP_j} = \frac{w_i}{w_j} \quad \forall i,j; \; i \neq j.$$

Marginal Rate of Technical Substitution

The ease with which a firm can substitute one factor **input** for another without changing **output**. If the firm's **production function** is $Q = f(x)$, where x is a vector of inputs of the factors of production, then the marginal rate of technical substitution between factor i and factor k is

$$MRTS_{ik} = \frac{\partial f(\mathbf{x})/\partial x_i}{\partial f(\mathbf{x})/\partial x_k}.$$

Marginal Revenue

The additional **revenue** that a firm receives from selling an additional unit of **output**. If the **inverse demand function** is denoted $P(q)$ then **total revenue** is $TR(q) = P(q).q$ and marginal revenue is $MR = dTR(q)/dq = P(q) + q.dP(q)/dq$ which can be written $MR = P(q)[1 + 1/\eta_q:P]$ where $\eta_{q:P}$ is the **elasticity of demand**. A firm maximizes its **profit** by choosing the output at which its marginal revenue equals its **marginal cost**.

Marginal Revenue Product

The additional **revenue** that is generated by employing an additional unit of a variable **factor of production**. If the **inverse demand function** is $P(q)$

and the firm's **production function** is $q = f(x)$, where x is a vector of factor **inputs**, then the marginal revenue product of factor i is

$$MRP_i = \partial(P(q)q)/\partial x_i = \left(q\frac{dP(q)}{dq} + P(q) \right)\frac{\partial q}{\partial x_i}.$$

Marginal Utility

The additional **utility** that a consumer obtains from consuming an additional unit of a good or service. If the consumer's **utility function** is $u(q)$ where q is a vector of the goods and services consumed, then marginal utility of good i is $MU_i = \partial u(q)/\partial q_i$. Suppose that the vector of product prices is p. Then a consumer maximizes utility by choosing a consumption bundle q such that

$$\frac{MU_i}{MU_j} = \frac{p_i}{p_j} \quad \forall i,j; \ i \neq j,$$

in other words, such that the ratio of marginal utilities for any two products i and j equals the ratio of the product prices of i and j.

Marginal Utility of Income

The additional **utility** that a consumer obtains from an additional unit of income. If the consumer's **indirect utility function** is $v(p, y)$, where p is a vector of goods prices and y is the consumer's income, then the marginal utility of income is $MU_y = \partial v(p, y)/\partial y$.

Marginal Willingness to Pay

For a given level of consumption of a product, a measure of consumers' valuation of consumption of the next unit of the good. This valuation is measured by the height of the demand curve, or the price, at the quantity of interest, and is used in the computation of **consumer surplus**.

Market

A gathering of sellers and buyers of goods or services and the mechanisms by which they can exchange these goods and services.

Market Clearing

The process by which a market achieves equality between the quantity demanded and the quantity supplied in the market in a given period of time. Typically this process works by causing price to fall when there is **excess supply** in a market and causing price to rise when there is **excess demand** in the market.

Market Concentration

A measure of the extent to which firms operating in a market are able to exercise **market power**. This is normally measured by a summary **concentration ratio** or by the **Herfindahl–Hirschman Index**.

Market Conduct

A description of the **strategies** that firms use in a market. Examples include their pricing, product and advertising strategies and investment in **research and development**. This is typically seen as part of the **structure–conduct–performance paradigm**.

Market Definition

A well-defined market includes all firms that compete with each other and excludes all non-competitors. One conceptual test used to determine whether a market is well defined is the **SSNIP criterion** used by the US **Department of Justice**. Suppose that all the firms in what is thought to be the market are allowed to merge. Would this lead to a small but significant nontransitory increase in price? If the answer is yes, the market is considered to be well defined. If the answer is no, presumably this is because there are competitors that limit the ability of firms within the market to increase their prices but that are not currently considered to be part of the market. So the market is not well defined.

Market Demand Curve

The relationship between the price of a good and the aggregate quantity of the good that consumers demand in the market in a specified period of time.

Market Failure

The inability of a market to work efficiently, perhaps because **property rights** are not well defined or tradable or because of other distortions in the market. The lack of property rights or the inability to trade property rights leads to **externalities**. If the market is for a **public good** then it is not possible to operate such a market privately since no private company will be able to operate the market at a **profit**.

Market for Corporate Control

A market that constrains the ability of senior management to pursue their own objectives at the expense of **shareholders** through the threat of **take-over** and the replacement of the senior management team. The argument is that inefficient management results in a stock price that is much lower than would be the case with efficient management. This creates an incentive for outsiders who believe that they can operate the company more effectively to seek to replace the inefficient management by taking over the company and replacing that management. See Manne (1965).

Market Foreclosure

See **foreclosure**.

Market for Ideas

A market in which a firm can sell its superior knowledge, perhaps embodied in **patents** and **trademarks**, for their full market value.

Market Portfolio

A financial portfolio that contains proportionate values of different assets in proportion to their aggregate proportion in the overall asset market.

Market Power

The power that a firm has to set price greater than **marginal cost**. One measure of market power is the **Lerner Index**. In **perfectly competitive** markets, firms are unable to exercise any market power: the Lerner Index is zero. In **monopolistically competitive** markets, firms have some market power because they each offer a **differentiated product**. In **monopoly**, market power derives from **barriers to entry** of potential competitors.

Market Share

The proportion of a market that is controlled by a particular seller.

Market Sharing Agreement

A collusive agreement in which the members of the **collusion** agree on the market shares that they will have in the relevant market.

Market Structure

A measure of the size distribution of firms in a market, typically summarized by a **concentration index** such as the **Herfindahl–Hirschman Index**.

Market Supply Curve

The relationship between the price of a good and the aggregate quantity of the good that firms supply in a specified period of time. In **perfectly competitive** markets the short-run market supply curve is the aggregation of the individual firms' **marginal cost** curves. The long-run market supply curve is the supply curve that results from the **entry** or **exit** of firms into or from the market.

Market Tipping

When there are competing systems in a **network industry**, once one system gains an advantage in consumer preferences then it becomes increasingly popular, driving out the rival systems. The market "tips" in favor of one of the competing systems. The market dominance of Facebook and Google are two examples. If a new product or service can be developed using competing technologies, then there will be competition to determine the technology standard, and the market will eventually tip in favor of one standard or the other. Competition between VHS and Betamax in video recorders is a classic example.

Mark-Up Pricing

A pricing system in which a firm determines the market price of a product by adding a mark-up to the product's **marginal cost**. Typically, the mark-up is determined by management taking an intuitive view of "what the market will bear". This pricing system can be justified from the profit-maximizing pricing rule $P = MC(1 + 1/\eta)$ where MC is marginal cost and η is the **elasticity of demand**. This can be interpreted as stating that the price is marginal cost marked up by a multiple determined by the elasticity of demand. See also **cost-plus pricing** and **inverse elasticity rule**.

Marshallian Demand Function

The **demand function** that is derived from maximizing the consumer's **utility function** subject to a **budget constraint**. Given the consumer's **indirect utility function** $v(p, y)$, the Marshallian demand function for commodity i is, by **Roy's Identity**,

$$x_i(\mathbf{p}, y) = -\frac{\partial v(\mathbf{p}, y)/\partial p_i}{\partial v(\mathbf{p}, y)/\partial y}.$$

Matrix Organization

An organizational structure in which employees are required to report to at least two sets of managers with different functional responsibilities. Suppose, for example, that a firm can be organized along functional lines, such as finance, manufacturing and service, and along product lines such as business and consumer products. A matrix organization has employees assigned to functional departments but also reporting to product-based subunits. The intent is to encourage employees to look at the organization as a whole rather than focus on their own functional specialties. A major disadvantage is that there are intersecting lines of authority, resulting in employees being confused as to their primary loyalties or focusing on the line manager who they believe has the greatest influence on the employees' rewards.

Maximum Differentiation

An outcome in two-person **location games** in which the players choose to maximally separate their locations. This can apply to location choices by political parties, geographic locations or locations in product **characteristics space**. Assume a linear **Hotelling line market**. If consumer transport costs are quadratic then duopolists playing a two-stage location–price game will choose locations at the opposite ends of the line.

Maximum Likelihood Estimation

A method of estimating the parameters of an econometric model based on maximizing the likelihood of observing the particular sample of data under analysis. The method formally maximizes the natural logarithm of a likelihood function that depends on the statistical distributional assumptions of the model and on the parameters. This method is used to estimate such non-linear models as the **logit** and **probit models**.

Measurement Costs

The costs that an economic agent incurs in improving his knowledge about the true **quality** of a good or service. These costs are usually incurred to improve the agent's bargaining position.

Measurement Error

The error that arises in the accuracy with which performance is measured in **incentive-based compensation** systems. According to the **incentive intensity principle**, the intensity of incentives in incentive compensation should be inversely proportional to measurement error.

Meet-the-Competition Clause

A guarantee offered by a retailer to its consumers that it will meet or beat any lower price charged for the same good by a rival retailer. Such clauses are usually justified by companies who offer them on the basis that they save consumers **search costs** and ensure that consumers are offered the best possible prices. By contrast, it is argued that such clauses actually result in higher prices. To see why, consider the pricing **game** in the following **payoff matrix**, where in each cell, the **payoff** to the row player is listed first, and the payoff to the column player is listed second. In the absence of a meet-the-competition clause, and given that the game is not a **repeated game**, the **Nash equilibrium** to this game is that both firms set a Low Price.

		Firm B	
		High Price	Low Price
Firm A	High Price	10, 10	5, 12
	Low Price	12, 5	6, 6

Now suppose that both firms offer a meet-the-competition clause. Firm A, for example, anticipates that moving from High Price to Low Price will gain no additional market share. As a result the game becomes

		Firm B	
		High Price	Low Price
Firm A	High Price	10, 10	6, 6
	Low Price	6, 6	6, 6

(High Price, High Price) is now a Nash equilibrium for this game.

Menu Costs

The costs that firms incur in changing their prices. The term derives from the costs that a restaurant incurs in printing new menus when the restaurant wishes to change its prices. If these costs are sufficiently great, the restaurant may choose to postpone the price increases. More generally, a firm incurs menu costs when it has to physically change price tags on items, conduct market research on what the new prices should be, and update its computer systems to incorporate the new prices. Suppose that the firm's profit-maximizing prices are p_1 when market conditions are described by some parameters a_1 and profit at these prices is $\Pi(a_1, p_1)$. Now suppose that there is a change in market conditions to a_2, with the resulting profit-maximizing prices being p_2 and profit $\Pi(a_2, p_2)$. The firm will choose not to change its prices if its menu costs are $M > \Pi(a_2, p_2) - (a_2, p_1)$. Menu costs are one explanation that is given for prices being "sticky" or unresponsive to relatively minor changes in market conditions.

Menu Pricing

See **second-degree price discrimination**.

Merger Guidelines

Guidelines issued and regularly updated by the United States **antitrust authorities** detailing the rules that they shall apply in assessing whether a proposed **merger** should be investigated to assess its competitive and **welfare** impacts. Typically these guidelines are based on the estimated impact that the merger will have on **market concentration**. See also **Horizontal Merger Guidelines**.

Merger

The act of combining the operations of two previously independent companies, usually enacted by one company acquiring a controlling interest in the other. Mergers can be **horizontal**, **vertical** or **conglomerate**.

Merger Paradox

The paradoxical result that the **merger** of firms producing **strategic substitutes** is unprofitable unless a sufficiently high proportion of the firms in the market are parties to the merger. Suppose that the market contains N **Cournot competitors** each with identical, linear **marginal costs** and each producing a **homogeneous product** for which demand is linear. Then for a merger of $a(N)$ of these firms to be profitable it is necessary that

$$a(N) > \frac{3 + 2N - \sqrt{5 + 4N}}{2N} > 0.8.$$

In other words, at least 80 percent of the firms have to merge for the merger to be profitable. The **merger guidelines** would typically result in such a merger being prevented. See Salant et al. (1983).

Merger to Monopoly

A series of **mergers** that results in a market being monopolized. Typically, but not always, the **antitrust authorities** will intervene to prevent such a series of mergers.

Merger Waves

The empirical regularity that **mergers** appear to occur in waves, with periods of high merger activity followed by lulls.

Method of Moments Estimation

An estimation method that uses sample moments, such as the sample mean or variance, in place of population moments, to estimate parameters of interest. **Ordinary least squares (OLS)** estimation is an example of method of moments estimation. In the **classical linear regression model**, for $y = \beta_0 + \beta_1 x_1 + \ldots + \beta_k x_k + u$, we assume that the expected value of the error term is zero, and that the error term is independent of the **explanatory variables**, implying the following moment conditions: $E(u) = 0$ and $E(X'u) = 0$, where X is the vector of **independent variables**. Expanding the expectation operators, and using the corresponding sample values, we can derive estimates for the β_i coefficients. See also **generalized method of moments**.

Minimax Strategy

A decision rule, typically for **zero-sum games** by which a player chooses a strategy that minimizes the worst possible outcome for that player. Take the following game in which the payoffs for Player A are:

	B1	B2
A1	+30	−20
A2	−10	0

and the payoffs for Player B are:

	B1	B2
A1	−30	+20
A2	+10	0

The minimax strategy for Player A is A2, for which the worst possible outcome is −10 as compared to −20 for A1, while the minimax strategy for Player B is B2, for which the worst possible outcome is 0, as compared to −30 for B1. The actual **Nash equilibrium** for this game is in **mixed strategies**.

Minimum Differentiation

An outcome in two-person **location games** in which the players choose the same locations. This can apply to location choices by political parties, geographic locations or locations in product **characteristics space**. Assume a linear **Hotelling line market**. If consumer transport costs are linear then Hotelling argued that duopolists playing a location-price game would choose locations close to the center of the line. It has subsequently been shown, however, that there is no **subgame perfect Nash equilibrium** to this game. Changing the transport cost function to quadratic costs restores equilibrium existence but leads to **maximum differentiation**. If, by contrast, firms play a location–quantity game in which they first choose locations and then compete as **Cournot competitors**, the principle of minimum differentiation applies, even with $n > 2$ firms, with the firms agglomerated at the market center.

Minimum Efficient Scale

The smallest level of **output** at which long-run average cost is minimized and so **economies of scale** are exhausted.

Minimum Wage

A government-enacted regulation governing the lowest wage an employee can be paid per unit of time worked.

Missing Markets

A situation in which no market exists to facilitate transactions in a particular good or service. Typically, missing markets arise because **property rights** are either not defined or not tradable.

Mixed Bundling

A strategy in which a firm offers consumers the choice of buying its products as a bundle, or buying the products individually. For example, a restaurant might offer a fixed price, set menu and an à la carte menu. Mixed bundling can increase the firm's **profits** when the firm knows that it is serving consumers with diverse tastes, with different groups of consumers ranking the products that the firm offers differently. See **bundling**.

Mixed Logit Model

An econometric model that extends the **multinomial logit model** to accommodate a **random-coefficients** specification, in which the parameters of interest are treated as **random variables**. This specification is an alternative to the **multinomial probit model**, with particular applicability to estimating **discrete choice models of demand**. The mixed logit model allows for variation in consumer tastes, as well as a range of consumer substitution patterns, that the independence of irrelevant alternatives (IIA) assumption in the multinomial logit model precludes. See Berry et al. (1995) for a seminal application to the automobile industry and Train (2009) for comprehensive coverage.

Mixed Strategy

A strategy in which a player selects the probabilities with which he will play his individual strategies. If the set of possible strategies is denoted by the vector $s = (s_1, \ldots, s_n)$ then a mixed strategy is a vector $p = (p_1, \ldots, p_n)$ such that p_i is the probability with which strategy i is played and

$$\sum_{i=1}^{n} p_i = 1.$$

A **pure strategy** can be thought of as a special case of mixed strategy in which one element of p is unity. Nash showed that any **game** with a finite number of players and a finite number of strategies always has a **Nash equilibrium** in mixed strategies.

Mixed-Strategy Nash Equilibrium

A **Nash equilibrium** in **mixed strategies**. All non-cooperative **games** with a finite number of players, each of which has a finite number of strategies, has at least one mixed-strategy Nash equilibrium. Consider a two-player game with the following **payoff matrix**, where in each cell, the **payoff** to the row player is listed first, and the payoff to the column player is listed second:

		Player B	
		I	II
Player A	I	A, a	B, b
	II	C, c	D, d

A mixed-strategy Nash equilibrium in which both players randomize between I and II is an equilibrium strategy when the following conditions are satisfied: (1) Player A chooses to play I with probability p and II with probability $1 - p$ with p chosen such that Player B is indifferent between playing I or II; (2) Player B chooses to play I with probability q and II with probability $1 - q$ with q chosen such that Player A is indifferent between playing I or II. In the game above, the mixed-strategy equilibrium is for Player A to play I with probability $p = (d - c)/(a + d - b - c)$ and II with probability $1 - p$, and for player B to play I with probability $q = (D - B)/(A + D - B - C)$ and II with probability $1 - q$.

Modigliani–Miller Theorems

Two theorems in financial markets. The first states that, but for taxes, the total market value of a firm's debt and equity is independent of the proportion of debt and equity it chooses in its financing. The second states that the total value of a firm's debt and equity is unaffected by its dividend policy. These theorems hold under the assumption that individual investors can undo a firm's financing or dividend policies by holding or constructing appropriate portfolios of financial assets.

Monitoring

An activity undertaken by one party to a **contract** that is intended to confirm whether the other party is meeting the contractual obligations specified in the contract. The cost associated with monitoring activity is considered a **transaction cost**.

Monitoring Intensity Principle

The principle that in an **incentive contract**, more resources should be devoted to **monitoring** in order to reduce error in performance measurement when the contract offers stronger performance incentives.

Monopolistic Competition

A competitive market characterized by perfect information, free **entry** and **exit** but in which the competing firms each offer a **differentiated product**. In such a market, each firm's **demand function** is downward sloping as a result of the **product differentiation**. In the long run, the process of entry and exit guarantees that each firm just breaks even. As a result, each firm has **excess capacity**, in the sense that each firm is operating on the downward sloping part of its **average total cost** curve, because in equilibrium the demand function for each firm must be just tangent to the firm's average total cost function and the demand function is downward sloping.

Monopolization

An offence under the **antitrust laws** by which a firm seeks to eliminate its rivals, and prevent **entry** of potential competitors in order to convert the market into a **monopoly** and seek to perpetuate that monopoly. There are two elements to monopolization. First, it must be shown that the firm has monopoly power. Second, it must be shown that this monopoly power has been attained and/or sustained through conduct that is determined to be unlawful. In other words, mere possession of monopoly power is not, of itself, a violation of antitrust laws. It could be, for example, that the monopoly results from product innovation by the firm that has come to dominate the market.

Monopoly

A market dominated by a single seller.

Monopoly Power

Market power resulting from the presence of only one seller in a market. Determining the size and extent of market power plays an important role in **antitrust law** enforcement. Measures such as the **Lerner Index** provide a baseline for assessing the extent to which a monopolist can mark up price relative to the marginal-cost pricing of a **competitive market**.

Monopoly Profit

The **supernormal profit** that can be earned by a firm with **market power**.

Monopsony

A market dominated by a single buyer.

Moral Hazard

A form of **post-contractual opportunism** that arises when the actions of a party to a **contract** are not perfectly observable by the other party to the contract, with the result that the former can exploit the terms of the contract without being found to be in breach of the contract. In insurance markets, a driver might become less careful as a result of being insured. In financial markets, a financial institution might take on excessive risk on the assumption it is insured by the Central Bank against failure. See also **principal–agent problem**.

Most-Favored-Customer Clause

A clause in a business-to-business transaction that contracts a seller to offer buyer *A* a rebate if the seller subsequently sells the same product or service to any other buyer *B* at a discounted price, below the price originally charged to *A*. This clause can take two forms: contemporaneous and retroactive. If contemporaneous, the clause is in effect during the duration of the contract between A and B. If retroactive, it is extended to cover some period after the contract between A and B has expired. It has been argued that such clauses reduce the intensity of competition by making price reductions more costly, in ways similar to **meet-the-competition clauses**, resulting in buyers actually paying higher prices than they otherwise would. On the other hand, these clauses offer early buyers the reassurance that later buyers, with whom the early buyers are in competition, will not be offered a better deal. See Cooper (1986).

Motivation Problem

The challenge of arranging economic transactions so that the decisions taken by self-interested individuals with **private information** take into account not only how the decisions affect their own well-being but also how their decisions affect others.

Multicollinearity

In **regression analysis**, the case in which some **explanatory variables** are strongly correlated. This condition lowers the precision of the coefficient estimates.

Multi-Divisional Organization

An organization that consists of multiple business units, each with autonomy over day-to-day operating decisions and with control over their functional departments such as accounting and marketing. **Coordination** and performance assessment of these units is the role of a central office. The units may be established as **cost centers**, **expense centers**, **investment centers**, **profit centers** or **revenue centers**.

Multi-Market Contact

A situation in which the same rival firms compete with each other in multiple markets. If the markets are asymmetric such contact can aid the maintenance of **tacit** or **explicit collusion** by allowing the firms to use slack enforcement power in one market to facilitate cooperation in other markets. Suppose, for example, that firms A and B are **Bertrand competitors** in markets 1 and 2 and that firm A has market (and profit) share s in market 1 and $1-s$ in market 2, with $s > \frac{1}{2}$. If the firms treat the two markets separately, for cooperation between them to be sustainable, their **discount factors** must be greater than $\max\{s, 1-s\} = s > \frac{1}{2}$. By contrast, if the firms treat the two markets together, for cooperation to be sustainable, their discount factors must be greater than $\frac{1}{2}$. The latter is a less stringent condition.

Multinational Corporation

A corporation that owns or controls production establishments or operations in more than one country. Such a corporation is typically formed as the result of **foreign direct investment** by the home corporation.

Multinomial Logit Model

An econometric model in which the decision maker chooses from among three or more discrete choices. The model depends on the strong assumption of independence of irrelevant alternatives (IIA), which requires that the relative probability the individual selects one option over another not be influenced by the presence of additional alternatives in the choice set. The IIA assumption can be problematic when the elements of the choice set include close substitutes. For example, a consumer, when faced with the choice of transportation mode, might choose from among taking a bus, train or Toyota sedan. If the same consumer instead faced the choice from among bus, train, Toyota sedan or a second sedan, produced by a different company, but with very similar features to the Toyota, the relative probability of taking the bus compared to taking either car remains the same as the initial bus–Toyota comparison; however, if the IIA assumption holds, to preserve these relative probability relationships between the bus and each car, the overall probability of taking the bus, out of all the available alternatives, will now change. For a comprehensive overview of this and related discrete choice models, including the **mixed** and **nested logit models**, see Train (2009).

Multinomial Probit Model

An econometric estimation method in a discrete choice setting that relaxes the independence of irrelevant alternatives (IIA) assumption in the **multi-**

nomial logit model, accommodating the inclusion of closely related choices in the choice set under study.

Multiperiod Game

A **game** that is repeated over a series of periods that can be either finite or infinite. See also **finitely repeated game** and **infinitely repeated game**.

Multi-Product Firm

A firm that produces a range of **differentiated products**.

Mutual Interdependence

A situation in which a firm recognizes that it must take account of the actions of other firms when it makes its own decisions. This can occur in non-cooperative situations; for example, Ford and Toyota are mutually interdependent and must take this into account when formulating their strategies. It can also call for cooperative behavior. For example, manufacturers of smartphones such as the iPhone are mutually interdependent, and must cooperate with companies that develop applications for the smartphones. Mutual interdependence characterizes **oligopoly** markets.

N

NAICS

See **North American Industry Classification System**.

Nash Bargaining Game

A two-person **game** that models **bargaining** interactions. In a non-cooperative setting, two players must choose the division of a fixed sum, s. Player i chooses a proportion of the sum, p_i, that player i will receive, such that player j receives the share $p_j = (1 - p_i)$, for $i, j = 1, 2$. If $p_i + p_j \leq 1$, then each player receives their respective share of the sum. However, if $p_i + p_j > 1$, then each player receives a share according to a disagreement point, such as $p_1 = p_2 = .5$, or an even split of the sum.

Nash Bargaining Solution

The solution to the **Nash bargaining game** in which player 1 (2) chooses x (y) to maximize $|u_1(x) - u_1(d)| (|u_2(y) - u_2(d)|)$ where $u_1(.)$ $(u_2(.))$ is the **utility function** for player 1 (2) and $u_1(d)$ and $u_2(d)$ are the utilities that the two players receive if they refuse to bargain. See Nash (1950a, 1953).

Nash Equilibrium

An equilibrium for a non-cooperative game in which each player has no incentive to change its strategy given that the other players do not change their strategies. In a Nash equilibrium each player is making a **best response** to the strategies of the other players. Let (S, f) be a non-cooperative game where S denotes the set of possible **strategy** profiles and f is the set of **payoff** profiles. Each player chooses a strategy x_i ($i = 1, \ldots, n$) giving the strategy profile $x = (x_1, \ldots, x_n)$ and the payoff to player i $f_i(x)$. Let x_{-i} be a strategy profile for all players except player i. A strategy profile $x^* \in S$ is a Nash equilibrium if no player can increase their payoff by choosing a different strategy given the other players' strategies: in other words, x^* satisfies: $f_i(x_i^*, x_{-i}^*) \geq f_i(x_i, x_{-i}^*)$ $\forall i$ and $\forall x_i \in S$. See Nash (1950b).

Nash Point

In a two-person **game** the intersection of the two players' **best response functions**.

Natural Monopoly

A market in which it is cheaper for one firm to supply the whole market than for the market to be supplied by two or more firms. In such markets **minimum efficient scale** exceeds the quantity demanded. In the context of **antitrust laws**, authorities will trade off the efficiency gains deriving from monopoly power against the ability of the monopolist to mark price up over marginal cost. One solution is for the government to regulate a natural monopoly in order to preserve the **welfare** benefits from efficient production, while softening the monopoly price effect with **rate-of-return regulation**.

Negative Advertising

Advertising that aims to attract consumers by emphasizing or exaggerating the defects of rivals' goods or services.

Negative Externality

An **externality** that harms someone, also referred to as an **external cost**.

Nested Logit Model

An econometric model in which the decision maker chooses from among several discrete choices, in which closely related choices are grouped into nests. For example, a consumer might face a leisure time allocation decision and choose from among volunteering locally, volunteering nationally, attending the opera, attending the theatre or watching a movie. A logical grouping of related activities into nests would be "volunteer activities", with local and national opportunities included, and "entertainment activities", with opera, theatre and film attendance included. This model provides a method for addressing the problem identified in the **multinomial logit model** when closely related options are present in a choice set. In the nested logit model, the assumption of independence of irrelevant alternatives (IIA) introduced in the multinomial logit model now applies within each nest rather than across the full set of choices.

Net Present Value

The value that is obtained by **discounting** an investment project's future net cash flows to their **present values**. Suppose that an investment project has a projected life of T periods, that the net cash flows in each period t are C_t, and that the firm's per-period **discount rate** is r, then the net present value of the project is

$$NPV = \sum_{t=0}^{T} \frac{C_t}{(1 + r)^t}.$$

Determining the net present value of an investment allows the investor to compare the value of that investment to alternative investment opportunities in present value terms. In the absence of capital constraints, all projects that are not mutually exclusive and that have positive net present values should be adopted. If projects are mutually exclusive, the firm should adopt the project with the greatest net present value.

Net Price

When a firm produces **differentiated products** the net price is the price paid by the buyer adjusted for the costs associated with the product differentiation.

Net Return

The total return from an investment project minus the initial outlay to set up the project.

Network Effect

A characteristic of certain **markets** in which the value to a potential consumer of the good or service being provided in the market is an increasing function of the number of other consumers who currently have bought the good or are using the service. Formally, the number of current adopters is an argument in the **utility** that potential consumer *i* gets from purchasing the good or service. Typical examples of goods and services exhibiting network effects are telephones, fax machines, particular types of computer operating systems, online auction sites such as eBay and social networking websites such as Facebook.

Network Externality

The indirect benefit that an individual consumer obtains when a good or service that exhibits **network effects** is bought or used by other consumers. For example, an individual's e-mail account becomes more valuable when other individuals also use e-mail. Network externalities are particularly important in computer technology, such as with common operating systems and platforms, and on the internet, through social networking websites such as Facebook. An important strategic implication of there being network externalities in a particular market is that they can create a **barrier to entry**, favoring a company that can establish a large installed base of users as has been the case, for example, with eBay.

Network Industry

An industry that is characterized by **network effects**.

Nexus of Contracts

In the literature on the **theory of the firm**, the concept that a firm can be viewed as comprising contractual relationships for hiring **factors of production**, raising financial capital and exchanging final goods and services with consumers. Such a formulation raises the question of how a **vertically integrated** firm can be distinguished from a firm that **outsources** much of its productive activities. Grossman and Hart (1986) suggest that a key distinction between the two derives from how firms address **contractual incompleteness** in assigning **residual rights of control**.

Niche Strategy

A **targeting strategy** in which a firm confines itself to producing a specific product for a specific market segment. This is a strategy that is often adopted by a new entrant in order to limit the willingness of **incumbent firms** to react aggressively to the new entrant.

Node

A decision point in an **extensive form game** at which a player or nature takes an action or at which the game ends. In games characterized by **imperfect information**, such as when a player must take an action following an unobservable prior action by their rival, the player will face uncertainty regarding the particular node the game has reached. The collection of all such possible nodes comprises an information set.

No-Entry Model

A model in which the number of rival firms is determined exogenously.

Nominal Rate of Return

The rate of return on an asset that has not been adjusted for inflation. See also **real rate of return**.

Non-Compete Clause

A clause in an employment **contract** stipulating that if the individual leaves the firm they may not directly compete with the firm for a number of years stipulated in the contract.

Non-Cooperative Game

A **game** in which the players choose their strategies without cooperation or coordination.

Non-Cooperative Oligopoly

An **oligopoly** in which the firms choose their strategies without cooperation or coordination. The assumption of non-cooperation among firms is essential to the concept of a **Nash equilibrium** and of a firm's **best response function**. Each firm determines, for each possible action of its rival(s), what its own **payoff**-maximizing action, or **best response** is; this optimization concept is inherently inward-looking, reflecting the assumption that firms take their opponents' actions as given, rather than trying to take into account the potential gains from cooperative action.

Non-Cooperative Strategic Behavior

Actions that a firm takes to increase its **profit** by improving its competitive position relative to its rivals.

Non-Drastic Innovation

A **process innovation** that gives a firm a **cost advantage** over its rivals that is not sufficient to allow the innovating firm to price at the **monopoly** price without fear of competition. Suppose that a market is supplied by **Bertrand competitors** each with **marginal cost** c_h and that **inverse demand** is linear, given by $P = A - B.Q$. Before the innovation, price would be c_h. Now assume that one firm innovates to obtain marginal cost c_l. If it acts as an unconstrained monopolist, it will set price $P_m = (A + c_l)/2$. The innovation is non-drastic if $P_m > c_h$ or $c_l > 2c_h - A$.

Non-Excludable

A situation in which once a good or service has been created, individuals cannot be excluded from consuming it even if they have not paid to do so. A classic example is national defense. A good that is both non-excludable and non-rival, such that consumption by one person does not preclude consumption by another, is a **public good**.

Nonlinear Pricing

A pricing policy such that the average price charged by the seller is a nonlinear function of the quantity demanded. Typical examples are **two-part tariffs** and the **bundling** of quantity and total expenditure that exhibits **quantity discounting**. With the former, the total charge to the consumer takes the form $T = A + p.Q$ so that the average price is $T/Q = A/Q + p$. With the latter, the firm offers to sell Q units for a total charge $T(Q)$ so that average price is $AP(Q) = T(Q)/Q$ and $dAP(Q)/dQ \neq 1$. Nonlinear pricing is a method for implementing **first-degree price discrimination** or, if consumer types are unobservable, **second-degree price discrimination**. Two-part pricing is common in the pricing of some amusement parks, where consumers pay a fixed fee to enter the park, and then are charged a per-ride fee. This pricing mechanism distinguishes customers by intensity of preference, and thus **willingness to pay**, for riding the amusement vehicles. Bundling is common in the sale of wine, which can be bought by the bottle or by the case, and in the sale of, for example, sports or opera tickets, where consumers can buy individual or season tickets.

Non-Price Competition

Competition using strategic variables other than price, such as **advertising**, **product differentiation** or location, expenditure on **research and development**, or marketing.

Nonprofit Organization

An organization whose primary organizational goal is not **profit** but rather the support of an objective or interest for non-commercial reasons. Typical examples are charities, religious institutions and organizations established to support the arts.

Nonspecific Human Capital

Human capital that is easily transferred from one employer or situation to another. Examples include reading, writing, general knowledge, and general skills in sales and marketing. Investment in nonspecific human capital is not subject to the **hold-up problem** that can result from **relationship-specific investment**.

Non-Tariff Barrier to Trade

A trade barrier that is not tariff-based but rather results from **regulations** or the imposition of **quotas**. Examples include the requirement that importers obtain an import license, or the imposition of product safety and labeling requirements specifically designed to make imported goods more costly or less desirable to domestic consumers.

Nonuniform Pricing

Charging different consumers different prices for the same good or service, or charging an individual consumer a price that varies with the quantity purchased. See **first-, second-** and **third-degree price discrimination** and **nonlinear pricing**.

Non-Zero-Sum Game

A **game** in which the total of players' gains and losses in a particular strategy combination need not sum to zero. For example, in a **coordination game**, such as with the selection of a common standard for technology in computer operating systems, total benefits are maximized when the players agree on one standard; the challenge in this case is in choosing the standard on which all parties will agree. This is in contrast to a **zero-sum game**, in which, for example, firms compete for **market share** in a market of fixed size; in this case, one firm's gain is at the direct expense of another competing firm.

Normal Good

A good for which the **income effect** is positive with the result that quantity demanded increases as income rises. Most goods are normal goods: see also **inferior goods**.

Normal Form Game

Representing a **game** with a finite number of players and a finite number of strategies as a matrix, where each cell in the matrix gives the **payoffs** to the players for the **strategy combinations** associated with that cell. Also known as the **strategic form of game**.

Normal Profit

A situation in which the **revenues** received by a firm just equal the **opportunity costs** of the **inputs** that the firm is using. If firms are earning above-normal profits in an industry, and the industry faces low **barriers to entry**, these profits will provide a signal for new firms to enter the market, since firms currently operating in the industry are outperforming firms in related industries.

Norms

Generally accepted forms of behavior in a society that are enforced by social sanctions.

North American Industry Classification System (NAICS)

A numbering system that is used by business and government in Canada, Mexico and the United States to classify and measure economic activity. It is based on a six-digit code. The first two digits identify the general business sector to which an activity belongs, the third digit the subsector, the fourth digit the industry group and the fifth the specific industry. The sixth digit identifies national industries. See also **Standard Industrial Classification**.

Number Portability

A regulation imposed on telecommunications that allows customers to keep the same telephone number when they change providers.

Numbers Equivalent

In an industry with a **Herfindahl–Hirschman Index (HHI)** of H, the number N of equally sized firms that would have the same HHI. This is given by the equation $N = 10,000/H$, where 10,000 is the HHI if the industry is a **monopoly**. The numbers equivalent is helpful in providing **antitrust authorities** a baseline for identifying the prevalence of **market power** in an industry. Consider the case of an industry comprising 10 firms. If each firm had equal **market share**, the HHI for the industry would be

$$\sum_{i=1}^{10} (10)^2$$

or 1000, corresponding to a numbers equivalent, N, of 10,000/1000, or 10. If, however, the size distribution in the market is in fact skewed, such that a dominant firm covers 50 percent of the market, the next firm covers 10 percent and the remaining firms split the rest of market equally, the HHI for the industry would be $50^2 + 10^2 + 8(5)^2$ or 2800, with a numbers equivalent for this case of 10,000/2800 or 3.57. The extent to which the numbers equivalent (3.57) is below the actual number of firms in the industry (10), provides guidance on the extent to which the leading firm(s) possesses market power.

O

Objective Performance Measure

A means of measuring performance that is accurate, quantifiable and confirmable.

Oligopoly

A market structure in which there is a relatively small number of inter-dependent firms. Because there is a small number of participants in an oligopolistic market, each firm in formulating its strategies must take account of their impact upon other firms and the likely responses of the other firms. As a result, analyzing equilibrium in oligopolistic markets typically requires the use of **game theory**.

Oligopoly Model

An economic model in which the firms are assumed to belong to oligopolistic markets.

Omitted Variables Problem

A statistical problem that arises when estimating an econometric equation without all of the relevant **explanatory variables**. If a missing variable is, in fact, a predictor of the **dependent variable**, and if it moves with at least one of the explanatory variables, a bias will be introduced into the **ordinary least squares (OLS)** coefficient estimates.

One-Fund Portfolio Theorem

For investors who care solely about the mean and variance of the returns on their investment, the proposition that the optimal portfolio consists of some combination of a riskless asset and predetermined propor-tions of other securities, with the proportions defining the one fund that is part of every efficient investment portfolio.

One-Shot Game

A **game** in which the players play the game on the assumption that they will not interact again after the game has been completed. As a result, strategies in one-shot games cannot be made dependent upon the history of play of the game. This type of game is to be contrasted with a **repeated game**.

OPEC

An international **cartel**, the Organization of the Petroleum Exporting Countries is made up of Iraq, Iran, Kuwait, Libya, Angola, Algeria, Nigeria, Qatar, Saudi Arabia, the United Arab Emirates, Ecuador and Venezuela, and accounts for approximately two-thirds of world oil reserves. Its principal aim is to try to control international oil markets by agreeing production targets and quotas among the members of the cartel. The effectiveness of the cartel has varied over time, on occasions being very effective in controlling oil prices and at other times being much less able to do so as a result of the temptation that each member of the cartel has to cheat on the agreed quotas.

Open Access

A situation in which **property rights** of particular resources are either not defined or not enforced, with the result that there is no control over the number of users of the resources or the extent to which the resources can be exploited, almost always resulting in overexploitation. See also **tragedy of the commons**.

Open Economy

An economy that imposes no restrictions, such as **tariffs** or **quotas**, on imports and exports, investment and cross-border flows of **factors of production**.

Operating Curves

Short-run total cost curves that are used to make short-term production and pricing decisions.

Opportunism

See **moral hazard**.

Opportunistic Behavior

The decision by a party to a **contract** to exploit **contractual incompleteness** by taking actions that better the position of the opportunistic party at the expense of the other parties to the contract, but in such a manner that the opportunistic party cannot be shown to have breached the contract and so cannot be subject to legal remedies. **Incentive contracts** can mitigate the costs of **opportunistic behavior** in **principal–agent** relationships by at least partially aligning the interests of principal and agent. In business-to-business transactions, opportunistic behavior is particularly troublesome when the contract requires the creation of **relationship-specific assets**.

Opportunity Cost

The value of the resources used to produce a good or service in terms of the next-best alternative use of the resources. For a resource **input** such as labor, opportunity cost is the income that would be received from the next-best employment opportunity.

Option

A financial **contract** that gives the holder a right that need not be exercised unless the holder considers it to be beneficial to do so.

Option Value

The expected increase in **net present value** that arises when a firm postpones making a **strategic commitment** in order to resolve some of the uncertainty surrounding the commitment. Suppose, for example, that a strategic commitment has a probability p of being successful, generating a net return R, and $1 - p$ of being unsuccessful, losing L. The expected value of the strategic commitment is $p.R - (1 - p)L$. Suppose that by delaying the commitment by one period the uncertainty regarding the commitment can be resolved and, if it is going to be unsuccessful, the firm can adopt an alternative project with a normal return of zero. The expected value of the commitment with one period's delay is then $D.p.R$ where D is the firm's **discount factor**. The option value of delay is then $D.p.R - p.R + (1 - p)L = (1 - p)L - (1 - D)p.R$. The option value is likely to be higher when the firm's **learn-to-burn ratio** is higher.

Ordered Probit Model

An econometric model that extends the **probit model**, in which the **dependent variable**, y, represents three or more categories, to which a natural ranking applies. For example, a firm might survey a sample of consumers to determine their responses to a new product, with choices including strongly negative, negative, neutral, positive and strongly positive. Each classification is assigned an integer value, which increases with ranking, where the underlying, unobserved variable measures product quality. The **logit model** can be similarly extended.

Ordinary Least Squares (OLS)

An estimation method for the **classical linear regression model** that provides coefficient estimates based on the criterion of minimizing the sum of the squared residuals from a given data sample. For each observation, the residual measures the difference between the observed value of the **dependent variable**, and the predicted value, based on the estimated coefficients and the values of the observation-specific **explanatory variables**.

Organizational Architecture

The structure of an organization defining the assignment of **decision rights** within the organization, the methods of rewarding individuals and the structure of systems to **monitor** and evaluate the performance of individuals and business units.

Organizational Complexity

A condition in which an organization consists of multiple autonomous but interrelated and interdependent sub-organizations. Complexity comes from the interrelationships between individuals in the organization; imperfect information flow between the individuals and sub-organizations; and complex interrelationships between the organization and its external environment.

Output

The number of units of a particular product that a firm produces in a specified period of time. This is the strategic variable that **Cournot competitors** are assumed to choose.

Output Agreement

An agreement by members of a **cartel** determining the total **output** that will be brought to market and the individual cartel members' output shares.

Outsourcing

A firm's decision to reassign the performance of non-core operations from an internal division to an external supplier, usually on the basis of a medium- or long-term **contract** between the firm and the supplier. The objective of outsourcing is usually to lower the costs of the outsourcing firm or to allow the firm to concentrate on its **core competencies**.

Overinvestment

If actions are **strategic complements** and a **strategic commitment** makes a firm **soft**, or if actions are **strategic substitutes** and a strategic commitment makes a firm **tough**, the firm should overinvest in such a commitment if by doing so it can constrain the actions of its rivals. See Tirole (1988, pp. 324–325).

Overlapping Generations

A set of economic models in which each generation of consumers is assumed to be finitely lived but to live simultaneously with at least one other generation of consumers.

Overserve

To offer consumers in a target consumer group costly **product attributes** that consumers in the group do not particularly value.

Overt Collusion

Collusive behavior with no attempt to hide the **collusion**. Such collusion is typically illegal unless, as in the case of *OPEC*, it involves nation states.

Ownership

When applied to assets, the possession of **residual rights of control** over the asset, as a result of which the owner has the right to make decisions regarding the use of the asset. When applied to publicly traded firms, ownership resides with the **shareholders** but this will not necessarily give them control over the operations of the firm.

Ownership Advantage

An advantage to a firm deriving from **residual rights of control** over an asset, potentially leading to **internalization**.

Own-Price Elasticity of Demand

See **price elasticity of demand**.

P

Panel Data

Data characterized by a set of repeat observations, on the same individuals, over time, where the number of individuals under study is large and the number of time periods relatively small. Such data are particularly valuable to empirical studies of dynamic competition, within a given industry, using individual firm-level data. **Pooled ordinary least squares (OLS) estimation** is appropriate when such data involve a small number of individuals and a relatively large number of time periods.

Parallel Import

Importing from country B to country A a product originally produced in country A and exported to country B. This usually occurs because the price charged for the product in country B is significantly less than the price in country A.

Parameter

In econometrics, a value that reflects a proposed underlying relationship between variables, such as the β_i coefficients in the **classical linear regression model**. Parameters are estimated using a variety of approaches, including **ordinary least squares (OLS), logit** and **probit models**.

Pareto-Dominated Allocation

An allocation of resources from which it is possible to find a reallocation of resources that increases the **welfare** of at least one person without reducing the welfare of anyone else.

Pareto Efficient

A resource allocation is Pareto efficient if there exists no other allocation of the available resources that makes at least one individual better off without making some other individual(s) worse off. See also **Pareto optimality**.

Pareto Optimality

An allocation of resources from which it is impossible to increase the welfare of one person without reducing the welfare of another person. The market outcome under **perfect competition** is Pareto optimal. If a competitive market becomes monopolized, and cost and demand conditions remain the same, the new market outcome under monopoly will not be Pareto optimal: **consumer surplus** will decline; a portion of this loss will be redistributed to **producer surplus**.

Partial Equilibrium Analysis

Economic analysis that focuses on an individual market or small groups of markets. For example, in the model determining the equilibrium price and quantity for a given **demand** and **supply curve**, all other factors influencing this market are held constant. Partial equilibrium analysis implicitly assumes that supply or demand changes in the market under study have limited impact on markets across the economy. This is in contrast to the **general equilibrium model**, which accounts for economy-wide feedback effects. See also **ceteris paribus**.

Participation Constraint

A constraint on an **incentive contract** that the party being offered the contract must expect to do at least as well from the present contract as from the next-best alternative. If the constraint is not satisfied, the contract will not be accepted. The participation constraint and **incentive compatibility constraint** are key elements of the **principal–agent model**.

Patent

An exclusive set of rights granted by a government agency – typically a Patent Office – to a patentee for a defined and finite period of time in return for the patentee disclosing the invention as part of the patent application process. Patent laws vary but typically involve that the product, service or process being patented be novel, useful and non-obvious.

Patent Breadth

A measure of the extent to which a new innovation must differ from an existing product or process in order for the new one to avoid infringement on an existing **patent** or to be itself patentable.

Patent Duration

The period of time for which a **patent** is granted. In the United States and the United Kingdom this is now 20 years from the date of filing the patent application.

Patent License

Permission granted by a **patent** holder to another party (the licensor), granting the licensor the right to exploit the patent under terms defined in the license agreement.

Patent Race

Competition between firms to be the first to develop new technologies or new goods to the point at which a **patent** application can be filed. These are examples of "winner-take-all" competition. Such competition can involve wasteful duplicated **research and development** efforts across firms, and lead to inadequate prior experimentation, as firms race to be the first to file for the patent.

Patent System

A system of granting and enforcing rights to inventions. See **patents**.

Payoff

The reward received by a player of a **game** at the end of the game.

Payoff Matrix

A matrix that details the **payoffs** to each player of a **game** from each **strategy combination** of the game. The payoff matrix is defined only if the number of strategies available to each player is finite.

Peak-Load Pricing

A form of **price discrimination** in which the price being charged varies with the demand for the good or with the time of day in which the good is provided. The rationale for this type of pricing is that it reduces demand during peak periods, leading to a related reduction in the capacity that the provider has to carry in order to be able to meet peak demand. Examples include pricing by electric utilities during peak usage hours, such as during early-evening hours, to avoid bringing on line significantly more expensive power sources.

Penetration Pricing

A strategy of setting the price for a new product deliberately low in order to gain rapid market penetration for the product. This strategy can be justified if the firm believes that there are strong learning effects, with the result that future production costs are expected to fall, increasing profit margins.

Perceived Benefit

The gross benefit consumers receive from a product minus the user cost of the product and minus any purchasing or **transaction costs** of acquiring the product, excluding the actual purchase price. A necessary, but not sufficient condition for a consumer to be willing to purchase a product is that its perceived benefit is greater than its price.

Perfect Capital Market

A capital market in which all individuals can borrow and lend on the same terms, with these terms being unaffected by the amount being borrowed or lent. Such a market is a theoretical ideal and underpins the **Fisher separation theorem** and the **Modigliani–Miller theorems**.

Perfect Competition

A market structure in which all firms offer **homogeneous products**, in which all agents – firms and consumers – are **price takers** with no strategic power and in which all agents have perfect information. There is **free entry** and **exit** to perfectly competitive markets. Under perfect competition, **total surplus** is maximized and the market achieves **allocative efficiency**.

Perfect Nash Equilibrium

A **Nash equilibrium** in which any strategies involving threats are credible. For this to be the case, a firm promising punishment in the event of specified behavior by a rival will find it in its best interests to implement the threat even if the rival takes the specified behavior.

Perfect Price Discrimination

See **first-degree price discrimination**.

Perfectly Contestable Market

A market in which an incumbent monopolist cannot raise price above marginal cost because of the threat of **hit-and-run** entry. The contestability of a market is an important consideration in **antitrust law** enforcement in assessing the potential **market power** of the monopolist.

Performance Contract

A compensation contract in which the amount to be paid is determined by an agreed measure of performance.

Performance Measure

Information on which an **incentive contract** is based, such as sales per period or, in chief executive officer (CEO) compensation, share price.

Performance Standard

A benchmark that is established measuring the output that a hardworking individual can be expected to achieve.

Perpetuity

A constant cash flow that is received each period forever. If the perpetuity is C and the **discount rate** is r then the **present value** of the perpetuity is C/r.

Per Se Rule

A ruling that a particular set of actions violates **antitrust law** no matter what the proposed defense of these actions might be. For example, a group of firms found to have collusively engaged in price-fixing can be found in per se violation of the **Sherman Act**.

Personalized Pricing

Prices that lead to **first-degree price discrimination** in which the seller is able to extract the full **willingness to pay** of each consumer, converting all **consumer surplus** into **revenues** to the firm.

Persuasive Advertising

Advertising that is intended to influence consumer perceptions of the product or service being advertised. This type of advertising aims to differentiate the product or service being advertised from its rivals, increasing consumer loyalty and softening **price competition**.

Pesky Little Brother Game

A technology game in which a large, dominant firm prefers incompatibility with a smaller rival, whereas the smaller rival prefers compatibility. The **payoff matrix** for this game looks as follows, where in each cell, the **payoff** to the row player is listed first, and the payoff to the column player is listed second:

		Small rival	
		Technology 1	Technology 2
Large incumbent	Technology 1	12, 4	16, 2
	Technology 2	15, 2	10, 5

There is no **Nash equilibrium** in **pure strategies** to this game if it is played simultaneously.

Peter Principle

The – not necessarily serious – principle that individuals are promoted to their levels of incompetence.

Phantom Freight

A shipping cost charged to a buyer that is not the same as the true delivery cost. This type of charge was characteristic of basing-point pricing where the seller added a freight cost from a **basing point** to the seller's location no matter where the product actually originated. See **basing-point pricing.**

Physical Capital

A tangible **capital asset**, such as machinery and buildings. Physical capital tends to depreciate with time and use.

Piece-Rate Contract

An **incentive contract** in which an employee is paid for each unit of a product that the employee produces in a specified period of time. Such a contract can create the incentive to produce higher quantities, potentially at the expense of product **quality**.

Pirating

The illegal copying of copyrighted material such as articles, books, movies and music. As the recording and copying capabilities of computers, smartphones and other personal electronic media devices improve, efforts to protect against piracy become increasingly costly.

Planned Obsolescence

Deliberately making a **durable good** short-lived as a way to limit the firm's ability or temptation to reduce the price of the good in the future. Regular software upgrades and regular issuing of new editions of textbooks are examples of such a strategy.

Planning Curve

A long-run average cost function that plays a key role in longer-run decisions relating to plant size and equipment acquisition. Since all inputs, including capital, are variable in the **long run**, the **long-run average cost** curve provides information on the optimal level of capital for a given set of market demand conditions.

Point Elasticity

See **elasticity**.

Poison Pill

A defense against **hostile takeover** that gives a **stockholder** the right to acquire shares in the firm being taken over, or some other financial claim on the firm, at a greatly reduced price should the hostile takeover be successful. Such a defense typically greatly reduces the value of the firm in the event of a hostile takeover bid being made.

Pooled Ordinary Least Squares (OLS) Estimation

An econometric model appropriate for data characterized by a set of repeat observations, on the same individuals, over time, where the number of individuals under study is small and the number of time periods is relatively large. This estimation method assumes that the regression coefficients are the same for each individual under study, then combines the data and uses **ordinary least squares** to estimate the coefficients. See **classical linear regression model** for an introduction to regression coefficients; see also **panel data**.

Pooling Equilibrium

An equilibrium in a **dynamic game** with **asymmetric information** in which all players choose the same strategies. An example would be where an incumbent monopolist who is high-cost sets the same price as an incumbent monopolist who is low-cost in the first period of an **entry** game, as a result of which the **potential entrant** learns nothing about the true type of the incumbent from the period 1 price. See, by contrast, **separating equilibrium**.

Pooled Interdependence

When two or more activities in a firm are not directly dependent upon each other but are associated through their independent contributions to the success of the firm.

Post-Contractual Opportunism

Opportunistic behavior that occurs after a **contract** has been signed. Two important examples are **moral hazard** and **hold-up**. In the case of moral hazard, an agent can take advantage of, for example, the unobservability of a **hidden action**, such as choosing to expend a low level of effort on a work activity. In the case of hold-up, a contracting party can take advantage of another's **relationship-specific investment**.

Posting of a Bond

Setting aside a sum of money or postponing a payment to guarantee performance under a **contract**.

Potential Entrant

A firm that poses a sufficiently credible threat of market **entry** as to impose constraints on the pricing and output choices of the **incumbent firms**. In

contestable markets, with low **barriers to entry**, the threat of entry significantly constrains the incumbent's behavior; the entry threat is less effective in cases of high **barriers to entry** or when the incumbent firm engages in **pre-emptive** tactics.

Pre-Contractual Opportunism

Opportunistic behavior by a party to a **contract** that is taken before the contract is signed and is intended to increase the **payoff** that the party receives from the contract. **Adverse selection** is one form of pre-contractual opportunism in which a party to a contract can exploit **hidden information**.

Predatory Conduct

Actions by a firm that are designed specifically to deter rivals from entering the firm's market or to drive existing firms from the market. Such actions, if proved to be predatory, typically violate **antitrust laws**.

Predatory Dumping

A strategy by a firm to set a **predatory price** in a foreign market in order to undercut the domestic firms in that market, taking away **market share** from those firms.

Predatory Pricing

A specific form of predatory conduct in which a firm sets its price low in the deliberate attempt to drive rival firms out of the market. In **antitrust law** enforcement it is typically difficult to prove that a firm has engaged in predatory pricing. The prosecution must establish that: the firm had **monopoly** power in the market; the firm charged a price below average variable cost (a price at which firms would choose to shut down in the short run); and that the firm had a reasonable expectation of recouping the losses experienced during the predatory period. Even if the first two conditions are demonstrated, it is difficult to prove that the firm could reasonably expect to sustain sufficiently high prices following the rival's exit, particularly in **contestable markets** with low **barriers to entry**. See also **Areeda–Turner test**.

Pre-emption

A strategy taken by an early first mover into a market to prevent later **entry** to the market. One such strategy is to crowd the product space sufficiently that a later entrant can find no profitable niche in the market.

Present Value

The value today of a flow of future revenues and/or costs. If the net cash flow in period t is C_t and the **discount rate** is r then the present value of C_t is $PV(C_t) = C_t/(1 + r)^t$.

Price Ceiling

An upper limit of price: see **price control**.

Price Competition

A non-cooperative **game** in which the strategy chosen by each rival firm is the price(s) it will charge for its product(s). This is often referred to as a **Bertrand game**. In the case of homogeneous goods and constant **marginal costs**, the **Bertrand equilibrium** is the competitive outcome of marginal-cost pricing, even when the number of firms in the market is small. This finding is in contrast to the expectation that, in an **oligopoly**, firms will use their **market power** to price above marginal cost. See also **Bertrand paradox**.

Price Control

A regulatory limit on the maximum price that firms can set for particular goods or services or on the minimum price that they can offer for specified inputs. Examples are **rent** control on rented accommodation and **minimum wages** for labor. When price controls are binding, they prevent the market from achieving equilibrium, potentially leading to **excess demand** and shortages in the case of **price ceilings**, and to **excess supply** and surpluses in the case of **price floors**.

Price–Cost Margin

The difference between price and marginal cost, expressed as a fraction of the price, defined by the equation $(P - MC)/P$. This is also known as the **Lerner Index** of **market power**. This measure is used in **antitrust law** enforcement to assess the potential harm from a monopolist's market power to **consumer surplus**.

Price Discount

An agreement, usually secret, to offer a product or service at a price lower than advertised or lower than agreed by colluding firms.

Price Discrimination

A pricing practice in which different varieties of a product are sold to different buyers at different **net prices**, where the net price is equal to the buyer's purchase price less the cost of **product differentiation**. Suppose that variety i costs C_i to make and is sold to a buyer at price P_i, while variety j costs C_j to make and is sold to a different buyer at price P_j. There is price discrimination between these buyers if $P_i - P_j \neq C_i - C_j$. On this definition, **free on board (fob) pricing** is non-discriminatory since the prices at different locations reflect the different transport costs to those locations. By contrast, **uniform delivered pricing** is discriminatory since there is no difference in delivered prices across locations despite the different transport costs to those locations. See additionally **first-**, **second-** and **third-degree price discrimination**.

Price Elasticity of Demand

See **elasticity of demand**.

Price Elasticity of Supply

See **elasticity of supply**.

Price-Fixing Agreement

A collusive agreement in which the members of the **collusion** agree on the prices that they will each set in the relevant market. Price-fixing agreements are difficult to achieve in practice; since collusion is illegal, members cannot enforce the agreements in courts, and each member has a strong incentive to cheat on the agreement by undercutting price and increasing quantity sold. See also **cartel instability**.

Price Floor

A lower limit on price: see **price control**.

Price Leadership

A market environment in which one firm controls price changes and price setting by setting its own price in the (correct) anticipation that the remaining firms in the market will follow suit. The firm initiating price changes is referred to as the price leader and the remaining firms are referred to as price followers. For the price leader to be able to exercise this type of leadership at least three conditions must be satisfied. First, the price leader is a dominant firm in the market – one with a relatively large market share. Second, the price leader is at a competitive advantage with respect to the remaining firms in the market. Third, the price followers accept the price leader's price because they feel that it is in their best interests to do so.

Price Rigidity

A situation in which prices do not change in response to fluctuations in costs or in demand. This may happen when the prices are **administered prices** or when there are **menu costs** associated with changing prices In markets characterized by price rigidity it is unlikely that prices are clearing these markets, leading to a possible loss of **efficiency**.

Price Squeeze

A strategy by a **vertically integrated** firm to sell its upstream products to outside firms but only at exorbitant prices.

Price Support

A regulatory policy in which the regulator guarantees to buy if price falls to some specified limit. This policy is often used in agricultural markets as a means to maintain farm incomes. They can have the unintended effect of creating large stockpiles of agricultural products.

Price Taker

A firm or consumer in a perfectly or imperfectly competitive market who believes that their actions will have no impact on the market price. In a perfectly competitive market, firms take the market **equilibrium price** as given, and thus operate under the assumption that their **marginal revenue** is equivalent to the market price. Since profit-maximizing firms choose the quantity at which marginal revenue equals **marginal cost**, it follows that price equals marginal cost under perfect competition.

Price War

A situation in which there is intense **price competition**, with competing firms continually trying to undercut each other. These types of wars can break out when a **cartel** agreement fails and can be thought of as progression towards the **Bertrand equilibrium**. They are good for consumers in the short term but can be harmful in the long term if they lead to the elimination of large numbers of firms in the market.

Principal

In an agency relationship the individual or group whose interests are intended to be served by the relationship. See **principal–agent problem**.

Principal–Agent Model

See **principal–agent problem**.

Principal–Agent Problem

A situation in which a **principal** hires an **agent** to perform an action for the principal but in which the principal is unable to confirm that the agent has fulfilled the terms of their agreement. Such a problem arises when there is **asymmetric information** between the principal and the agent and when the incentives of the principal and the agent are not fully aligned. To reduce the impact of the problem, the principal needs to find some mechanism that will motivate the agent to work on the principal's behalf. The model typically assumes that the principal is **risk neutral** and that the agent is **risk averse**. The challenge in devising the optimal **contract** is to provide sufficient incentives for the agent to work hard, by, for example, basing compensation on a share of the **profits**, while accounting for the agent's risk aversion and preference to avoid uncertainty in compensation. The optimal contract must be **incentive compatible** and must satisfy the **participation constraint**, such that the agent will choose to work for the principal as opposed to at his next-best alternative employment opportunity.

Principle of Minimum Differentiation

See **minimum differentiation**.

Prisoners' Dilemma Game

A **duopoly** game in which the two players mutually benefit from cooperation but in which the **dominant strategy** for each player is defection. The **Nash equilibrium** to this game is **Pareto dominated** by another strategy combination. A **payoff matrix** typical of a prisoners' dilemma game looks as follows, where in each cell, the **payoff** to the row player is listed first, and the payoff to the column player is listed second:

		Player 2	
		Cooperate	Defect
Player 1	Cooperate	10, 10	4, 12
	Defect	12, 4	6, 6

This type of game arises in many non-prisoner-type games. For example, a collusive agreement between two firms typically has this form and so is unstable in the absence of enforcement or **monitoring** mechanisms. Alternatively, if the game is repeated an indefinite number of times, cooperation can be sustained by a **trigger strategy**.

Private Good

A good that can be consumed by one consumer at the exclusion of all other consumers and so is **rivalrous** in consumption.

Private Information

Information that is held by an individual or organization but that others know at best imperfectly. This may relate to product design or performance, **quality**, or the true characteristics of the individual such as ability. Such **asymmetric information** can give rise to problems of **adverse selection**.

Privatization

The decision by a government to sell publicly owned companies. Public utilities such as gas, electricity, water and telecommunications have been privatized in many countries.

Probit Model

A **latent variable model** in which the **dependent variable**, y, takes on the value zero or one, depending on the value of an underlying latent variable, y^*. The probit estimation assumes that the probability that y equals one, conditional on the values of the **independent variables**, follows the standard normal distribution. This specification is useful when the researcher observes an outcome variable, such as whether or not a firm serves a particular market, when the choice is determined by an unobserved variable, such as the firm's expected profits from doing so. The **logit model** assumes a logistic distribution instead.

Process Innovation

The discovery of new, typically cheaper methods for producing existing goods or services.

Produce to Order

A system in which a firm waits for an order before producing the good or service.

Produce to Stock

A system in which firms produce without necessarily having received an order, hold the produced goods in **inventory**, and sell finished goods from inventory.

Producer Surplus

For the individual firm, the difference between the total amount received in payment for a given quantity of a good and the total marginal cost of producing that quantity. Suppose that the firm's supply function is given by $q = 0$ for $0 \leq P < P^{min}$ and $Q = S(P)$ for $P \geq P^{min}$. Suppose further that the good is offered at a unit price of P. Producer surplus at price P is

$$PS(P) = \int_{P^{min}}^{P} S(p)\,dp.$$

It follows that producer surplus increases as the price is increased. For a market, the aggregate producer surplus for all firms active in the market.

Product Attributes

The specific characteristics of a product. See also **characteristics space** and **discrete choice model of demand**.

Product Differentiation

Producing several varieties of a good, where each product variant is aimed for a specific target market. The product variants can be differentiated by **quality (vertical product differentiation)** or by the individual product characteristics such as shape, color, location, style and timing (**horizontal product differentiation**). A key distinction between **monopolistically com-**

petitive and **perfectly competitive** markets is that products are differentiated in the former, and homogeneous in the latter.

Product Innovation

Innovation that leads to the creation of new goods or services.

Product Life Cycle

The various stages through which a product passes over its life. The life cycle is typically characterized as having four stages: introduction, growth, maturity and decline. Demand usually increases rapidly through the growth phase, levels off with maturity and drops in the decline stage. See **life cycle – product**.

Product Performance Characteristics

The characteristics that a product offers consumers and that determine consumer attitudes towards the product and towards potential substitutes. One way of defining **substitute goods** is in terms of their product performance characteristics.

Product Proliferation

A **strategy** by an **incumbent firm** to try to cover the product market space, thereby preventing potential competitors from exploiting profitable market niches in order to be able to enter the market. See also **pre-emption**.

Product-Specific Economies of Scale

A measure of how **total costs** of a **multi-product firm** change as the output of only one product is varied. It is defined for product i as the **average incremental cost** of product i divided by the **marginal cost** of product i: $PS_i = AIC_i/MC_i$.

Product Standardization

The process of adopting mutually agreed and uniform characteristics for particular goods and services. In high-technology industries, agreeing on the technical standards that are to be adopted. The advantage of such standardization for consumers is that it strengthens competition among product or service providers and, when there are potentially competing standards, avoids the risk of adopting the "wrong" standard as, for example, happened in the video recorder industry with the competition between VHS and Betamax. For producers, a disadvantage is tougher competition. An advantage is that standardization facilitates new product adoption by consumers. A further advantage for both consumers and producers is that standardization reduces risk for firms that offer complementary products, for example with DVD players, the risk of firms that produce DVDs.

Product Tying

A strategy in which a seller forces a buyer of one of the seller's goods to purchase another of the seller's goods. For example, IBM required users of its computer punch-card machines to purchase only IBM-produced cards. More recently, manufacturers of computer printers design their printers to take only specific types of ink cartridges. See also **tie-in sales**.

Product Variety

A measure of the number of different product variants that are supplied to a particular market. See **product differentiation**.

Production Function

A function that specifies the efficient relationship between a firm's **inputs** and its **outputs**. This is typically written as $q = f(\mathbf{x})$, where q is output and $\mathbf{x}$ is a vector of factor inputs. The **constant elasticity of substitution (CES)** and **Cobb–Douglas production functions** are commonly used in the theoretical analysis of firms' **profit-maximizing** behavior.

Production Possibility Frontier

The feasible combinations of the numbers of brands and the quantities of each brand that a society can produce given the society's available **inputs** and state of technical knowledge.

Profit

The difference between a firm's **total revenue** and the firm's **total cost**. Historical or accounting profit measures the difference between total revenues and monetary costs. **Economic profit**, a standard measure in economic models, includes in total cost all **opportunity costs** (including monetary costs). See also **normal profit** and **supernormal profit**.

Profit Center

A business unit whose performance assessment is based upon the reported **profits** of the unit. A profit center is usually given **decision rights** over input and output mix and selling prices.

Profit Function

Suppose that the firm's **production function** is $y = f(\mathbf{x})$ where $\mathbf{x}$ is the vector of factor inputs, and that the vector of input prices is $\mathbf{w}$. Then the profit function is the maximum-value function that solves the programming problem

$$\pi(p, \mathbf{w}) = \max_{p, \mathbf{w} \geq 0} py - \mathbf{w} \cdot \mathbf{x}$$

subject to $f(\mathbf{x}) \geq y$. Applying the **envelope theorem** to the profit function generates the proposition that the supply curve (that is, the production function evaluated at the solution for the **factor demand functions**) is upward-sloping in output price, p. See also **Hotelling's Lemma**.

Profit Maximization

The choices that a firm makes that lead to the firm making the greatest possible **profit**. Denote the **total revenue** function for a multi-product firm as $TR(q_1, q_2, \ldots, q_i \ldots, q_n)$ and its **total cost** function as $TC(q_1, q_2, \ldots,$

$q_i \ldots, q_n$). Profit maximization is the output combination that maximizes $TR(..) - TC(..)$. This requires

$$\frac{\partial TR(..)}{\partial q_i} = \frac{\partial TC(..)}{\partial q_i}$$

for $i = 1, \ldots, n$. This can be written $MR_i = MC_i$: the **marginal revenue** from product i should equal the **marginal cost** of product i. For a single product firm total revenue can be written $TR = Q.P(Q)$. Marginal revenue is then $MR = P(Q) + Q.dP(Q)/dQ$, which can be rewritten

$$MR = P(Q)[1 + \frac{Q}{P(Q)} \cdot \frac{dP(Q)}{dQ}] = P(Q)[1 + 1/\eta_{Q:P}].$$

Profit maximization requires that $P(Q)[1 + 1/\eta_{Q:P}] = MC(Q)$, which can be rewritten

$$P(Q) = \frac{\eta_{Q:P}}{1 + \eta_{Q:P}} MC(Q),$$

giving a form of **mark-up pricing**.

Profit Sharing

An **incentive contract** in which some part of the employee's compensation is tied to the profit that the firm makes. See **principal–agent problem**.

Promotion Tournament

A situation in which promotion within an organization is determined by competition between the current employees of the organization.

Property Rights

Ownership or exclusive rights to use an asset such as a good or service. Others must pay you if they wish to use the asset. An individual has property rights in their time, the car that they own or the house that they own. The individual does not have property rights in a public highway, even if the highway is paid for and maintained by tax revenues.

Proprietary Information

Private and sensitive information that a firm holds regarding issues such as its procurement policies, product design and performance. The firm will typically be reluctant to share this information with potential suppliers.

Proximity–Concentration Hypothesis

The hypothesis that a firm serving multiple geographically distinct markets has to balance the advantage/cost of production concentration against the advantage/cost of placing production facilities in proximity to some of the target markets. An advantage of production concentration is that this allows the firm to benefit from **economies of scale** and **economies of scope**. A disadvantage is that production concentration increases the transport, distribution and other costs of supplying distant markets: for example tariff and non-tariff barriers to trade across national boundaries. An advantage of proximity to the target markets is that it reduces the transport, distribution and other costs of supplying the distant markets, but at the cost of dispersing production, sacrificing economies of scale and scope. This hypothesis is particularly important in the analysis of **foreign direct investment**.

Public Corporation

A corporation whose shares are bought and sold in a legally organized exchange, such as the London or New York Stock Exchanges, and so whose shares can be held by any investor.

Public Enterprise

See **state-owned enterprise**.

Public Good

A good that is non-rival, in that consumption by one individual does not reduce the amount of the good available for consumption by others, and **non-excludable**, in that once the good is created individuals cannot be excluded from consuming it. National defense, radio broadcasts and information are examples of public goods. Hospital services and education services are not, even if they are publicly provided.

Puppy Dog Strategy

Suppose that actions are **strategic complements** and that a proposed investment makes a firm a tougher competitor. Then the firm should **underinvest** so as not to induce an aggressive response from its rival(s). See Fudenberg and Tirole (1984), **fat-cat effect**, **lean-and-hungry look** and **top dog strategy**.

Pure Bundling

The practice of selling two or more goods as a package with fixed amounts of each good in the package, but not offering to sell the goods individually.

Pure Strategy

In **game theory**, a strategy that is played with probability unity. A pure strategy can be seen as a special case of a **mixed strategy**.

Pure Strategy Nash Equilibrium

A Nash equilibrium in which all players are playing **pure strategies**. This is a special case of a **mixed-strategy Nash equilibrium**.

Put Option

A financial **contract** that guarantees the option to sell a particular asset at a specified price on a certain date if it is European, or on or before a certain date if it is American.

Q

Quadratic Cost Model

A spatial model in which transport costs are assumed to be quadratic in distance. In the duopoly case of the **Hotelling spatial model** introducing the assumption of quadratic transport costs guarantees the existence of a **subgame perfect Nash equilibrium** to the location–price game. In a **Hotelling line market** quadratic transport costs result in duopolists **maximally differentiating** – locating at opposite ends of the line market.

Quality

A measure of the superiority or usefulness of a good or service. It indicates the extent to which the inherent characteristics of a good or service meet the user's requirements. When the quality of a good is observable prior to purchase we are dealing with **search goods**. The primary issue with such goods is what quality to offer at what price. By contrast, if quality is unobservable prior to purchase we are dealing with **experience** or **credence goods**. In these cases the main problems are: How do consumers learn the true quality of the goods on offer? What incentives do firms have to supply truly high-quality goods?

Quality Competition

A non-cooperative **game** in which the strategy chosen by each rival firm is the **quality** of its product. This is often referred to as a **vertical product differentiation** game.

Quality Discrimination

Selling different qualities of a product to different buyers at different **net prices**, where the net price is the price paid by the buyer adjusted for the cost of the change in quality.

Quality Premium

The additional margin that a high-quality product must command in order for a monopolist to prefer to offer a high-quality product rather than "cheat" and offer a low-quality product. Suppose that a monopolist can offer a product of low quality $s = 0$ or high quality $s = 1$. The low quality costs c_0 to produce and the high quality c_1 such that $c_1 > c_0$. Quality is observable to consumers only after purchase and consumers base their beliefs regarding the reputation of the monopolist in period t on the basis of the observed quality in period $t - 1$. If consumers believe that the quality is low in period t they will not purchase in this or any future period. If they believe that the quality is high they will purchase (this implies a lower limit on the consumer **reservation prices**) so long as quality stays high. The market is of infinite duration.

If the monopolist begins with a high-quality good, priced at p_1, and continues to provide such a good his expected profit is:

$$\pi_1 = (p_1 - c_1)(1 + d + d^2 + \ldots) = \frac{p_1 - c_1}{1 - d} = \left(\frac{1 + r}{r}\right)(p_1 - c_1)$$

where d is the monopolist's **discount factor** and r is the **discount rate**. If instead the monopolist "cheats" and offers a low-quality good in the first period at price p_1 his expected profit is $p_1 - c_0$. For the monopolist to behave honestly and offer the high-quality good requires that: $p_1 - c_1 \geq r(c_1 - c_0)$. The right-hand side is the quality premium in this simple model. See Tirole (1988, p. 122).

Quantity Competition

A non-cooperative **game** in which the strategy chosen by each rival firm is the quantity it will supply of each of its products. This is often referred to as a **Cournot game**. Typically, with quantity competition, the quantities chosen by the competing firms are **strategic substitutes**.

Quantity Discount

Suppose that a monopolist serves n different types of consumer but does not know the type of each consumer and so adopts **second-degree price discrimination**, offering n "bundles" (q_i, T_i) $(i = 1, \ldots, n)$, where q_i is the quantity intended for purchase by a consumer of type i at a total charge of

T_i. Order the bundles such that $q_1 < q_2 < \ldots < q_n$. These bundles exhibit quantity discounting if $q_1/T_1 < q_2/T_2 < \ldots < q_n/T_n$.

Quantity Fixing

A constraint, usually imposed by a manufacturer on a retailer, specifying the amount to be bought by the retailer. This generally takes one of two forms: **quantity forcing** or **quantity rationing**.

Quantity Forcing

A **quantity fixing** agreement setting a minimum quantity that the retailer must purchase from the manufacturer. If the retailer is not allowed to dispose of the product rather than sell it, quantity forcing is equivalent to the manufacturer establishing a **price ceiling**.

Quantity Rationing

A **quantity fixing** agreement setting a maximum quantity that the retailer will be supplied by the manufacturer. If the retailer is not allowed to dispose of the product rather than sell it, quantity rationing is equivalent to the manufacturer establishing a **price floor** or to **resale price maintenance (RPM)**.

Quasi-Linear Utility Function

A **utility function** that is linear in at least one of its arguments and additive in the utilities derived from the remaining goods. Such a function is of the form

$$U(q_0, q_1, \ldots, q_n) = q_0 + \sum_{i=1}^{n} V_i(q_i).$$

Good 0 is the numeraire and the functions V_i are increasing and concave. Maximizing $U(q_0, q_1, \ldots, q_n)$ subject to the **budget constraint**

$$q_0 + \sum_{i=1}^{n} p_i q_i \leq I$$

where I is the consumer's income gives the inverse demand functions $p_i = V_i'(q_i)$ for $i = 1, \ldots, n$.

Quasi-Rents

See **asset specificity**.

Quota

When applied to imports, a restriction on the quantity that can be imported into a country over a specified period of time.

R

R-Squared

In **ordinary least squares (OLS)** estimation, a measure, ranging from zero to one, of the goodness-of-fit of the estimated relationship between the **dependent variable** and the **explanatory variables** compared to the sample data. The R-squared value uses as a baseline the variation in the dependent variable within a given sample, and measures the proportion of this variation attributable to the explanatory variables, based on the model's predicted values of the dependent variable.

Raising Rivals' Costs

Strategies that are designed to **deter entry** by increasing a **potential entrant's** production costs. Typical mechanisms are increasing **advertising**, expenditures to strengthen brand image, and lobbying to impede entry of foreign firms to a domestic firm's market.

Ramsey Pricing

A policy rule that requires a monopolist to set prices that maximize social **surplus** subject to a **profit** constraint. Suppose that the monopolist sells N goods in separate markets, with the demand for good i being given by $q_i(p_i)$ and inverse demand $p_i(q_i)$. Assume also that the firm's total cost is $C(q_1, \ldots, q_N)$. Then the Ramsey prices solve the programming problem: maximize total surplus

$$W(\mathbf{p}, \mathbf{q}) = \sum_{n=1}^{N} \left(\int_0^{q_i(p_1)} p_n(z) \, dz \right) - C(\mathbf{q})$$

subject to the constraint that profit equal a given fixed value, or

$$\sum_{i=1}^{N} p_i q_i(p_i) - C(\mathbf{q}) = \Pi^0.$$

See Ramsey (1927) and Boiteux (1964).

Random-Coefficients Model

An econometric model in which the coefficients in the regression equation are treated as random variables. (See **classical linear regression model** for an introduction to regression coefficients.) This model permits each observation, in the sample under study, to have an idiosyncratic response to a change in the corresponding **explanatory variable**, rather than assuming that all individual observations experience the same marginal response. In a **discrete choice model of demand**, such as the **mixed logit model**, this specification allows for variation in consumers' tastes.

Random Variable

A variable whose **expected value** is determined by the probability distribution that describes the distribution of values that the variable can take.

Ratchet Effect

A **moral hazard** problem that confronts **principals** rather than **agents**. (1) In a regulatory setting, the incentive of regulators to lower the price cap on a regulated firm in response to the firm's efficiency gains, thereby undermining the firm's incentive to reduce production costs. To avoid such potential efficiency losses, price-cap determinations should be made independent of any observed productivity gains. (2) Within firms, the temptation that an employer has to increase targets for employees on **incentive contracts** when employees exceed their stated targets, again with the effect of undermining the employees' incentives to continue exerting effort once stated targets have been achieved.

Rate Base

The valuation of a regulated firm's invested capital that is used to allow the regulator to measure the firm's profit. See **rate-of-return regulation** and **Averch–Johnson effect**.

Rate of Return

The ratio of the amount gained or lost on an investment to the amount of money invested over a given period of time, expressed as a percentage.

Rate-of-Return Regulation

A constraint imposed on pricing for a regulated **monopoly** based on an allowable **rate of return** on the firm's capital or **rate base**. See **Averch–Johnson effect**.

Rate of Time Preference

A measure of the extent to which present consumption is preferred to future consumption. A high rate of time preference is equivalent to the agent having a higher **discount rate**.

Rate Structure

In a regulatory setting, the determination of price for each market segment served by the regulated firm. See, for example, **fully distributed cost pricing** and **peak-load pricing**; see also **rate-of-return regulation**.

Rational Agent

An economic agent who takes actions that maximize their **utility** given their knowledge of the environment within which the actions are being taken. In **game theory**, for example, it is typically assumed that all agents are rational.

Rationing Rule

Suppose that there are two firms and that firm 1 charges the lower price p. Suppose further that firm 1 has insufficient capacity to meet all demand at price p. Then the rationing rule determines how the **residual demand** for firm 2 is determined. Two such rules have been considered: efficient rationing where the rule maximizes **consumer surplus**, and proportional rationing in which all consumers have an equal probability of being rationed. See Tirole (1988, pp. 213–214).

Ray Average Cost

A method of defining average cost for a **multi-product firm**. Suppose that a firm has a technology that allows it to produce n products and that its **total cost** function is $C(q_1, \ldots, q_n)$. Total output q is defined implicitly by the equations $q_i = \lambda_i q$ $(i = 1, \ldots, n)$ with

$$\sum_{i=1}^{n} \lambda_i = 1,$$

where the λ_i defines the proportions in which the n products are produced. Then ray average cost is total cost divided by q, or

$$RAC(q) = \frac{C(\lambda_1 q, \ldots, \lambda_n q)}{q}.$$

An important limitation of this measure of average costs is that the measure of ray average cost is sensitive to the assumed proportions in which the firm's outputs are produced.

Reaction Function

See **best response function**.

Real Option

The right by a decision maker to tailor a decision, typically a capital investment decision, in response to information that will be received some time in the future.

Real Option Pricing

The method by which **real options** are valued.

Real Rate of Return

The rate of return adjusted for the effects of inflation. See also **nominal rate of return**.

Real Value

The value of a good or service adjusted for inflation and expressed in terms of its value in exchange for a representative basket of market goods.

Rebate

A promotion technique in which the buyer is offered a reduction in price, usually by mailing in a rebate coupon.

Reciprocal Buying

A request by a large **conglomerate** that its suppliers purchase some of their inputs from another of the conglomerate's divisions. This technique can be used by the conglomerate to strengthen the **market power** of its divisions at the expense of smaller independent firms.

Reciprocal Dumping

Dumping by firm i in firm j's market(s) and by firm j in firm i's market(s).

Reciprocal Interdependence

Exists between groups of workers when these groups depend on each other for the effective completion of their work.

Refusal to Deal

The decision by a firm to prevent sales to another market participant. Refusal can involve restrictions on retail sales, as in **exclusive dealing**, or on the willingness of the firm to supply a monopolized input to rival producers. Such monopolizing behavior can violate **antitrust laws**. See **exclusive dealing**.

Regression Analysis

An econometric technique that seeks to identify the relationship between a **dependent variable** and a specified set of **independent variables**. See **classical linear regression model**.

Regression Equation

See **regression analysis**.

Regulation

Legal restrictions imposed by governmental authorities governing what actions by individuals and organizations should be judged to be illegal. Regulation of industries can involve oversight of product prices, levels of production, market entry conditions and operations of natural monopolies. In the case of monopoly, regulators may determine the **rate base**, in **rate-of-return regulation**, as well as the prices charged to each market, according to the **rate structure**. Regulatory agencies in the US provide oversight on safety and environmental standards through the Occupational Health and Safety Administration (OSHA) and the Environmental Protection Agency (EPA). See **Becker model of regulation** for a model of political influence in the context of regulation. See also Viscusi et al. (2005).

Regulatory Capture

A situation in which an agency set up to regulate a group of firms or other organizations ends up coming under the control of the group(s) whose actions they were intended to control.

Regulatory Lag

If a utility is regulated it cannot change its prices in response to a change in costs until it has received permission to do so from the regulator. Between regulatory hearings, when prices are fixed, a reduction in production costs will increase profits during the lag period, before regulators can adjust prices downward, to maintain the previously specified **rate of return** under the new, and lower, costs.

Related Acquisition

The purchase of one firm by another firm when the two firms operate in significantly overlapping lines of business.

Relationship-Specific Asset

An asset that is intended to support a specific transaction. Typically the asset is essential to the effectiveness of the transaction. Moreover, the asset cannot be redeployed to another transaction without some reduction in the asset's productivity. For physical assets, relationship specificity arises if the asset is designed for a specific purpose or client, or is located geographically to serve a particular client, or is dedicated to serve the needs of a particular client. When these conditions arise, the value of the asset is much higher in its intended use than in its next-best use. For human capital it results from an individual's investment in acquiring or developing specialized knowledge or skills that are imperfectly transferable from their intended use to their next-best use. As a result the creation of a relationship-specific asset gives rise to **quasi-rents** and the **hold-up problem**.

Relationship-Specific Investment

Investment in the creation of a **relationship-specific asset**.

Relative Performance Evaluation

A performance evaluation system that uses the output of other employees to adjust an employee's compensation in an **incentive-based compensation** contract.

Remedy

In the event of a successful antitrust prosecution a requirement that the violators change their business practices, for example requiring divestiture of some divisions or requiring the firms to stop **tying arrangements** or **price discrimination**.

Renegotiation

The attempt by one party to a **contract** to change the contract conditions after the contract has been signed. Renegotiation is typically feasible because of **contractual incompleteness**. The risk of renegotiation is particularly acute when one party to the contract has to invest in **relationship-specific assets** to support the contract, giving rise to a **hold-up problem**.

Renewable Resource

A resource that has the ability to reproduce itself with the result that if resource use is less than the reproduction rate the resource is self-perpetuating.

Rent

A payment to an owner of a resource over and above the amount that needs to be paid to induce the owner to agree to allow the resource to be used.

Rent Gradient

A measure of the rate at which land rents decline with distance from the central business district.

Rent-Seeking

The expenditure of resources by individuals, organizations or firms in order to manipulate the economic and/or legal environment in ways that generate **rent** for these individuals, organizations or firms rather than using the resources directly to make profit or produce wealth. An extreme form of rent-seeking arises when firms compete to obtain a **monopoly** position in a market. Such competition will lead the firms to incur wasteful expenditures equal to the **monopoly profit** that they expect to make. With such rent-seeking the **deadweight loss** of monopoly should be increased to include the monopoly profit.

Repeated Game

A **game** in which the interactions between the players are repeated over a number of periods, where the number of repetitions of the game may be defined, indeterminate or infinite. For some **non-cooperative games**, such as the **prisoners' dilemma game**, cooperation can be sustained by **trigger strategies** when the game is repeated, even though in the **one-shot** version, players will always choose not to cooperate. Whether or not repetition of the game leads to cooperation being **subgame perfect** is dependent upon several factors: (1) if the game is a **finitely repeated game** repetition will sustain cooperation for some of the periods of play only if the game has more than one **Nash equilibrium** (see **Selten's theorem**); (2) if the game is repeated indefinitely cooperation is sustainable only if the probability of repetition of the game is "sufficiently high"; (3) cooperation is sustainable only if the **discount factor** is sufficiently close to unity (see the **folk theorem**).

Replacement Cost

A valuation method in which an asset is valued at the amount that would have to be paid today to replace the asset.

Replacement Effect

The property that **research and development** by a monopolist that leads to the creation of a new process or product will lead to the displacement of some or all of the monopolist's existing processes or products. The replacement effect causes the monopolist to place a lower value on innovation than a competitive firm, unless the monopolist includes the strategic value that the innovation might have in maintaining its monopoly, which is captured by the **efficiency effect**. To see why, take the following example. Consider a market in which aggregate demand is $Q = D(p)$.

Assume that this market is supplied by Bertrand competitors, each with constant marginal cost c_h. Now suppose that one of these firms can make a **non-drastic innovation** that lowers its marginal cost to c_l. The per-period value that the innovator places on the innovation is $v^b = (c_h - c_l)D(c_h)$. Suppose, by contrast, that the market is supplied by a monopolist that faces no threat of entry. The value placed on the innovation by the monopolist is

$$v^m = \int_{c_l}^{c_h} MC(c)\,dc.$$

Since $MC(c) \le D(c)$ we have $v^m < v^b$. See Tirole (1988, pp. 391–392).

Representative Consumer Model

A **monopolistically competitive** model in which consumers are assumed to be identical and to view all products as being equally good substitutes.

Reputation

The opinion that a group holds of an individual, group or organization. Individuals may wish to gain a reputation for being honest, or firms a reputation for being fair or tough. For example, an **incumbent firm** might engage in costly **predatory conduct** in order to develop a reputation for toughness and so **deter entry** by **potential entrants**.

Requirements Contracts

See **tie-in sales**.

Requirements Tie-In Sale

A constraint imposed on a buyer of one good from a firm that requires the buyer to make all their purchases of another good from the same firm. IBM, for example, required users of their computer punch card machines to buy the punched cards from IBM. See also **tie-in sales**.

Resale Price Maintenance (RPM)

An agreement between a manufacturer and a distributor according to which the distributor must sell the manufacturer's product at a set price (RPM), or at or above a price floor (minimum RPM), or at or below a price ceiling (maximum RPM). Such agreements have been argued as being necessary to encourage distributors to offer potential consumers costly promotional and distribution services but have been criticized as being anticompetitive by effectively limiting competitive pricing among distributors.

Research and Development

Creative activities that are undertaken systematically with the intention of increasing the stock of knowledge and applying these advances to developing new applications, new and improved production processes, or to introducing new products.

Research Joint Venture

A **joint venture** that is established to coordinate the **research and development** activities of the parties to the joint venture and to ensure that the products of the research and development activities are made available to these parties. One advantage of research joint ventures is that they allow the partners to the joint venture to exploit synergies in their research capabilities. Another is that the joint venture avoids wasteful research expenditures when the partners to the joint venture would otherwise be involved in a **patent race**. See Grossman and Shapiro (1986).

Reservation Price

The maximum price that a consumer is willing to pay for a unit of a particular commodity. **Consumer surplus** from buying this unit is the difference between the reservation price and the actual price that the consumer pays. In a given market, the reservation price of the last consumer along the demand curve to purchase the product is equal to the market-clearing price.

Reservation Price Method

A market research method for identifying consumers' **reservation prices** for new products.

Reservation Wage

The lowest wage that an individual has to be paid in order to accept an offer of employment.

Residual Claimant

The individual who is entitled to receive whatever is left from the **revenues** a firm or other asset produces once all debts, expenses, wages and other contractual obligations have been paid. For privately owned companies the residual claimant is typically the owner of the company. With publicly traded companies the residual claimants are the shareholders, but they have limited ability to exercise their residual rights. For a **franchise** the residual claimant is the franchisee.

Residual Demand

The demand curve facing a particular firm that is market demand minus the quantity supplied by rival firms at any given price. If market demand is $D(p)$ and rival firms' supply is $S_{-i}(p)$, then residual demand for firm i is $D(p) - S_{-i}(p)$.

Residual Return

Income from an asset or business that remains after all fixed and contractual obligations have been met.

Residual Right of Control

The right to make decisions regarding an asset's use or disposal that are not explicitly assigned to other parties by law or by a contract between the parties. The need for assigning residual rights of control arises from

contractual incompleteness. The individual or group that has the residual right of control of an asset is the individual or group that has the greatest interest in maintaining the value of the asset. See Grossman and Hart (1986).

Resource Allocation

A description of how the goods, assets and endowments of individuals in an economy are allocated. An efficient resource allocation is such that no reallocation can make any one individual better off without making at least one other individual worse off. See also **Pareto efficient**, **Pareto optimality** and **allocative efficiency**.

Resource-Based Theory of the Firm

A theory that posits that for a firm's **competitive advantage** to be sustainable it must be based on the firm having control of **resources** that are valuable, rare, difficult to substitute and difficult to imitate. In the absence of resources with these characteristics any competitive advantage a firm has will be short-lived as a result of competition from rivals. See Wernerfelt (1984).

Resources

Firm-specific assets such as **patents**, **trademarks**, **brand name**, **reputation**, installed base in a **network industry** or the firm's organizational culture. These resources underpin the firm's ability to create more value than its competitors and so to have a **sustainable competitive advantage**. For such value creation to be feasible, the firm must also have **capabilities** that are consistent with its resources.

Retailing

The sale of goods, merchandise or services directly to consumers. This may occur in fixed locations such as shops or department stores, or in virtual locations such as over the Internet or by post. Retailers occupy the final stage in the supply chain.

Retail Services

Services provided by a retailer to potential consumers. These might include expert advice, pre-purchase demonstrations or training, post-purchase support activities, or **warranties**.

Retained Earnings

Profit earned by a publicly traded firm that is held for further investment in the company rather than distributed as dividends to stockholders. See also **free cash flow problem**.

Returns to Scale

The rate at which **output** changes in response to proportional changes in all **inputs**. If returns to scale are: (1) decreasing, output increases less than proportionately; (2) constant, output increases proportionately; or (3) increasing, output increases more than proportionately with inputs. In the case of a **Cobb–Douglas production function**, where total output is

$$Q = \prod_{i=1}^{n} x_i^{\alpha_i},$$

$$\text{if } \sum_{i=1}^{n} \alpha_i \text{ is less than one,}$$

the production process exhibits decreasing returns to scale; if greater than one, increasing returns; and if equal to one, constant returns.

Revealed Preference

A method that is used to determine the underlying preferences of individuals by looking at their actual choices. If a bundle A is chosen by an individual when another bundle B is affordable, then A is revealed preferred to B, and we can assume that A will also be chosen in preference to B whenever both are affordable. This method allows the economist to chart **indifference curves** that behave according to the standard assumptions of consumer theory.

Revelation Principle

The principle that regulators can design mechanisms that induce privately informed individuals to act true to type. Formally the principle states that for any Bayesian **Nash equilibrium** of a **game** of **incomplete information**, there is an associated revelation mechanism whose equilibrium results in players revealing their true preferences. See Dasgupta et al. (1979).

Revenue

The total amount of money that a firm receives from the sale of its goods or services.

Revenue Center

A business unit that is allocated a fixed budget and asked to maximize revenue. The unit manager typically has limited discretion over the prices that can be charged. Prices usually must be kept within a defined range. Examples are selling, distribution and occasionally servicing business units.

Revenue Equivalence Theorem

Assume that there are N risk-neutral bidders, each of whom has a privately known valuation v of an item to be sold at **auction**, with v drawn from a continuous distribution $F(v)$ that is strictly increasing over the range $[\underline{v},\bar{v}]$. Any auction in which the item always goes to the individual with the highest value of v, and in which any bidder with valuation $\underline{v}$ expects to receive zero surplus, results in exactly the same payment for each bidder v and results in exactly the same **revenue** to the seller. If these conditions are met, then auction design is not an issue. See Riley and Samuelson (1981) and Myerson (1981).

Reverse Auctions

An **auction** in which a potential buyer of a good or service seeks competing bids from a group of potential sellers. In this type of auction, competition is between sellers, as compared to a typical auction in which competition is between buyers. The auction proceeds by sellers offering lower and lower prices until only one seller is left willing to bid.

Reverse Engineering

Discovering how a product or system works and can be manufactured by analyzing its structure and properties, usually by taking it apart in order to reveal its essential design and functional mechanisms.

Rising Stars

Products with significant potential for future growth in sales. See **growth share matrix**.

Risk-Adjusted Rate of Return

The **rate of return** earned by competitive firms undertaking projects that have the same degree of risk as that of the firm being analyzed.

Risk Averse

An individual who values a sure thing more highly than a risky outcome with the same expected value. If the individual's **coefficient of absolute risk aversion** is $r(I)$ then for a risk averse individual $r(I) > 0$. In the **principal–agent model**, the agent is often assumed to be risk averse. Risk aversion complicates the design of **incentive-based compensation** contracts. Such contracts are intended to align the agent's interests with those of the principal. However, incentive-based contracts also introduce uncertainty into the agent's expected compensation, which has to be offset by offering the agent a **risk premium**.

Risk Loving

An individual who values a sure thing less highly than a risky outcome with the same expected value. If the individual's **coefficient of absolute risk aversion** is $r(I)$ then for a risk-loving individual $r(I) < 0$.

Risk Neutral

An individual who is indifferent between a sure thing and a risky outcome with the same expected value. If the individual's **coefficient of absolute risk aversion** is $r(I)$ then for a risk-neutral individual $r(I) = 0$. In the **principal–agent model**, the principal is typically assumed to be risk neutral.

Risk Premium

The extra payment that must be made to a **risk-averse** individual to induce that individual to accept a risky outcome rather than a sure thing with the same expected value. The risk premium is the expected value of the risky outcome minus its **certainty equivalent**. If the expected value of the risky outcome is I with variance $Var(I)$ and the individual's **coefficient of absolute risk aversion** is $r(I)$, then the risk premium is approximately $Var(I).r(I)/2$.

Risk-Sharing Contract

A **contract** that guarantees an **agent** some payment but has sufficiently strong incentive components to encourage the agent not to shirk on the contract.

Risk-Sharing Principle

The principle that the cost of pooling independent risks reduces the cost of bearing these risks.

Risk Tolerance

A measure of an individual's willingness to bear risk. If the individual's **coefficient of absolute risk aversion** is $r(I)$ then the individual's risk tolerance is $1/r(I)$.

Rivalrous

A situation in which the consumption of a good or service by one individual reduces the amount of that good or service that is available to other individuals. Most goods and services are rivalrous but some, such as knowledge or street lighting, are not. When a good is non-rival and **non-excludable**, it is a **public good**.

Robinson–Patman Act

A US federal law passed in 1936 that prohibited particular practices that were considered to be anticompetitive, in particular **price discrimination**, if the effect of these practices was "substantially to lessen competition or tend to create a monopoly in any line of commerce".

Routines

Standardized rules for decisions and actions that an organization adopts and imposes with very little scope being allowed for variation.

Royalties

The payment from one party, the licensee or franchisee, to another party, the licensor or franchisor, that gives the first party the right to use an asset of the second party. Typically the asset in question will be an **intellectual property right** – for example the right to use a **patent**, **copyright** or **trademark**, or the right to operate under the name of the licensor, for example the right to operate a McDonald's **franchise**.

Roy's Identity

Given the consumer's **indirect utility function** $v(p, I)$, Roy's Identity states that the **demand function** for commodity i is given by

$$x_i(p, I) = -\frac{\partial v(p, I)/\partial p_i}{\partial v(p, I)/\partial I}.$$

Ruinous Competition

Competition between rival firms that is so aggressive that no firm is able to cover its costs of production. This type of competition is unsustainable for the firms involved but may be pursued strategically by a firm that believes it is strong enough to outlast its competitors. See also **war of attrition**.

Rule of Reason

A rule applied by **antitrust authorities** that balances the pro- and anti-competitive effects of a business practice in order to judge whether the practice violates **antitrust laws**. This contrasts with the **per se rule** that deems particular business practices always to be illegal. Under the rule of reason, the prosecution must establish evidence of both monopoly **market power** and deliberate and willful engagement in monopolizing tactics. The latter condition is to be contrasted with attaining monopoly position through successful product development and operational advantage.

Rule-of-Thumb Pricing

The use of a set formula by a firm in order to determine its prices. Examples are setting a target **rate of return** on invested capital or setting prices as a fixed mark-up over some measure of costs.

S

Sales Revenue

The product of the price that a firm charges and the quantity that is demanded at that price. If the firm's **demand function** is $Q = D(p, \alpha)$ then its sales revenue at price p is $p.\ D(p, \alpha)$. If the firm adopts simple **linear pricing** then the price that maximizes sales revenue is such that the absolute value of the **price elasticity of demand** is unity.

Sales Revenue Maximization

An objective given to managers that they choose their strategies to maximize **sales revenue**, usually subject to some specified minimum **profit** constraint. In the absence of the profit constraint, the manager will increase production to the point where **marginal revenue** falls to zero.

Salop's Circle Model

A **spatial model** of **monopolistic competition** in which firms and consumers are assumed to be distributed over the circumference of a one-dimensional circular market, in contrast to the **Hotelling spatial model** in which the market is assumed to be a one-dimensional line. An advantage of Salop's circle model as a model of monopolistic competition is that in equilibrium all firms in the market can be assumed to be symmetric. By contrast, in the **Hotelling line market** the firms at each extremity of the market face different market conditions than firms that are interior to the market. See Salop (1979).

Satisficing

Behavior that sets a minimum acceptable level of performance below which the individual does not wish to go rather than trying to maximize **profit** or **utility**. This type of behavior might be chosen when the environment in which choices are being made is complex or noisy.

Scale Economies

A measure of the way in which **total cost** varies with **output**. Scale economies are measured for a single output firm by the index $S = AC(q)/MC(q)$
where AC is **average total cost** and MC is **marginal cost**. For a **multi-
product firm** the index of scale economies is

$$S = C(q_1, \ldots, q_n) / \sum_{i=1}^{n} q_i MC_i$$

where MC_i is the marginal cost of product i. If the scale economy index
$S > 1$ there are **economies of scale** and if $S < 1$ there are **diseconomies of
scale**.

Scarce Resources

Resources that are limited in supply with the result that firms will compete
with each other to acquire them.

Schumpeterian Hypothesis

A conjecture first articulated by Joseph Schumpeter that **research and
development** expenditures are more likely to be undertaken by large firms
than by small firms. Schumpeter further hypothesized that monopolistic
or oligopolistic firms would pursue innovative activity more aggressively
than would firms with little or no **market power**. The underlying intuition
is that the large firm has more to lose from failing to innovate than the
small firm has to gain. See also the **efficiency effect** and the **replacement
effect**

Scope Economies

See **economies of scope**.

Scorched Earth Policy

A **takeover** defense in which the managers of a firm deliberately lower its
value to a hostile bidder.

SCP Paradigm

See **structure–conduct–performance paradigm**.

Screening

Offering a menu of options or **contracts** that is intended to lead to **self-selection** by the individuals to whom the menu is offered. **Second-degree price discrimination** is one form of screening in which the different packages are designed to be bought by different types of individual. Using different types of signals, such as education, in determining employment offers is another. Offering a range of products of different **quality** is a third. Screening is necessary when the individual offering the menu has **imperfect information** about the true types of the individuals to whom the menu is being offered, but wants each individual to act true to type in selecting from the menu. For screening to be effective the menu must satisfy individual **incentive compatibility constraints**.

Sealed-Bid First-Price Auction

An **auction** in which bidders submit bids simultaneously and privately so that each bidder knows only the value of their own bid. The highest bidder wins the auction at the price of their bid. There is no rebidding.

Sealed-Bid Second-Price Auction

As in the **sealed-bid first-price auction**, bidders submit bids simultaneously and privately so that each bidder knows only the value of their own bid. In this auction, however, while the highest bidder wins the auction, the winner pays the price submitted by the second-highest bidder. This is also referred to as a **Vickrey auction**.

Search Costs

Costs incurred by buyers in order to obtain information regarding the prices and characteristics of **substitute goods**.

Search Good

A product or service whose features, characteristics and **quality** are easily and accurately observable prior to purchase. They are so named since buyers of search goods are likely to make their purchase decisions by searching for the lowest price. They are to be contrasted with **experience goods**.

Seasonal Pricing

Setting prices to take account of variations in demand at different times of the day, week, month or year.

Second-Best Optimum

The best possible outcome given that there is a constraint that prevents attainment of the **first-best** outcome.

Second-Degree Price Discrimination

A type of price discrimination that is employed when the seller knows that they are serving consumers of different types but is unable to determine the actual type of each consumer. With this type of price discrimination the seller bundles quantity and total charge. Suppose that there are n different consumer types. The bundle designed for consumers of type i offers a quantity q_i for a total charge of T_i. The bundles on offer must satisfy the **incentive compatibility constraint** that the bundle designed for each consumer type is actually bought by that type. Typically this requires that a **quantity discount** is offered to higher-demand consumers. It also means that all consumer types other than the lowest demand type are left with some consumer **surplus**. Third, while the bundle designed for the highest-demand type offers the **socially optimal** quantity, the bundles designed for all other consumer types contain suboptimally low quantities.

Securities and Exchange Commission

A federal agency charged with regulatory oversight of trading in securities, including stocks, bonds, and other financial instruments in the United States.

Self-Managed Team

A group of individuals who work together as a **team** and who set the common objectives that they will pursue.

Self-Selection Constraint

See **incentive compatibility constraint**.

Selten's Theorem

A theorem for **repeated games** stating that if a game with a unique equilibrium is played finitely many times, its solution is that equilibrium played each and every time. Take a standard **prisoners' dilemma game** such as that in the following **payoff matrix**, where in each cell, the **payoff** to the row player is listed first, and the payoff to the column player is listed second:

		Player 2	
		Cooperate	Defect
Player 1	Cooperate	10, 10	4, 12
	Defect	12, 4	6, 6

If this game is played once the **Nash equilibrium** is (Defect, Defect). Selten's theorem states that if this game is played a finite number of times, known in advance to both players, (Defect, Defect) remains the only equilibrium. To see why, suppose that this game is played 20 times. In the final play, any attempt to deviate from (Defect, Defect) fails since this is the last play and so is, effectively a **one-shot game**. But this means that the 19th play is effectively the last play, with the result that again (Defect, Defect) is the only equilibrium for that play. This logic can be continued right through to the first play. It is important to note that Selten's theorem rests on two assumptions: that the number of plays is finite and known to all the players, and that the Nash equilibrium is unique. If either of these assumptions does not hold then it may be possible to maintain other strategy combinations as **subgame perfect Nash equilibria**. See, for example, **finitely repeated game** and **repeated game**.

Semi-Fixed Costs

Costs that are fixed and independent of **output** over certain ranges of output but which are variable over other ranges. These costs are typically incurred when certain **inputs** come in indivisible sizes. For example, a refrigerated truck might have a capacity of 5000 liters. The cost of trucks to a delivery service is fixed for any delivery capacity up to 5000 liters, between 5000 liters and 10,000 liters, and so on. So these costs are fixed in each 5000-liter interval, but variable between such intervals.

Semi-Strong Form Efficient Market Hypothesis

The hypothesis that stock prices fully reflect all publicly available information. This version of the **efficient market hypothesis** implies that an investor cannot be expected to make better returns from an active investment policy than from holding a fully diversified market portfolio, unless the investor has inside information that is not publicly available.

Separating Equilibrium

An equilibrium in a **dynamic game** with **asymmetric information** in which the different types of players choose different strategies. An example would be where a high-cost and a low-cost incumbent monopolist each sets different prices in the first period of an **entry** game, as a result of which the **potential entrant** learns the true type of the incumbent from the period 1 price. See, by contrast, **pooling equilibrium**.

Separation of Ownership and Control

A feature of a corporation in which the decision-makers – the managers – are not the owners of the corporation. It has been suggested that this type of separation allows managers to pursue objectives that are in their own interests rather than in the interests of the owners. Such self-serving behavior is constrained by the **market for corporate control**. See Fama and Jensen (1983).

Sequential Game

A game in which the players choose their strategies in sequence, with the choices made by earlier players being observable by later players. Such games can give early movers a **first-mover advantage** in that they can anticipate and so endogenize the choices of later players. However, in some cases, for example in pricing games, the first-mover may actually be at a disadvantage in that firms moving later can undercut the first mover's price. Sequential games are usually represented as **extensive form games**.

Sequential Interdependence

A situation in which the performance of one individual or group depends upon the performance of another individual or group, but not vice versa. A typical example is production using modern assembly lines.

Serial Correlation

In time-series **regression analysis**, the case in which the error term is correlated across periods. For example, when estimating the demand for a firm's product using a sample of weekly observations, an unobservable factor that decreases demand in one period, such as a decline in consumers' perception of product quality, can continue to impact demand over the next several periods.

Shareholders

Individuals, groups or companies that have legal **ownership** of the shares of stock of a publicly traded, or joint stock company. The shareholders collectively own the company but may not be able to control it as a result of the **separation of ownership and control**.

Share Strategy

A strategy in which a firm uses its **benefit** or **cost advantage** to obtain a higher **market share** than its competitors. If the firm has a **benefit advantage**, this can be done by charging a price equal to that of its rivals. If it has a cost advantage, the firm can undercut its competitors. A share strategy is more likely to be effective as compared to a **margin strategy** if the good or services on offer exhibit highly elastic demand implying that consumers are willing to shop around and to switch suppliers.

Shephard's Lemma

Given the consumer's **expenditure function** $E(\mathbf{p}, u)$, Shephard's Lemma states that the **compensated demand function** for good i is $x(\mathbf{p}, u) = \partial E(\mathbf{p}, u)/\partial p_i$.

Sherman Act

A United States antitrust act passed in 1890 stating that: Section 1, "Every contract, combination in the form of trust or otherwise, or conspiracy, in restraint of trade or commerce is illegal"; Section 2, "Every person who shall monopolize, or attempt to monopolize, or combine or conspire with any other person or persons to monopolize any part of the trade or commerce among the several States . . . shall be deemed guilty of a felony" (15 U.S.C. § 1 and 2).

Shop Goods

Consumer goods and services that are relatively expensive items in the shopper's budget and that tend to be infrequently purchased. They are so called because consumers will tend to "shop around" for the best deal. Examples are automobiles, up-scale furniture and medical procedures.

Short Run

A period of time in which a firm cannot vary the quantity of some of the **factors of production** that it employs.

Short-Run Average Total Cost

Short-run total costs divided by total output.

Short-Run Total Costs

The costs that a firm incurs in the **short run**. Any such costs associated with invariant factors of production are fixed, independent of the firm's level of **output**.

Short-Run Equilibrium

The profit-maximizing decisions that a firm makes in the **short run**. In a competitive market, an equilibrium that equates aggregate demand and aggregate supply but in which **incumbent firms** may be making excess profits because new firms have not yet had the chance to **enter** the market or economic **losses** because some existing firms have not yet **exited** the market.

Shutdown Price

The price at which it is better for a firm to shut down operations, even in the short run, rather than continue in business. Typically this is a price that is just less than the firm's minimum **average variable cost**. More accurately, the shutdown price is equal to **average avoidable cost**.

Signaling

In **principal–agent problems** the idea that the **agent** tries to convey useful information about the agent's true type to the **principal**. In **advertising**, the idea that an important motive for advertising **experience goods** is to inform consumers of the true qualities of these goods.

Simultaneous Game

A game in which the players choose their strategies simultaneously or, more generally, without being able to observe the choices of the other players.

Simultaneity

In **regression analysis**, a form of **endogeneity** in which an **explanatory variable** and the **dependent variable** are determined together. For example, in a study of firm profitability across industries, the number of firms within each industry would be expected to influence profitability, while profitability would be expected to influence the number of firms in each industry. If firm profitability is the dependent variable, with number of firms as an explanatory variable, this econometric specification would be characterized by simultaneity.

Single-Product Firm

A firm that is assumed to produce only one product or service.

Site-Specific Asset

An asset that has a higher value in a particular location than in any other location. For example, a major supplier's production facility is of greater value if it is located close to the assembly plant that it intends to supply than if the two are located a considerable distance apart. When assets are site-specific, their creation opens the asset owner to the **hold-up problem**. For example, the supplier, having established its production facility close to the assembler, but distant from any other potential buyer, runs the risk that the assembler will attempt to **renegotiate** the agreed supply price.

Slacking

Managers or workers who knowingly do not exert their best effort on behalf of their employer.

Sleeping Patent

A **patent** that is held by a firm but that the firm chooses not to develop into a finished product or process. These patents provide the firm with a buffer of protection around a core patent that the firm does intend to develop, making it more difficult for rival firms to invent around the core patent.

Slutsky Equation

An equation that relates **Hicksian demand** and **Marshallian demand**. If the Hicksian demand function for good i is $h_i(p, u)$ and the Marshallian demand function is $x_i(p, y)$ where p is price, u is utility and y is income, then the Slutsky equation is

$$\frac{\partial x_i(p, w)}{\partial p_i} = \frac{\partial h_i(p, u)}{\partial p_i} - \frac{\partial x_i(p, w)}{\partial w} x_i(p, w).$$

The first term is the **substitution effect** of a price change and the second term is the **income effect**. While the substitution effect is unambiguously negative, the income effect is ambiguous, its sign being determined by whether good i is **normal** or **inferior**.

Small Business Administration

A government agency in the United States charged with helping entrepreneurs and small businesses to succeed. This support can take the form of loans, directing federal contracts to small businesses, and business advising.

Social Benefit

The internal and external benefits associated with an economic activity. If an activity produces products and services that are valued by the society and for which the activity is paid, but also produces additional benefits, for example from aesthetic design, for which no payment is received, the activity's social benefits are the sum of these two sets of benefits.

Social Cost

The internal and external costs associated with an economic activity. If an activity produces products and services that are valued by the society but also produces pollution, the firm's social costs would be the sum of its production costs and the costs imposed on others by the pollution.

Social Optimum

A **Pareto-efficient** allocation of resources that maximizes aggregate **surplus**, taking into account all internal and external costs and benefits.

Social Welfare

The aggregate welfare in a society, measured as the sum of aggregate **consumer surplus** and **producer surplus**.

Social Welfare Function

A function that is intended to represent the aggregate preferences of individuals in a society and to allow the society to make judgments about the **social welfare** implications of different policy proposals. Such a function provides a ranking of alternative social states, potentially allowing the analyst to compare different economic policies in terms of their impact on aggregate social welfare.

Soft Commitment

A **strategic commitment** that results in a firm behaving much less aggressively than it would have done without the commitment, no matter what its competitors do. In a **Cournot game** such a commitment results in the firm producing relatively less output, while in a **Bertrand game** it results in the firm charging a relatively higher price.

Sole Proprietorship

A firm that is owned by a single individual who is personally liable for any debts that the firm incurs due to **unlimited liability**.

Spatial Price Discrimination

A form of **price discrimination** in which a seller sells to consumers at different locations at prices that differ by other than the difference in transport costs to these different consumers. Suppose that consumers are uniformly distributed across a linear market, that all consumers have the same, linear demand for the firm's product given by $q = a - bp$ and that transport costs to consumers distance x from the firm are tx. Suppose further that the firm has constant **marginal costs** of c. Then the firm maximizes **profit** from consumers at x by choosing p to maximize $(p - tx - c)(a - bp)$, giving the price $p(x) = (a + c)/2b + tx/2$. In other words, the firm absorbs

50% of the transport costs. More generally, suppose that inverse demand is given by

$$q(p) = (\gamma(a - bp))^{\frac{1}{\gamma}} \, (\gamma > -1)$$

if $\gamma \neq 0$ and $q(p) = a.e^{-bp}$ if $\gamma = 0$. If $\gamma = 1$ this is a linear demand function, if $\gamma < 1$ it is convex and if $\gamma > 1$ it is concave. If $\gamma < 0$ demand is more convex than the exponential demand $a.e^{-bp}$. The profit-maximizing price charged to consumers at x is:

$$p(x) = \begin{cases} \dfrac{a\gamma + bc}{b(1 + \gamma)} + \dfrac{tx}{1 + \gamma} & \text{if } \gamma \neq 0 \\[2mm] \dfrac{1}{b} + c + tx & \text{if } \gamma = 0 \end{cases}.$$

If $\gamma < 0$ the firm passes on more than 100 percent of transport costs to consumers, if $\gamma > 0$ the firm absorbs some proportion of transport costs, this proportion increasing in some proportion of transport costs, this proportion increasing in γ. Only for the exponential demand function is there no spatial price discrimination.

Spatial Model

See **Hotelling spatial model**.

Specialized Assets

Assets that are designed for particular purposes or to support particular relationships and that have much lower value in any alternative use. Given that **contracts** are **incomplete**, a contract that requires one or other party to the contract to invest in creating specialized assets exposes that party to the risk of a **hold-up problem**.

Specific Human Capital

Human capital that is created when individuals are trained in the routines that a firm uses to perform particular activities or produce particular goods. This kind of human capital is not easily transferable from one firm to another. As a result, an individual who invests in specific capital runs the risk of the returns on that investment being expropriated by the employer. Consequently, it is usually the case that such investment is paid for by the employer rather than the employee.

Spillovers

In **research and development** (R&D) a situation in which the results of one firm's R&D expenditures benefit other firms without the latter having to compensate the former. If spillovers are strong enough they can reduce the amount of R&D that firms undertake because of the temptation that firms have to **free-ride** on the research activities of others.

Spot Market

A market in which transactions are made immediately at the current market price and with no expectation of a long-term commitment between buyer and seller.

Spread

In financial markets the difference between the buyer's **bid price** and the seller's **ask price**.

Spurious Product Differentiation

A situation in which consumers mistakenly believe that identical goods are actually differentiated. **Persuasive advertising** has been claimed to give rise to this type of mistaken belief, leading consumers to purchase more expensive branded goods than cheaper but identical generic goods.

SSNIP Criterion

A method, also known as the **hypothetical monopolist test**, used by **anti-trust authorities** to define the relevant market. The test asks whether the firms in a hypothetical market would benefit from a 5 percent increase in price for at least one year. If the answer to this test is yes, the implication is that buyers have few **substitute goods** and so the hypothetical market is well defined and can be taken as the relevant market. If the answer is no, then buyers are able to switch to other products and the hypothetical market does not accurately define the relevant market. (SSNIP is "Small but Significant Non-Transitory Increase in Prices.")

Stackelberg Followers

In the **Stackelberg model**, the firm(s) that move second, having observed the choice(s) of the **Stackelberg leader(s)** who moved first.

Stackelberg Leaders

In the **Stackelberg model**, the firm(s) that move first. The leaders potentially have a strategic advantage in that they can correctly anticipate the responses of followers to the leaders' actions. For example, in a duopoly setting, under quantity competition, with **homogeneous products** and identical costs, the leader will produce a larger quantity, and earn larger profits, than the follower, simply as a result of moving first.

Stackelberg Model

An **oligopoly model** in which firms choose their strategies in sequence. The firm that moves first is usually referred to as the market, or **Stackelberg, leader**.

Stag Hunt Game

A game in which the players face a conflict between playing safe and cooperating. An example of such a game is as follows, where in each cell the **payoff** to the row player is listed first, and the payoff to the column player is listed second:

		George	
		Stag	Gather
Richard	Stag	10, 10	0, 8
	Gather	8, 0	4, 4

The two players can choose either to hunt for a stag or to gather produce from the forest. Gathering does not need cooperation to be successful but if both gather they share the resulting bounty. A stag hunt, by contrast, is successful only if both players participate in the hunt. There are two **Nash equilibria**, (Stag, Stag) and (Gather, Gather). The former is preferred to the latter by both players. However, if there is uncertainty about whether the other player will actually choose to cooperate in the hunt, (Gather, Gather) might emerge as the equilibrium since it is less risky.

Stakeholders

Individuals and groups who have an interest in the continued profitable operation of a firm. These will include employees, **shareholders**, lenders, customers, suppliers and communities in which the firm employs workers.

Standard

An agreed metric by which the **quality** of a good can be evaluated.

Standard Industrial Classification

A numbering system that is used by business and government to classify and measure economic activity. The most widely used codes are the three-digit and four-digit codes. The first two digits identify the general business sector to which an activity belongs, the third digit the subsector and the fourth digit the industry group. In the United States this classification is being replaced by the **North American Industry Classification System (NAICS)**.

Standard Setters

Industry groups that are appointed to certify that certain products meet agreed **standards**.

State of Nature

See **uncertainty**.

State-Owned Enterprise

An enterprise that is owned by a governmental authority and whose strategies are designed to meet objectives set by that authority. This form of **ownership** has been used to regulate the actions of **natural monopolies**. A government might choose to create such a **public enterprise** as an alternative to **regulation**, with resulting production and pricing decisions motivated by **social welfare** optimization. This form of organization can mitigate adverse efficiency effects, such as the **Averch–Johnson effect**, arising from regulation.

Static Analysis

Economic models of markets that are assumed to last for just one period.

Static Efficiency

The efficient allocation of a society's resources at a specific point in time.

Static Game

A **game** that is played only once and in which the players choose their strategies simultaneously.

Stigler–Peltzman Model of Regulation

A model of regulation based on seminal papers by Stigler (1971) and Peltzman (1976), providing a framework for the supply of and demand for regulation. The model assumes that both interest groups and elected officials act rationally in their efforts to influence the extent and nature of the state's regulatory activities. Interest groups are motivated by receiving the highest possible transfer of wealth, while elected officials seek political favor, including from interest groups, to ensure longevity in their elected positions. The model provides a theoretical basis for regulatory activity, with a broad set of empirical implications, explaining a wide variety of observed regulatory outcomes.

Stockholders

See **shareholders**.

Stock Option

A **contract** that gives an individual the right to purchase shares of stock in a company at an agreed price (the exercise price) at any point up to an agreed expiry date. These options are often used as part of **incentive-based compensation** to align the interests of employees with those of the firm granting the option.

Straight-Line Depreciation

An accounting technique in which an asset is assumed to last for a fixed period of time and in which the value of the asset is depreciated in equal increments over that period.

Strategic Alliance

An alliance in which two or more firms agree to collaborate on a project by committing resources to the project while the firms remain independent legal entities.

Strategic Barriers to Entry

Behavioral choices that are made deliberately to prevent **entry** and that would not be implemented if there were no threat of entry. For these choices to have the desired **entry-deterring** effect they must be credible.

Strategic Behavior

A set of actions that a firm takes in order to influence market outcomes and increase the firm's **profit**, taking into account the likely reactions of rival firms.

Strategic Commitments

Decisions that have long-term impacts on a firm and its rivals and that are expensive to reverse. For such commitments to have their desired strategic effects on the rival firms they must be visible, comprehensible and **credible** to the rivals.

Strategic Complements

In **game theory** strategies are strategic complements if they mutually reinforce each other. For example, an increase in price by one firm might be expected to lead to an increase in the price of a rival. The firms' **best response functions** are upward sloping. In the **duopoly** case, suppose that player i's **payoff** function is $\pi_i(s_1,s_2)$ where s_i represents player i's decision ($i = 1, 2$). Then s_1 and s_2 are strategic complements if $\partial^2\pi_1/\partial x_1\partial x_2, \partial^2\pi_2/\partial x_1\partial x_2 > 0$. See Bulow et al. (1985).

Strategic Fit

Activities that exhibit **complementarities** are said to exhibit strategic fit.

Strategic Form of Game

A game that is represented by a game matrix identifying the players, their strategies and the payoffs to each player in each **strategy combination**. The strategic form of a game, also known as the **normal form**, does not indicate the timing of moves and so is most appropriate for **simultaneous games**. **Sequential games** are better represented in **extensive form**.

Strategic Investments

(1) Investments whose benefits are enjoyed by many parts of an organization, including, in particular, business units that have made no contribution to the investments. (2) Investments that are made to create a **strategic commitment** and that are intended to influence the behavior of rival firms.

Strategic Substitutes

In **game theory** strategies are strategic substitutes if they mutually offset each other. For example, an increase in output by one firm might be expected to lead to a decrease in the output of a rival. The firms' **best response functions** are downward sloping. In the **duopoly** case, suppose that player i's **payoff** function is $\pi_i(s_1, s_2)$ where s_i represents player i's decision ($i = 1, 2$). Then s_1 and s_2 are strategic substitutes if $\partial^2\pi_1/\partial x_1\partial x_2, \partial^2\pi_2/\partial x_1\partial x_2 < 0$. See Bulow et al. (1985).

Strategic Trade Policy

Government trade policies that are intended to increase domestic **welfare**, even if this decreases welfare overseas. These policies typically are formulated to benefit domestic firms over their international rivals.

Strategy

A long-term plan of action that is designed in order to achieve a specified goal. For a firm, the objectives, policies and plans intended to achieve set purposes or goals, stated in a way that defines what business the firm is in and the kind of company it is or should be.

Strategy Combination

In **game theory** a set of strategies, one for each player, from which the **payoffs** to each player from that set of strategies can be identified.

Strong Form Efficient Market Hypothesis

The hypothesis that stock prices fully reflect all information, whether this information is publicly available or held by insiders.

Structural Barriers to Entry

Features of a market that create **barriers to entry** without the need for the **incumbent firm** to create **strategic barriers to entry**. Typical structural barriers are **economies of scale** and **scope**.

Structural Equation

In econometrics, an equation from among a set of equations comprising a structural model of economic activity, in which the **dependent variable** in one equation can appear as an **explanatory variable** in another equation and, more generally, in which variables across equations can mutually influence each other. The value of a structural approach lies in its formal modeling of equilibrium conditions. For example, in a structural model of price and quantity determination in a product market, one structural equation for demand, one for supply, and one for a market-clearing condition, will determine the equilibrium price and quantity. Such simultaneous equations models address the problem of **endogeneity** arising from **simultaneity** and can be estimated using **instrumental variables estimation**.

Structural Parameter

In **structural equation** models, the coefficient of interest from one of the underlying structural equations, such as a **parameter** from the demand equation in a model of supply and demand.

Structure–Conduct–Performance Paradigm

The view of early industrial organization economists that **market structure** determines the conduct of firms in the market and that conduct in turn determines outcomes or market performance in terms of economic **efficiency** or general **social welfare**. A major limitation of this paradigm is that it ignores the importance of feedback loops, for example from market performance to market structure.

Stuck in the Middle

The suggestion that if a firm attempts to pursue both a **benefit advantage** and a **cost advantage** it will fail to be effective in pursuing either.

Subgame

A part of an entire **game** that can stand alone as a game itself.

Subgame Perfect

A strategy combination such that the behavioral strategy it specifies for each player is a best response against the behavioral strategies of the other players in every **subgame**.

Subgame Perfect Nash Equilibrium

A **Nash equilibrium** in which the strategies are Nash equilibria for every **subgame**.

Subjective Performance Evaluation

Performance evaluation that is based upon the subjective opinions of the supervisor rather than on some more objectives measures. Such evaluation systems encounter several problems: shirking by supervisors who are reluctant to criticize employees; forced distributions that assign fixed proportions of employees to each category; **influence costs** as employees try to influence their appraisers; and reneging by employers on the rewards that have been promised for good performance, in that the employer falsely claims that subjective targets have not been met.

Subsidy

Financial or other assistance to a firm to encourage the production of goods and services supplied by the firm. The subsidy can take the form of direct financial assistance such as grants or tax breaks, and indirect assistance such as trade barriers to protect the firm against import competition.

Substitute Goods

Goods or services that provide the same services to consumers, with the result that the consumer will choose between these goods in terms of the relative **consumer surplus** they offer. One measure of whether two goods are substitutes is if the **cross-price elasticity** of demand for the two goods is positive. In these circumstances, an increase in the price of one good will cause consumers to increase their consumption of the other, substitute good.

Substitution Effect

When the impact on the quantity demanded of a good, resulting from an increase in the price of a related good, is positive. If the **demand function** is written $Q = D(p_i, \boldsymbol{p}_{-i}, y, \mathbf{a})$ where p_i is the price of the related good, $\boldsymbol{p}_{-i}$ is a vector of prices for all other goods, $\mathbf{a}$ includes all determinants of demand other than the price and income, and y is income, then the substitution effect is $\partial D()/\partial p_i$. See also **Slutsky equation** for discussion of a negative own-price substitution effect

Sunk Cost

Cost that has been incurred by an economic agent and that cannot be recovered should the agent choose to cease operations. Sunk costs should not affect decision-making after they have been incurred, but may affect the decision on whether or not to **enter** a market before they have been incurred. A non-refundable airline ticket is an example of a sunk cost. If an investment project requires the creation of **specialized assets**, then at least part of the investment expenditure is a sunk cost.

Sunk Cost Effect

A situation in which a firm continues to use its existing production processes or offer its existing product range even though a superior process or product technology is available that would be used or offered by a *de novo* firm because the existing firm is reluctant to write off the **sunk costs** associated with its current operations.

Supergame

Repeated games in which players know their rivals' previous actions and determine their own actions in each period based on this knowledge.

Supermajority Rule

A rule that any change of control of an organization must be approved by more than a simple majority of the voters. This is a form of **takeover** defense when the organization is a publicly traded company.

Supernormal Profit

Profit in excess of **normal profit**. See also **monopoly profit**.

Supplier Power

The ability of **input** suppliers to negotiate supply contract terms that extract **surplus** from their buyers. One of Porter's **five forces**.

Supply Curve

A curve in (Q, P) space describing the function $Q = S(P; \alpha)$ that gives the relationship between the price of a good and the quantity of the good that a firm is willing to supply, all else, α, remaining equal. The "all else" are typically number of competitors, **input** prices, expected prices and the prices of other goods.

Supply Elasticity

A measure of the sensitivity of quantity supplied to a change in price. If the supply function is $Q = S(P; \alpha)$ where α includes all other determinants of supply other than the price, then the supply elasticity is

$$\eta_P = \frac{\partial S(P,\alpha)}{\partial P} \frac{P}{S(P,\alpha)}.$$

Supply Function

The **output** choice that maximizes a firm's profit. Suppose that the output price is p, the vector of factor prices is $\mathbf{w}$ and the firm's **production function** is $y = f(\mathbf{x})$ where $\mathbf{x}$ is the vector of factor **inputs**. The supply function $y(p, \mathbf{w})$ solves the programming problem

$$\max_{p,\mathbf{w} \geq 0} py - \mathbf{w} \cdot \mathbf{x}$$

subject to $f(\mathbf{x}) \geq y$. Let the firm's **profit function** be $\pi(p, \mathbf{w})$, then Hotelling's Lemma states that the firm's supply function is $y(p,\mathbf{w}) = \partial \pi(p,\mathbf{w})/\partial p$.

Surplus

See **consumer surplus** and **producer surplus**.

Survivorship Studies

A method for identifying the efficient plant size in an industry by studying trends in plant sizes over time, based on the idea that if a particular plant size is efficient then all plants in the industry should approach that size over time.

Sustainability

A **natural monopoly** that can prevent **entry** is sustainable. A single-product natural monopoly is sustainable if there are **economies of scale** at all **outputs**.

Sustainable Competitive Advantage

A **competitive advantage** that a firm can sustain over time despite attempts by rivals to undermine or copy the firm's strategy. See also **resource-based theory of the firm**.

Switching Costs

The costs that are incurred in switching from one supplier to another. Examples include investments made by a consumer in order to purchase from a current supplier that have to be duplicated if the consumer switches to an alternative supplier: learning how to use new software, or a different brand of mobile telephone; switching from one social network site to another. Other examples are exit fees or the search, negotiation and learning costs that firms incur in changing suppliers. A firm that can create switching costs may exploit these as a **barrier to entry**.

SWOT Analysis

A management technique that seeks to identify the strengths (S), weaknesses (W), opportunities (O) and threats (T) associated with a proposed course of action or **strategy**.

Symmetric Information

In **game theory** the assumption that all players have the same information at any point in the game.

Synchronization Problem

The problem that arises when efficient operation requires that the timing of the activities involved have to be closely coordinated. This is one example of a system that has **design attributes**, where use of the price system to achieve the desired coordination is less effective than using command and control. The sport of crew rowing exhibits a synchronization problem: it is more important that the individual rowers row at the same speed than that they each row as fast as they can. The design of a mass production line must take into account the ways in which the different assembly operations should be organized.

Systems Competition

Competition between different technologies that offer the same services to consumers. In such competition, each firm is keen to have its technology declared or chosen as the **industry standard**. See **coordination game**.

T

Tacit Collusion

A situation in which firms in an **oligopoly** successfully coordinate their actions without any explicit **cartel**-like agreement. This type of agreement requires that the firms play a **repeated game** so that they can use the implicit threat to punish deviation from the agreement, perhaps by using a **trigger strategy**, as a means to sustain the agreement without the need for explicit communication. When airlines sustain high prices over extended periods of time, **antitrust authorities** could view this as evidence of tacit collusion.

Take-or-Pay Contract

A **contract** between a supplier and a purchaser requiring that the purchaser either uses the full input quantity originally contracted or, if it orders less than the contracted quantity, makes some payment, usually less than the full contract price, for the quantity outstanding.

Takeover

The **acquisition** of a publicly traded company (the target company) by another company (the acquirer). See also **hostile takeover**.

Takeover Premium

The extent to which the amount paid for a firm's shares in a **takeover** exceeds the total market value of the firm being taken over in the absence of the takeover.

Tapered Integration

A combination of **vertical integration** and market sourcing by which a company produces some proportion of an **input** in-house and sources the remainder from outside suppliers.

Targeting Strategy

A strategy by which a company selects the market segments it intends to supply (target) and develops the product line needed to supply those market segments.

Tariff

A tax imposed by a country on goods imported from another country. Tariffs take one of two broad type: an ad valorem tariff is a percentage of the value of the good being imported, while specific tariffs do not relate to value but are related to measures such as weight or volume.

Task Interdependence

Production processes in which one group of activities depend for their efficiency on other production activities.

Task-Specific Learning

Learning how to perform specific tasks. The skills obtained are typically not firm-specific and so allow the individual who has acquired the task-specific learning to bargain to capture some of the value created in higher compensation.

Taxes

Duties imposed by regulatory authorities on individuals and companies. Income taxes determine what proportion of earned income is deducted while **profit** taxes determine what proportion of a company's profit is deducted.

Team

A group of individuals within a firm who are charged with performing a defined set of tasks. See **teammates' dilemma** and **team production**.

Teammates' Dilemma

A **prisoners' dilemma game** played between members of a **team**. If such a game is played once then the members of the team will be tempted to shirk on the effort that they put into the team, attempting to **free-ride** on the effort of other members of the team.

Team Production

A production process in which individuals work in **teams** and in which the contribution of each individual to the team cannot be identified or measured. Such processes are prone to the **free-riding problem** unless individuals are motivated by appropriately designed **incentive contracts**. A benefit to team production derives from the synergies and efficiencies that can arise from well-matched team members with complementary **human capital** and talent.

Technical Efficiency

The extent to which a company maximizes the **output** it produces from a given set of **inputs**. More generally, a measure of whether the firm is employing least-cost production techniques. In resolving the **make-or-buy decision** on whether a particular activity should be left to the market or **vertically integrated**, the technical efficiency of market provision is typically greater (less costly) than the technical efficiency of vertical integration. The market firm is able to exploit economies of scale and scope more than the internal division since the market firm has a wider range of customers than the internal division.

Technological Innovation

See **innovation**.

Technology

A broad description of a society's state of knowledge, which determines the types of production processes that can be employed and the types of goods and services that can be produced by the society's **factors of production**.

Technology Change

The ways in which a society's **technology** alters over time.

Technology Licensing

Permitting a licensee to use the **technology** of the licensor in return for an agreed fee and under agreed restrictions.

Telecommunications Act (1996)

A United States Act designed to open telecommunications markets, including phone service, cable service, and broadcasting, thereby increasing competition. The Act required local phone companies, or local exchange carriers, to allow network access to entrants at prices commensurate with the carriers' costs. The Act also allowed local exchange carriers to expand into long-distance service provision to the local market once the local market achieved a sufficient level of competitiveness.

Territorial Restrictions

A **contract** between a seller and a distributor of the seller's products that constrains the geographic areas and/or customers to which the distributor can sell.

Theory of the Firm

A theoretical construction that investigates the behavior of firms operating in imperfectly competitive markets. A central question in the theory of the firm literature is whether a firm can appropriately be viewed as a **nexus of contracts**. This approach raises the question of how a **vertically integrated** firm would thus be distinguished from a firm that turns to outside markets for much of its productive activity. Grossman and Hart (1986) identified the essential roles of **contractual incompleteness** and the assignment of **residual rights of control** in this distinction.

Third-Degree Price Discrimination

A type of price discrimination that is employed when the seller knows that they are serving consumers of different types, is able to determine the actual type of each consumer, and can prevent **arbitrage** between consumers of different types but not between consumers of the same type. With this type of price discrimination the seller charges a uniform, **linear price** to each consumer type by equating **marginal revenue** to **marginal cost** for each consumer type. If the absolute value of the **elasticity of demand** for consumer type i is η_i then the ratio of the price charged to consumer type i and the price charged to consumer type k under third-degree price discrimination is given by

$$\frac{P_i}{P_k} = \frac{\eta_i(\eta_k - 1)}{\eta_k(\eta_i - 1)}.$$

This implies that price is higher to consumer types with less elastic demand.

Tie-In Sale

A business practice that makes the purchase of one good (the tying good) conditional on the purchaser also buying a second good (the tied good). When tie-in sales are required by **contract** they are typically regarded as an attempt by the seller to extend **market power** from one market to another and thus in violation of **antitrust laws**. Firms may, however, achieve tying technologically, for example by designing a computer printer in such a way that it takes only one type of ink cartridge. Products might be tied for obvious **technical efficiency** reasons, such as when car sales require that consumers also purchase the attached tires.

Time-Based Pricing

A pricing system in which the price contracted between seller and buyer is determined by the time at which the good or service is consumed. Typical examples in which the price varies by the time of day are prices charged for cell phone use and electricity consumption. The tourist industry makes extensive use of time-based pricing where prices vary with the seasons. See also **peak-load pricing**.

Tit-for-Tat Strategy

A strategy in **repeated games** in which a player follows the rule "I will do in the next period whatever you have done in this period". This rule is intended to facilitate the maintenance of **tacit collusion**.

Tobin's q

The ratio of the market value of a firm (as determined by the market value of its stocks and outstanding debt) divided by the **replacement cost** of the firm's assets. Tobin argued that a q greater (less) than one would encourage (discourage) firms' decisions to invest in new capital.

Tobit Model

A **latent variable model** in which the **dependent variable**, y, is censored or truncated due to a constraint preventing observed values beyond a threshold value. The threshold value is often zero, with observations limited to non-negative values; however, the model can be generalized to allow for threshold values other than zero. For example, in a study of factors that improve productivity, a manufacturing firm might gather data on variations in management methods and labor usage, and in factory output as a measure of productivity. However, the upper values of output will be constrained by the physical capacity constraints of the factory. A tobit model would be an appropriate econometric specification.

Toehold Merger

A **merger** between a large firm that has a dominant position in one market with a small firm in another market that allows the large firm to gain entry – a toehold – to the small firm's market.

Top Dog Strategy

Suppose that a proposed investment makes a firm a tougher competitor. Then the firm has an incentive to **overinvest** in this type of commitment, become a "top dog", if the choice variables are **strategic substitutes**. See

Fudenberg and Tirole (1984), **fat-cat effect**, **lean-and-hungry look** and **puppy dog strategy**.

Total Cost

The aggregation of all of a firm's fixed and variable costs in a defined time period. In the **short run**, total costs increase with output and eventually increase at an increasing rate, due to **diminishing returns**. In the **long run**, **average total cost** eventually increases due to **diseconomies of scale**.

Total Quality Management

A management strategy that aims to make all individuals and groups within an organization aware of and committed to **quality** and customer satisfaction.

Total Revenue

The aggregation of all of a firm's revenues in a defined time period.

Total Surplus

The sum of **consumer surplus** and **producer surplus**. This is the primary measure that is used to evaluate the efficiency of a proposed government policy.

Total Variable Cost

The aggregation of all costs that vary with output over a defined period of time. In the **short run**, the capital costs are not included; in the **long run**, all costs are variable.

Tough Commitment

A **commitment** made by a firm that makes it act more aggressively with respect to its rivals than it would have done without the commitment. In a **Cournot game** such a commitment will lead the firm to produce more output than it would have done, while in a **Bertrand game** the firm will set a lower price than it would have done.

Tourist–Native Model

A model in which some potential consumers have limited information about prices. The market contains a number of uninformed buyers (tourists) who have to incur **search costs** to find out about prices, and a number of informed buyers (natives) who have perfect information about prices. Such a model will support the **competitive equilibrium** if there are enough informed buyers, but can also support equilibria with prices above the competitive level.

Tournament

An organizational structure in which individuals in the organization compete against each other for promotion. Typically this involves ranking employees against each other and promoting the hardest-working or most effective. Rewards are based on an ordinal ranking of individuals rather than on absolute performance.

Trade Association

An organization financed and run by the companies in a particular industry. Such associations may be used to coordinate support activities such as public relations and lobbying for the companies. The trade association is more generally involved in setting standards and helping to control access to the industry by attempting to persuade consumers that buying from non-association members is risky.

Trademark

A distinctive and unique symbol that an organization uses to identify its products or services and to distinguish these from the products or services of its rivals. Trademarks typically take the form of distinctive names, for example Coca-Cola, or logos, for example the McDonald's "golden arches". Trademarks are considered to be intellectual property and are usually protected from imitation.

Trade Secret

A process or practice used by a firm in order to give it a competitive edge but which the firm chooses not to **patent**. For example, Coca-Cola has always kept secret the formula of its syrup. The strategy of keeping knowledge secret rather than patenting it is appropriate when the knowledge is expected to be long-lived and the product or process is difficult to **reverse engineer**.

Tragedy of the Commons

See **common resource problem**.

Transaction

(1) The transfer of goods or services from one individual to another. (2) The largest unit of economic activity that cannot be subdivided for performance by several individuals.

Transaction Costs

Costs incurred in using the price system, excluding the product price. Typical transaction costs are the costs of searching for suppliers, negotiating the contract terms for the purchase, **monitoring** contract compliance and enforcing penalties for any contractual breach. For a firm, if transaction costs are sufficiently high, a firm might choose to **vertically integrate** to avoid incurring the costs of engaging in market exchanges for productive activity, assuming the benefits from internalizing operations are sufficiently high.

Transfer Price

The price at which a product or service is transferred from one division within an organization to another division. Transfer prices can affect the distribution of **profit** across divisions. If the divisions are established as **profit centers**, transfer pricing can reduce aggregate profit by introducing **double marginalization** unless the transfer prices are set by negotiation between the divisions or by reference to market prices. When the transfer is between divisions, one of which is in a low-tax location and the other a high-tax location, transfer prices can be used to reduce taxable profits.

Trans-Ray Convex

A **cost function** for a multi-product firm is trans-ray convex at a particular point if the cost of producing a linear combination of two output vectors is less than the weighted cost of producing the output vectors separately.

Treble Damages

Three times the actual damages; a penalty frequently used in settling antitrust and **patent** infringement cases, for example.

Trigger Price

A price agreed by a **cartel** such that if the market price falls below the trigger price, the cartel members will abandon the cartel agreement and increase their **outputs**.

Trigger Strategy

A strategy in *n*-person **repeated games** that guarantees punishment of some form in the event of any player deviating from an initial cooperative strategy. The punishment is triggered by the deviation. The punishment strategy must be **subgame perfect** if it is to be effective and rational. A trigger strategy can be shown to sustain cooperative agreements so long as each player's **discount factor** is sufficiently close to unity – see the **folk theorem** and **grim trigger strategy**.

Triopoly

An **oligopoly** containing three firms.

Truncated Regression Model

See **tobit model**.

Truth in Advertising

Government regulation intended to prevent false or deceptive claims by those advertising their products or services. **Advertising** is regarded as false when it includes implied or actual claims about a product that are demonstrably untrue. Deceptive advertising is more complex. It occurs when consumers are judged to interpret an advertisement as making claims that they subsequently find to be false and that result in harm from the purchasing decisions that are made in response to the advertising.

Turnover

(1) **Total revenue**. (2) A measure of the speed with which **inventory** is sold. (3) The speed with which a firm gains and loses employees.

Tweedledum and Tweedledee Game

A technology **game** in which competing firms prefer to adopt incompatible technologies than compatible technologies. The **payoff matrix** for this game is as follows, where in each cell, the **payoff** to the row player is listed first, and the payoff to the column player is listed second:

		Firm 2	
		Technology 1	Technology 2
Firm 1	Technology 1	8, 8	16, 22
	Technology 2	20, 13	10, 10

There are two **Nash equilibria**, (Technology 1, Technology 2) and (Technology 2, Technology 1), in **pure strategies** to this game if it is played simultaneously but no agreement on which should be chosen. The competing firms are likely to battle to have their choice of technology adopted as the **industry standard**.

Two-Part Price

A pricing policy in which the total charge that a consumer pays consists of a fixed fee independent of the quantity being purchased and a unit price or usage fee that is charged for each unit that the consumer actually buys. This pricing policy is one method by which a selling firm can implement **first-degree price discrimination**, by setting the unit price to marginal cost and the fixed fee to **consumer surplus** at that unit price.

Two-Part Tariff

See **two-part price**.

Two-Thirds Rule

A source of **economies of scale** when productive capacity is largely determined by the volume enclosed by the machinery being used, such as pipelines, tanks or storage facilities. The argument is that from the laws of geometry the cost of the equipment increases roughly as the surface area (the square) while its capacity increases roughly as the volume (the cube). In general in such cases, if capacity increases by a factor of x then capital costs will increase by a factor of approximately $x^{0.67}$.

Tying Arrangements

See **tie-in sales**.

U

U-Form Organization

An organizational structure in which the activities of the functional departments are under the direct control of top management, with limited or no functional autonomy. While most firms start their lives as U-form they will tend to change to **multi-divisional organizations** as they grow, in response to the need for greater decentralization of decision-making authority.

Umbrella Branding

The strategy of offering a broad product line under a single **brand name**. Companies such as Samsung and Sony follow this strategy. It is effective if consumers use information regarding the **quality** of one of the firm's products to infer the quality of the firm's other products since this then allows the firm to economize on **advertising** costs and benefit from **economies of scope**. Umbrella branding can also be viewed as the firm offering its consumers quality insurance, since it puts pressure on the brand owner to maintain a consistent level of quality across the full brand spectrum of existing and new products. A risk with umbrella branding is that a mistake in one part of a firm's product range will affect consumer perception of the entire product range offered by the firm.

Uncertainty

A situation in which economic agents do not have perfect information about some states of the world, for example with respect to product **quality** or with respect to potential outcomes from actions that the agents can take.

Underinvestment

If actions are **strategic complements** and a **strategic commitment** makes a firm **tough**, or if actions are **strategic substitutes** and a strategic commitment makes a firm **soft**, the firm should underinvest in such a commitment. In the case of strategic complements, a strategic commitment that makes the firm tougher is likely to induce an aggressive response from rivals, undermining the value of the commitment. In the case of strategic substitutes, a strategic commitment that makes the firm softer is also likely to induce an aggressive response from rivals, again undermining the value of the commitment. See Tirole (1988, pp. 324–325).

Undifferentiated Products

Products that consumers consider to be identical in **quality** and characteristics, even if they are offered by different firms. See also **homogeneous products**.

Uniform Delivered Pricing

A pricing policy under which a firm sells its goods at the same price in every selling location even if the firm incurs transport costs that vary by selling location. This type of pricing is an example of **spatial price discrimination**, since the firm is absorbing all the transport costs, and can take one of two broad forms. With single-zone pricing the firm charges the same price at every selling location. Under multi-zone uniform delivered pricing the firm sets a uniform delivered price in each zone but may divide its market area into a number of zones, for example setting different uniform delivered prices in different countries or other geographically well-defined regions. Multi-zone pricing is constrained by the possibility of consumer **arbitrage** across the different zones.

Uniform Distribution

A distribution of economic agents (consumers or firms) that has the same density at every point in the economic space.

Unit Cost

See **average total cost**.

Unit Pricing

Providing consumers with information on price per unit, for example price per kilogram, for products that are offered in different package sizes.

Unitary Elasticity

A **demand function** that has an **elasticity of demand** equal in magnitude to 1 at every price. The demand function has the form $q = f(\mathbf{a})/p$ where q is quantity demanded, p is price and $\mathbf{a}$ is a vector of all non-price factors that influence quantity demanded, such as income and the prices of other goods. **Total revenue** is constant at $f(\mathbf{a})$ for this demand function no matter what price is set. A limitation of this form of the demand function in the analysis of **monopoly** is that the profit-maximizing price and quantity are undefined.

Unlimited Liability

A proprietorship, partnership or other organization in which the owners' liability for debts incurred by the organization is not limited to their investment in the organization and can extend to the owners' personal assets.

Unobservable Actions

Actions taken by one economic agent that cannot be observed perfectly by other economic agents. In a **principal–agent** relationship, the **principal–agent problem** arises when actions of the agent are unobservable by the principal. In post-contractual situations, **moral hazard** arises when the actions of some parties to the contract are not observable by other parties to the contract. Pre-contract, **adverse selection** arises when a party to a potential contract can hide their true nature and behavior from other parties to the potential contract. See also **hidden action**.

Unobservable Contract

A **contract** offered by a seller to one buyer that cannot be observed by any other buyers.

Unrelated Acquisition

The purchase of one firm by another where the two firms are active in different lines of business. This type of acquisition leads to **diversification** of the acquiring firm. See also **conglomerate merger**.

Up-or-Out Rule

An employment policy in which employees who are not promoted or made partners are required to leave the firm.

Upstream Firm

In a vertically related market structure, a firm that operates early in the production sequence and supplies **intermediate goods** to **downstream firms**.

Upstream Integration

See **backward integration.**

Upstream Process

In manufacturing processes, those processes that arise earlier in the production sequence and that supply intermediate products to **downstream processes**.

Utility

An index of personal well-being. Consumers are usually assumed to derive utility from the consumption of goods.

Utility Function

The relationship between an individual's consumption decisions and the individual's **utility**. In consumer theory the individual consumers are typically assumed to maximize their utility functions subject to their **budget constraints**. See also **indifference curve**.

V

Value Added

The incremental value that is created at each stage of the **vertical chain** of production. For example, if at a particular stage of assembly, **inputs** valued at $2000 are used to create an intermediate product valued at $2500, then the value added by this stage is $500. The sum of the value added at each stage in production of a final good is the value of this final good.

Value-Added Analysis

A method for analyzing the additional value created by different parts of the **value chain** using market prices of finished and **intermediate goods**.

Value Capture

Strategies that a firm can adopt to allow it to retain the additional value that it creates rather than have this value eliminated by competition and imitation by rival firms.

Value Chain

A method of depicting the firm as a set of vertically related activities, identifying the interconnections between each activity and the additional value that each activity creates for the firm.

Value Creation

Strategies that create additional value by discovering new and more efficient ways of using existing resources.

Value Map

A graphical method for comparing products in terms of the price–value combinations that they offer. The map is drawn in a two-dimensional space with **quality** on the horizontal axis and price on the vertical axis. Goods that lie on the same **indifference curve** in this space are goods with price–quality combinations that offer the consumer the same **consumer surplus**.

Value Net

A counterpoint to a **five-forces analysis** that assesses the opportunities that are available from (legal) cooperation between suppliers, customers and competitors.

Variable Costs

Costs that change in proportion to a firm's chosen level of activity. Raw material and labor costs are typical variable costs in the **short run**; all costs, including capital costs, are variable in the **long run**.

Variable Proportions Production (Utility) Function

A **production (utility) function** for which the **elasticity of substitution** is non-zero. For such a function the **factors of production** being employed, or the goods being consumed, can be substituted for each other. The proportions in which the factors will actually be employed, or goods will actually be consumed, are sensitive to the relative prices of the factors of production. If the function is denoted $f(\mathbf{x})$, then an optimal production, or consumption, plan satisfies the condition

$$\frac{\partial f(\mathbf{x})}{\partial p_i} \bigg/ p_i = \frac{\partial f(\mathbf{x})}{\partial p_j} \bigg/ p_j$$

where p_i, p_j are the prices of factors or goods i and j.

Variety

See **product variety**.

Vertical Boundaries of the Firm

The set of activities in the **vertical chain** that the firm chooses to perform for itself rather than buy these activities from outside suppliers. See **theory of the firm**.

Vertical Chain

A production process that begins with raw materials and ends with the distribution and sale of final goods and services. **Intermediate goods** move along this chain from **upstream** to **downstream**.

Vertical Foreclosure

See **foreclosure**.

Vertical Integration

The decision by a firm to perform some **upstream** or **downstream** activities in-house rather than pay to have these activities performed by an outside firm. See also **backward** and **forward integration** as well as **theory of the firm**.

Vertical Merger

Vertical integration that is implemented by the **acquisition** of an **upstream** supplier or **downstream** buyer.

Vertical Product Differentiation

Product differentiation in which products are viewed by consumers to be differentiated in **quality**, with general agreement among consumers of the relative qualities of the goods being offered.

Vertical Restraints

Contractual agreements between organizations at different levels in the **vertical chain** of production limiting the actions that they can take. Typical vertical restraints are **exclusive dealing** agreements, **resale price maintenance** and **tie-in sales**. While many such restraints have been found to break **antitrust laws** they are usually evaluated according to the **rule of reason**.

Vickrey Auction

See **sealed-bid second-price auction**.

Virtual Firm

A network of small, autonomous firms whose behavior, through their communications and interactions in the network, approximates that of a larger firm.

Visibility

A necessary property of a **strategic commitment** that the commitment must be visible to those whose behavior it is intended to affect if the strategic intent of the commitment is to be successful.

W

Wage Compression

A phenomenon in which new hires are paid more than current employees recruited some years earlier.

Wage Rate

The per-period compensation paid to an employee.

Waiting Time

The time that buyers have to wait to obtain a good or service that they wish to purchase. One strategy for **value creation** is to find ways to reduce waiting time.

Walras's Law

A principle in **general equilibrium** theory that the sum of excess demands across all markets must equal zero, whether or not the economy is in general equilibrium. Suppose that an economy contains n goods, that demand for good i is $d_i(\mathbf{p})$ and supply of good i is $s_i(\mathbf{p})$ where $\mathbf{p} = (p_1, p_2, \ldots, p_n)$ is the vector of goods prices. Then Walras's Law states that at any price vector p it must be that

$$\sum_{i=1}^{n} p_i(d_i(\mathbf{p}) - s_i(\mathbf{p})) = 0.$$

An important implication of Walras's Law is that in any such economy one commodity can be chosen as the numeraire with its price set to unity.

Walrasian Output

Suppose that market demand is given by $Q = D(p)$ and that each firm has a U-shaped average total cost function with minimum average total cost c. Then the Walrasian output of this economy is $Q^* = D(c)$.

War of Attrition

The expenditure of resources by competing firms to gain control of a market. The survivor of the war gains the entire market while the loser gets nothing. A **price war** is an example of a war of attrition.

Warrant

A right issued by a firm that entitles the holder of the warrant to purchase shares of stock in the issuing company at a specified price provided that the warrant is exercised before a specified date.

Warranty

A guarantee offered by a seller to a buyer that the item being traded is as described, and providing for a remedy such as repair or replacement if the item breaks down within a period specified in the warranty.

Wastefulness Postulate

The assertion that firms' expenditures on attempting to obtain the **monopoly profit** have no socially valuable by-products. One implication of the wastefulness postulate is that the **deadweight loss** of monopoly should be increased to include the monopoly profit in situations in which there is competition to acquire the monopoly, since such competition will lead to **rent-seeking** in which all potential monopoly profits are dissipated wastefully.

Weak Form Efficient Markets Hypothesis

The hypothesis that current stock prices fully incorporate all information embodied in past prices. As a result, observing past prices cannot help in predicting future prices. Under this hypothesis, price changes are not correlated over time and do not exhibit any predictable patterns.

Weakly Dominant Strategy

A strategy for a player that provides a **payoff** that is no lower than any other strategy the player can adopt no matter the strategies that are played by the player's rivals. Suppose that player I has two strategies A and B and player II has two strategies a and b, and denote the payoff to player I from strategy combination X, y as $P(X, y)$. Then A weakly dominates B for player I if $P(A, a) \geq P(B, a)$ and $P(A, b) \geq P(B, b)$. See also **dominant strategy**.

Weakly Dominated Strategy

A strategy that provides a **payoff** that is no greater than any other strategy no matter the strategies that are played by the player's rivals. Suppose that player I has two strategies A and B and player II has two strategies a and b, and denote the payoff to player I from strategy combination X, y as $P(X, y)$. Then A is weakly dominated by B for player I if $P(A, a) \leq P(B, a)$ and $P(A, b) \leq P(B, b)$. The order in which weakly dominated strategies are eliminated can affect the determination of the equilibrium to the underlying **game**. See also **dominated strategy**.

Wealth Effects

The change in the amount that a consumer is willing to pay for a good or service, or the change in the quantity of the good or service the consumer is willing to buy at a given price, as a result of a change in the consumer's wealth.

Weighted Average Cost of Capital

The cost of capital that is financed by a combination of debt and equity, reflecting the cost of debt, the cost of equity and the relative amounts of debt and equity. If, for example, the cost of equity is 18 percent, the cost of debt is 10 percent and the firm's capital structure is 60 percent equity and 40 percent debt then the weighted average cost of capital is 14.8 percent $(0.6 \times 18\% + 0.4 \times 10\%)$.

Welfare

See **social welfare**.

Welfare Theorems

The first welfare theorem states that a **competitive equilibrium** is **Pareto efficient**. The second welfare theorem states that if there are no **economies of scale**, any Pareto-efficient allocation can be supported by appropriately chosen prices and an appropriate redistribution of consumer incomes.

Wetware

The knowledge held by the individuals employed by a company. Wetware is the private property of the employees and is lost if the employees leave.

White Knight

A **takeover** defense in which an individual or firm is invited by senior management to gain control of a corporation facing a **hostile takeover**, usually with the understanding that the white knight will leave the senior management in place after the transfer of control is effected.

Widely Held Corporation

A corporation in which no single **shareholder** controls more than 10 percent of the shares.

Willingness to Pay

See **marginal willingness to pay**.

Winner's Curse

The prediction that in a **common value auction**, in which bidders have **incomplete information** about the value of the item being auctioned, the winner of the auction will tend to overpay relative to the true value of the item. The winner of such an auction is the highest bidder. On the assumption that the average bid is the best estimate of the true value, the winning bid overvalues the item.

Within-Firm Performance

A **relative performance evaluation** system that uses other employees' performance within the same firm to estimate the average error with which a particular employee's performance is measured.

Work Sampling

A form of time and motion study that bases the assessment of how long employees take to perform specified tasks upon a large sample of observations taken at random intervals.

X

x-efficiency

A measure of the effectiveness with which a firm is using its **inputs** in order to produce **output**. If the firm is producing the maximum output of which it is capable given the resources and technology that it has at its disposal, then it is x-efficient. Otherwise it is x-inefficient. In firms where there is a separation between ownership and control it is likely that the employees and management of the firm will not necessarily act in the best interests of the **shareholders**, leading to x-inefficiency. An argument against allowing a monopolist to operate in an uncontested market is that the monopolist will be x-inefficient, since it does not face competitive cost pressure. However, it is reasonable to expect that the monopolist will still seek to maximize profits, which implies an incentive to be x-efficient.

Y

Yardstick Competition

A method of assessing an agent's individual performance by comparing it with that of other agents who have been placed in similar circumstances. One form of yardstick competition is to base managerial compensation on the firm's performance relative to the performance of its competitors.

Yield Management

A set of practices used in particular by airlines and hotels to increase the **revenues** they earn per seat or room sold. Yield management techniques are based on complex mathematical and forecasting models that determine prices, the number of seats or rooms to be allocated to particular price categories, and adjustments in inventory to reflect forecast changes in demand. Such techniques usually result in extensive **price discrimination**.

Z

Zero Economic Profit

A condition that characterizes **perfectly competitive** and **imperfectly competitive** firms, that **free entry** and **exit** result in such firms earning exactly normal returns on the assets they employ. When the zero **economic profit** condition is achieved in a **competitive market**, the market achieves **long-run competitive equilibrium**, as no firm has an incentive to exit or enter the market.

Zero-Profit Condition

In markets where there are no **strategic barriers to entry** an equilibrium condition that **entry** continues until the **incumbent firms** are earning just **zero economic profit**.

Zero-Sum Game

A **game** in which in each strategy combination, one player's gain or loss is equal to the loss or gain of the other players. A typical two-person zero-sum game is as follows, where in each cell, the **payoff** to the row player is listed first, and the payoff to the column player is listed second:

		Player 2	
		Strategy 1	Strategy 2
Player 1	Strategy 1	A, −A	−B, B
	Strategy 2	−C, C	D, −D

See also **non-zero-sum game**.

Zero Wealth Effects

A decision has zero wealth effects for a decision maker when three conditions are satisfied: (1) given any two alternative decisions y_1 and y_2 there is a finite amount of money x that would compensate the decision-maker for switching from y_1 to y_2; (2) if the decision maker is given additional wealth, the compensation required for the consumer to make the switch remains x; and (3) the decision maker has sufficient resources to be able to absorb any wealth reduction necessary to pay for the switch from the less desired alternative to the more desired alternative.

Zone of Indifference

The set of issues over which the wishes of an individual with the power to exert formal authority usually prevail.

Zone Pricing

A form of **price discrimination** in which a seller defines a set of geographic zones and sets the price in each zone to reflect geographic, demographic and local competitive conditions.

REFERENCES

Akerlof, George A. 1970. "The Market for 'Lemons': Quality Uncertainty and the Market Mechanism", *Quarterly Journal of Economics*, Volume 84, pp. 488–500.

Averch, Harvey, and Johnson, Leland L. 1962. "Behavior of the Firm Under Regulatory Constraint", *American Economic Review*, Volume 52, pp. 1052–1069.

Bain, Joe S. 1941. "The Profit Rate as a Measure of Monopoly Power", *Quarterly Journal of Economics*, Volume 55, pp. 271–293.

Bain, Joe S. 1951. "Relation of Profit Rate to Industry Concentration: American Manufacturing, 1936–1940", *Quarterly Journal of Economics*, Volume 65, pp. 293–324.

Becker, Gary S. 1983. "A Theory of Competition Among Pressure Groups for Political Influence", *Quarterly Journal of Economics*, Volume 98, pp. 371–400.

Berry, Steven, Levinsohn, James, and Pakes, Ariel. 1995. "Automobile Prices in Market Equilibrium", *Econometrica*, Volume 63, pp. 841–890.

Boiteux, Marcel. 1964. "Marginal Cost Pricing", in Nelson, James R. (editor), *Marginal Cost Pricing in Practice*, Prentice Hall, Englewood, NJ.

Bulow, Jeremy I., Geanakoplos, and Klemperer, Paul D. 1985. "Multimarket Oligopoly: Strategic Substitutes and Complements", *Journal of Political Economy*, Volume 93, pp. 488–511.

Coase, Ronald H. 1937. "The Nature of the Firm", *Economica*, Volume 4, pp. 386–405.

Coase, Ronald H. 1972. "Durability and Monopoly", *Journal of Law and Economics*, Volume 15, pp. 143–149.

Cooper, Thomas E. 1986. "Most-Favored-Customer Pricing and Tacit Collusion", *RAND Journal of Economics*, Volume 17, pp. 377–388.

Dasgupta, Partha, Hammond, Peter, and Maskin, Eric. 1979. "The Implementation of Social Choice Rules: Some General Results on Incentive Compatibility", *Review of Economic Studies*, Volume 46, pp. 185–216.

Demsetz, Harold. 1968. "Why Regulate Utilities?" *Journal of Law and Economics*, Volume 11, pp. 55–65.

Dunning, John H. 1981. "Explaining the International Direct Investment Position of Countries: Towards a Dynamic or Developmental Approach", *Weltwirtschaftliches Archiv*, Volume 117, H. 1, pp. 30–64.

Fama, Eugene F., and Jensen, Michael C. 1983. "Separation of Ownership and Control", *Journal of Law and Economics*, Volume 26, pp. 301–325.

Fudenberg, Drew, and Tirole, Jean. 1984. "The Fat-Cat Effect, the Puppy-Dog Ploy and the Lean and Hungry Look", *American Economic Review*, Volume 74, pp. 361–366.

Galbraith, John K. 1952. *American Capitalism: The Concept of Countervailing Power*. Houghton Mifflin, Boston, MA.

Gastwirth, Joseph L. 1972. "The Estimation of the Lorenz Curve and Gini Index", *Review of Economics and Statistics*, Volume 54, pp. 306–316.

Ghemawat, Pankaj. 1993. "Commitment to a Process Innovation: Nucor, USX, and Thin-Slab Casting", *Journal of Economics and Management Strategy*, Volume 2, pp. 135–161.

Greene, William H. 2012. *Econometric Analysis*, seventh edition, Prentice Hall, Upper Saddle River, NJ.

Grossman, Gene M., and Shapiro, Carl. 1986. "Research Joint Ventures: An Antitrust Analysis", *Journal of Law, Economics, and Organization*, Volume 2, pp. 315–337.

Grossman, Sanford J., and Hart, Oliver D. 1986. "The Costs and Benefits of Ownership: A Theory of Vertical and Lateral Integration", *Journal of Political Economy*, Volume 94, pp. 691–719.

Harsanyi, John C. 1967. "Games with Incomplete Information Played by 'Bayesian' Players, I–III. Part I. The Basic Model", *Management Science*, Volume 14, Theory Series, pp. 159–182.

Harsanyi, John C. 1968a. "Games with Incomplete Information Played by 'Bayesian'

Players, I–III. Part II. Bayesian Equilibrium Points", *Management Science*, Volume 14, Theory Series, pp. 320–334.

Harsanyi, John C. 1968b. "Games with Incomplete Information Played by 'Bayesian' Players, I–III. Part III. The Basic Probability Distribution of the Game", *Management Science*, Volume 14, Theory Series, pp. 486–502.

Hotelling, Harold. 1929. "Stability in Competition", *Economic Journal*, Volume 39, pp. 41–57.

Kwoka, John E., Jr. 1977. "Large Firm Dominance and Price–Cost Margins in Manufacturing Industries", *Southern Economic Journal*, Volume 44, pp. 183–189.

Lorenz, Max O. 1905. "Methods of Measuring the Concentration of Wealth", *Publications of the American Statistical Association*, Volume 9, pp. 209–219.

Manne, Henry G. 1965. "Mergers and the Market for Corporate Control", *Journal of Political Economy*, Volume 73, pp. 110–120.

McFadden, Daniel L. 1984. "Econometric Analysis of Qualitative Response Models", in Griliches, Zvi, and Intriligator, Michael D. (editors), *Handbook of Econometrics*, Handbooks in Economics series, Volume II, Book 2, North-Holland, Amsterdam, pp. 1396–1457.

Milgrom, Paul R. 1988. "Employment Contracts, Influence Activities, and Efficient Organization Design", *Journal of Political Economy*, Volume 96, pp. 42–60.

Milgrom, Paul R., and Roberts, John. 1992. *Economics, Organization, and Management*, Prentice-Hall, Englewood Cliffs, NJ.

Myerson, Roger B. 1981. "Optimal Auction Design", *Mathematics of Operations Research*, Volume 6, pp. 58–73.

Nash, John F., Jr. 1950a. "The Bargaining Problem", *Econometrica*, Volume 18, pp. 155–162.

Nash, John F., Jr. 1950b. "Equilibrium Points in n-Person Games", *Proceedings of the National Academy of Sciences of the United States of America*, Volume 36, pp. 48–49.

Nash, John F., Jr. 1953. "Two-Person Cooperative Games", *Econometrica*, Volume 21, pp. 128–140.

Nevo, Aviv. 2000. "Mergers with Differentiated Products: The Case of the Ready-to-Eat Cereal Industry", *RAND Journal of Economics*, Volume 31, pp. 395–421.

Peltzman, Sam. 1976. "Toward a More General Theory of Regulation", *Journal of Law and Economics*, Volume 19, pp. 211–240.

Porter, Michael E. 1979. "How Competitive Forces Shape Strategy", *Harvard Business Review*, Volume 57, pp. 137–145.

Ramsey, Frank P. 1927. "A Contribution to the Theory of Taxation", *Economic Journal*, Volume 37, pp. 47–61.

Riley, John G., and Samuelson, William F. 1981. "Optimal Auctions", *American Economic Review*, Volume 71, pp. 381–392.

Salant, Stephen W., Switzer, Sheldon, and Reynolds, Robert J. 1983. "Losses from Horizontal Merger: The Effects of an Exogenous Change in Industry Structure on Cournot–Nash Equilibrium", *Quarterly Journal of Economics*, Volume 98, pp. 185–199.

Salop, Steven C. 1979. "Monopolistic Competition with Outside Goods", *Bell Journal of Economics*, Volume 10, pp. 141–156.

Selten, Reinhard. 1978. "The Chain-Store Paradox", *Theory and Decision*, Volume 9, pp. 127–159.

Smith, Adam. 1776. *An Inquiry into the Nature and Causes of the Wealth of Nations*, Cannan, Edwin (editor) 1904, reprinted 1976, University of Chicago Press, Chicago, IL.

Stigler, George J. 1971. "The Theory of Economic Regulation", *Bell Journal of Economics*, Volume 2, pp. 3–21.

Tirole, Jean. 1988. *The Theory of Industrial Organization*, MIT Press: Cambridge, MA.

Train, Kenneth E. 2009. *Discrete Choice Methods with Simulation*, second edition, Cambridge University Press, Cambridge.

Viscusi, W. Kip, Harington, Joseph E. Jr., and Vernon, John M. 2005. *Economics of Regulation and Antitrust*, fourth edition, MIT Press, Cambridge, MA.

Wernerfelt, Birger. 1984. "A Resource-Based View of the Firm", *Strategic Management Journal*, Volume 5, pp. 171–180.